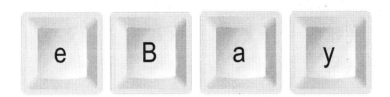

eBay Income

How *ANYONE* of *Any* Age, Location, and/or
Background Can Build a Highly Profitable
Online Business with eBay

REVISED 2ND EDITION

By John Peragine and Cheryl Russell

EBAY INCOME: HOW ANYONE OF ANY AGE, LOCATION, AND/OR BACK-
GROUND CAN BUILD A HIGHLY PROFITABLE ONLINE BUSINESS WITH
EBAY REVISED 2ND EDITION

Copyright © 2011 Atlantic Publishing Group, Inc.
1405 SW 6th Avenue • Ocala, Florida 34471 • Phone 800-814-1132 • Fax 352-622-1875
Web site: www.atlantic-pub.com • E-mail: sales@atlantic-pub.com
SAN Number: 268-1250

Library of Congress Cataloging-in-Publication Data

Russell, Cheryl L. (Cheryl Lynn), 1967-
  eBay income : how anyone of any age, location, and/or background can build a highly
profitable online business with eBay / by Cheryl L. Russell and John N. Peragine. -- Rev. 2nd
ed.
      p. cm.
  Includes bibliographical references and index.
  ISBN-13: 978-1-60138-441-6 (alk. paper)
  ISBN-10: 1-60138-441-6 (alk. paper)
  1. eBay (Firm) 2. Internet auctions. 3. Electronic commerce. I. Peragine, John N., 1970- II.
Title.
  HF5478.R87 2010
  658.8'7--dc22
                           2010005821

Printed in the United States

PROJECT MANAGER: Kim Fulscher • PEER REVIEWER: Marilee Griffin
ASSISTANT EDITOR: Brad Goldbach • INTERIOR DESIGN: Samantha Martin
FRONT & BACK COVER DESIGN: Jackie Miller • millerjackiej@gmail.com

Printed on Recycled Paper

We recently lost our beloved pet "Bear," who was not only our best and dearest friend but also the "Vice President of Sunshine" here at Atlantic Publishing. He did not receive a salary but worked tirelessly 24 hours a day to please his parents. Bear was a rescue dog that turned around and showered myself, my wife, Sherri, his grandparents Jean, Bob, and Nancy, and every person and animal he met (maybe not rabbits) with friendship and love. He made a lot of people smile every day.

We wanted you to know that a portion of the profits of this book will be donated to The Humane Society of the United States. *–Douglas & Sherri Brown*

The human-animal bond is as old as human history. We cherish our animal companions for their unconditional affection and acceptance. We feel a thrill when we glimpse wild creatures in their natural habitat or in our own backyard.

Unfortunately, the human-animal bond has at times been weakened. Humans have exploited some animal species to the point of extinction.

The Humane Society of the United States makes a difference in the lives of animals here at home and worldwide. The HSUS is dedicated to creating a world where our relationship with animals is guided by compassion. We seek a truly humane society in which animals are respected for their intrinsic value, and where the human-animal bond is strong.

Want to help animals? We have plenty of suggestions. Adopt a pet from a local shelter, join The Humane Society and be a part of our work to help companion animals and wildlife. You will be funding our educational, legislative, investigative and outreach projects in the U.S. and across the globe.

Or perhaps you'd like to make a memorial donation in honor of a pet, friend or relative? You can through our Kindred Spirits program. And if you'd like to contribute in a more structured way, our Planned Giving Office has suggestions about estate planning, annuities, and even gifts of stock that avoid capital gains taxes.

Maybe you have land that you would like to preserve as a lasting habitat for wildlife. Our Wildlife Land Trust can help you. Perhaps the land you want to share is a backyard— that's enough. Our Urban Wildlife Sanctuary Program will show you how to create a habitat for your wild neighbors.

So you see, it's easy to help animals. And The HSUS is here to help.

THE HUMANE SOCIETY
OF THE UNITED STATES.

2100 L Street NW • Washington, DC 20037 • 202-452-1100
www.hsus.org

Trademarks

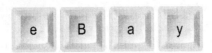

Dedication

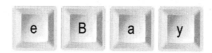

I dedicate this book to my beautiful wife, Kate, and to my shining daughters, Sarah and Loreena. Their tolerance and support of my writing exploits is epic.

— John Peragine

In memory of Ella Mae Drury Leibforth: great-grandmother, poet, and writer. To Mike Pratley, English teacher, and to Sarah Kay, my firstborn.

— Cheryl Russell

Table of Contents

Chapter 2: On Your Mark…Get Set… Auction   63

Chapter 3: Plan Ahead for Success   85

Chapter 4: Keeping Track   125

Chapter 5: Stuff to Sell   163

Chapter 6: Nail Down the Details   191

Chapter 7: Advertising — Toot Your Own Horn   229

Chapter 8: Join the Club   257

Foreword

S tarting a business on eBay is fairly easy; creating an eBay business that will make money and support your family is quite another undertaking.

As a business consultant, eBay PowerSeller, and certified education specialist trained by eBay, I am keenly aware of the pitfalls people encounter when starting their eBay business. I have personally made most of the mistakes that can be made. I started on eBay in March 1998 as a buyer. My husband and I wanted to expand our collection — and eBay did that beyond our wildest dreams. The first items I listed were three vintage sideshow postcards from the 1930s. I listed each one separately, and they collectively brought in more than $86. I only paid 50 cents for all three! I was hooked and set about learning all I could about selling on eBay.

Since my business started as a hobby, in the beginning I didn't think much about the business of eBay. When I did decide to make eBay a real business, I found little help. Many of the business questions I had either went unanswered or were answered by trial and error. What I needed was a guide to help me make the decisions I needed to make and map my path to success. This book is the guide I needed when I was creating my eBay business.

Cheryl Russell walks beginners and seasoned professionals alike through the maze of the business of eBay and e-commerce. John Peragine, who updated the book for its second edition, helps the reader understand eBay's perpetually changing services and options. It's important to understand these new concepts, and Peragine guides you through the newest information available. For business newbies, Russell and Peragine explain the basic concepts of business in easy-to-understand terms, help you understand eBay and the tools available to you, and show you concrete ways you can build a business and earn a living on eBay.

The difference between this book and others I have read is the emphasis on applying business basics to your eBay endeavors. You must have a solid understanding of business and good business practices in order to be a success on eBay. By following the map that Russell and Peragine have laid out, anyone can and will be able to create a successful online e-commerce business on eBay and beyond. I am recommending this book to all my students.

MARDI TIMM
Business consultant, eBay PowerSeller, and certified education specialist trained by eBay
www.youcansell2.com
E-mail: mardi@youcansell2.com

Introduction

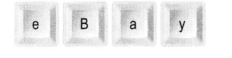

Welcome to eBay

It looked like one more forgettable Saturday garage sale, like so many others that day. Lots of clothes with stretched-out necks or worn spots in the knees, the usual supply of pots and pans past their prime, maybe a videotape or two. That is what Joe surmised as he slowed and pulled up to the curb. Was it even worth getting out of the car to look closer?

Deciding that he had room in his trunk for a bit more inventory, Joe, who started his eBay™ business (**www.ebay.com**) by selling his used VHS tapes, ambled over to the tables and began to scan them for anything interesting. He spied mostly boring merchandise of little or no value to a seasoned seller who can spot a good-old song-and-dance film 10 yards away.

Wandering through the mishmash of wobbly card tables and boards propped up on sawhorses, something caught Joe's eye. He had no idea what they were, but they looked old; that alone merited a closer investigation. The box contained old cards of some sort.

Joe had not ever seen anything like these before: turn-of-the-century scenes on finely pressed paperboard. Most of them were dated in the 1890s and were made by a company called Underwood & Underwood. They had images from all over the world; pyramids in Egypt, old warships, the Vatican, and the Philippine Islands. Each card had two of what appeared to be identical images on it — kind of like seeing double. Now that was odd.

Even though antiques were not exactly Joe's interest, he had enough gut instinct to suspect he had stumbled across something that might be worth obtaining. There was no price on the box, so he asked.

"How much do you want for the cards?"

"I don't know; how much will you give me?"

Not wanting to offend the owner, he scrambled to think of a fair price.

"Five dollars?" he offered.

"Tell you what. Take both boxes and pay me $10."

Both? Joe had not even seen the second box nearby. Nodding his agreement, he paid for the horde and headed home to do some research. No vintage videos to be had at that sale, but within days he would be thanking his lucky stars that he stopped at this garage sale.

If you have not already guessed, Joe (eBay user ID "whitebears") had stumbled across a cache of mint-condition stereoview cards. Popular in the late 1800s and into the 20th century, the Victorian-era cards were put into a binocular-type holder called a stereoscope that combined the slightly different images, making them three-dimensional — sort of like an early version of Mattel's View-Master® toys that first appeared in the 1940s and are still marketed today.

Joe picks up his story:

"Having researched the cards, I knew I had made a good find, and thought I might get $100 or even $150 for them," he said. "I listed them, not knowing I had hit the mother lode of stereoview cards."

The 200 or so cards were split up into lots, groups of one to 30 cards with a similar theme. The first lot listed included 30 cards with pictures from an exposition in Omaha, Nebraska, in the late 1890s. Bidding was fierce in the late hours of the auction, and Joe's excitement grew exponentially as the bids soared. When it was all said and done, that auction alone netted Joe nearly $1,100.

Some of the other cards fetched $50 apiece, and by the time he had exhausted his supply, Joe was giddy from his foray into the antiques market. He was more than $1,800 richer, too. Not bad for a $10 investment.

Joe has since become a PowerSeller, who are eBay sellers who sell large amounts of stock, and while he still sells old VHS tapes, this experience helped catapult his diversity: Suddenly, he had become a mini-expert at a new type of merchandise. Joe had inadvertently expanded his knowledge, his product line, and his reach to buyers on his favorite marketplace: eBay.

Does the thrill of the hunt before a Saturday of rummage sales and flea markets excite you to heights your spouse just does not comprehend? What about new merchandise: Do you see products lying lackluster on a store's clearance shelves, begging you to buy — and resell them — for a profit? Have you always thought someday you would start your own business, complete with wholesale suppliers, a storefront, and a huge customer base?

If so, then this book is for you.

This book will guide you through the basic principles of starting your own small business, using eBay as your primary selling tool. In order to use this book most effectively, you should already have at least a little experience using eBay, either to browse or purchase items.

Having some experience as a buyer is a great way to feel confident about becoming a seller, so go ahead and buy a few items to add to your collection or buy holiday gifts early this year. And, of course, having some feedback to your credit before you begin selling is always a good idea. *Learn more about feedback in Chapter 9.*

With that in mind, let us take a brief stroll down memory lane and revisit a time when eBay, and the Internet as we know it, did not even exist.

Understanding eBay

Many people have heard the simplistic — and not all-encompassing — story that eBay started as a way for the founder's wife to add to her collection of Pez dispensers. Pierre Omidyar admits now this tale is not entirely true. Although it does have some basis in truth — his then-girlfriend (later wife) was one of his inspirations for an online auction and one of the first sellers — the entire story is far more interesting and inspiring.

The original site, AuctionWeb, was hosted along with Omidyar's informational page about the Ebola virus. The first listing was a broken laser pointer. This first auction item was intended to be a test of the system; Omidyar really never expected it to sell, but it did, for $14.83. From that point on, Omidyar knew that he was onto something. The first buyer just happened to be a collector of broken laser pointers.

Omidyar was born in France in 1967 and immigrated to the United States with his family when he was a young boy. He was in junior high school when the first personal computers from companies such as Radio Shack came on the market. Immediately, Omidyar had found his life's passion and what would become his life's work: the world of computers. In fact, his fascination with computers was too strong to resist; he frequently skipped physical education classes to sneak off and use a teacher's computer during those early years. Even before finishing college in 1988, Omidyar began an early career in programming and was involved in various businesses that specialized in programming for Macintosh computers.

In the early 1990s, "the Internet" was a catch phrase that was spreading like wildfire on the lips of every computer geek in Silicon Valley. The epicenter of all things computer in those days — southern California en masse — swooned at the thought of how the Internet was going to change the world and all the money there was to be made doing it.

Omidyar, too, was caught up in the excitement, and even had some early Web sites devoted to such onerous subjects as the Ebola virus and a university alumni site. But when it came to making money via the Internet, his ideals about business and the free market inspired him to pursue equality for the common man in purchasing. For instance, he had become wealthy at a young age by buying stocks prior to an initial public offering (IPO) and then benefiting when the stock gained greatly just before the public had a chance to purchase it. This led Omidyar to wish that everybody would have the opportunity to buy low or bid the price up if the demand was there. He had been lucky with his shortcut to financial success but wanted to even the odds for everyone else.

Though Omidyar could not do much to change the way the stock markets operate, he could — and did — incorporate his ideals into his own hobby that turned into the world's largest business foray the Internet would know in its early days.

eBay, interestingly enough, was born in a quiet home office with very little fanfare. Over Labor Day weekend in 1995, Omidyar wrote the basic programming that would operate a simple auction site and named it Auction-Web. The site was hosted on his Web site, **www.eBay.com**, and shared space with the previously mentioned Ebola virus information, as well as a couple of pages used by his fiancé and the alumni Web site.

The auction format was simplistic and far from the neat and slick eBay most people think of today. The block lettering and grey background was rather boring, frankly, and there were only a few options: List an item, bid on an item, and view an item. It was plain-Jane functionality at its best. However, aesthetics aside, users immediately fancied the new way to buy and sell.

The first months of AuctionWeb were not blockbusters by today's standards, but by posting information about his new site on other Web sites and Usenet newsgroups (some of the earliest sites on the Internet), business slowly picked up. Within four months, thousands of auctions had been set up on AuctionWeb, and the buzz about this new marketplace was spreading as quickly as the Internet itself.

Not content to merely provide a forum for buyers and sellers to do business, Omidyar made sure all users were aware of the ethical way he wished the site's users to treat each other. He posted a list of desired behaviors, such as being courteous and settling disputes politely. Thus were born the Community Values that today are still prominently featured in eBay's pages and discussion boards. A list of those values follows:

1. We believe people are basically good.
2. We believe everyone has something to contribute.
3. We believe that an honest, open environment can bring out the best in people.
4. We recognize and respect everyone as a unique individual.
5. We encourage you to treat others the way you want to be treated.

Initially, AuctionWeb charged no fees to the users, but when Omidyar's Internet service provider started complaining about his site's traffic, they forced him to bump up to a business account costing $250 per month. Hobby or not, that was a far cry from the $30 he had been spending, so he began charging just the sellers, not the buyers, starting in February 1996. Users paid Final Value Fees only, through mail, sending checks, paper bills, or even coins taped together. Right from the start, the collected fees covered the new expenses and even turned a small profit.

Omidyar knew he was on to something, and by the end of summer of 1996, he quit his full-time job and devoted himself entirely to turning his hobby into a thriving business. Others who came on board, including Jeff Skoll, helped shape the site in its early years. One of Skoll's most notable contributions was convincing Omidyar to drop the other Web pages that existed on eBay.com and stick just to auctions. It was difficult, but Omidyar gave in and removed his prized Ebola virus page, along with the other non-auction pages, from the site. From then on, AuctionWeb became known by the handle eBay.

By the end of 1996, AuctionWeb had sold more than a quarter of a million items. By September 1997, AuctionWeb became eBay. In 1998, eBay became a public company with its stock traded on the NASDAQ. As of September 30, 2009, eBay reported they had 89.2 million active users worldwide. In the fourth quarter of 2009, eBay announced its revenue was $2.4 billion.

A recent study indicated that nearly 750,000 people in the United States rely on eBay for some or all of their income. While eBay has branched out to foreign countries, the United States is its most seasoned group of users and an important piece of its selling "pie." The gamut of eBay sellers runs from stay-at-home parents wanting to pad the family's budget to retired folks who know a thing or two about antiques. College students unload their old textbooks, and computer junkies hawk their outdated equipment. But the fastest-growing segment of eBay sellers seems to be those who are making it into a real business, steadily earning at least a portion of their necessary income without ever leaving the comfort of their homes.

Becoming the Icon

eBay has helped countless people realize their dreams of owning a business and being their own boss. Although it may not be like the business their father's generation opened — and certainly is far different from what their grandfather's generation could have ever imagined — it is still nonetheless a business. But why is this type of business so wildly popular?

Selling on eBay can be done with little or no overhead, inventory, and space. It is not necessary to rent an office, hire employees, or encounter many of the other traditional business headaches. Instead, there can be as little as a computer screen and a post office box, at least initially. Primarily, there is freedom, prestige, and a sense of accomplishment every bit as strong as those who operate more traditional (often referred to as "brick-and-mortar") businesses.

Sure, there are still the same responsibilities as any other business. You must have a source of merchandise to sell (a product stream), and you must find ways to have a constant income (by generating sales). And despite popular myth, selling online does not release you from following all the laws that regulate businesses, such as reporting income and paying the appropriate taxes.

But if you were going to go into business anyway, the Internet — and eBay specifically — has made it entirely possible for you to make yourself a big business with relatively little investment compared to traditional methods of breaking into this world. There will still be investment needed on your part: a current computer, some basic software, a reliable Internet connection, and some basic office supplies, to begin with. But compared to the tens of thousands of dollars required to start a traditional business, the few thousand dollars you will need to start this one are attainable to most people today.

Ordinary people are not the only ones who are clued in to the huge potential of eBay. Even big businesses are using the power of eBay to market their products. Some companies use eBay to unload surplus stock or launch new products, while others use eBay to promote their business while not ever selling a single item.

One such company is the Golden Palace Casino, an online-only casino that has made itself a household name by purchasing outrageous items on eBay, such as the vehicle once owned by Pope John Paul II. Even though they pay mightily for some of these offbeat items, the publicity they get is worth more than any ad campaign they could have bought for the same number of dollars. By standing out from the crowd of online gambling sites, they have managed to use eBay in a way that even Pierre Omidyar probably never imagined.

Other imaginative ways to do business and make money have cropped up with the help of, or because of, the success of eBay. eBay has helped shape the way we donate to charity, buy vehicles, rent apartments, and even hire employees. Countless Web sites have sprung to life in the past decade that takes these everyday tasks to new levels.

The World's Online Marketplace, as eBay's motto proclaims, also cares about global issues. Charity auctions are highlights of the Giving Works site (**www.ebaygivingworks.com**). Current events have inspired waves of charity auctions, and eBay makes it easy to access these special auctions, often right at the top of the home page.

In 1998, before going public with its stock offering, eBay set aside more than 100,000 shares of stock to be put into the eBay Foundation, a charitable fund that provides grants of more than $2 million to non-profit charitable organizations all over the world.

The eBay Foundation is considered one of the San Francisco Bay Area's top corporate foundations and to date has donated more than $18 million.

Purchasing a vehicle will never be the same after eBay. Though there are many sites on the Internet that specialize in vehicle sales, one of the first places it happened was on eBay. Back when there was no category for listing a vehicle for sale, trend-setting sellers listed them under the category where toy cars were sold. eBay eventually clued in and created eBay Motors, which advertises many motorized vehicles other than automobiles and now accounts for a tidy share of their sales.

The Web site's growth did not stop at just at auction sites and philanthropic pursuits. The following is a list of most eBay's business acquisitions. You may recognize the name of some of these as ones you use every day:

Name of Company	Type of Company	Web Address
Up4Sale.com	Online auction	www.up4sale.net
Butterfield & Butterfield	Auction house	www.bonhams.com
Billpoint	E-commerce payment systems	Phased out due to Paypal
Alando	Auction house	
Half.com	Online marketplace	www.half.com
Precision Buying Service	E-commerce payment systems	Absorbed by eBay
Internet Auction Co.	Online auction	Absorbed by eBay
iBazar	Online auction	Absorbed by eBay
PayPal	E-commerce payment systems	www.paypal.com
CARad.com	Online auction	www.carad.com
EachNet	Electronic commerce	Absorbed by eBay
Baazee.com	Online auction	www.eBay.in
Craigslist	Classified advertising	www.craigslist.org
Marktplaats.nl	Classified advertising	www.marktplaats.nl
Rent.com	Classified advertising	www.rent.com
Loquo	Classified advertising	www.loquo.com
Gumtree	Classified advertising	www.gumtree.com
Shopping.com	Online shopping	www.shopping.com
OpusForum.org	Classified advertising	Absorbed by eBay
Skype	Voice over Internet protocol	www.skype.com
Meetup.com	Social network service	www.meetup.com
Tradera	Online auction	www.tradera.com
StubHub	Electronic commerce	www.stubhub.com
GittiGidiyor	Electronic commerce	www.gittigidiyor.com
StumbleUpon	Browser plugin	www.stumbleupon.com
Bill Me Later	Electronic commerce	www.billmelater.com
dba.dk & bilbasen.dk	Classified advertising	www.bilbasen.dk

Looking for a new apartment? Rent.com (**www.rent.com**) is your answer. This site can even help match you with potential roommates and moving services. Half.com (**www.half.com**) boasts one of the largest fixed-price purchasing sites on the Internet. Though these two sites are "eBay" sites, they started out as eBay's competition — capitalizing on the amazing advances in online selling and servicing pioneered by their future parent company.

Using a strategy common to many large corporations, eBay has acquired other companies that provide services that are complementary to their own. This has given eBay an extremely broad range of appeal for sellers, buyers, and investors alike. In addition to owning all or a stake in many foreign auction sites, eBay acquired PayPal™ in 2002 to help facilitate auction payments. The software is so seamlessly integrated with eBay that it is almost silly to use anything else.

Another company eBay has acquired and put to work servicing its own users is Kurant, a leading-edge company that specializes in software for e-commerce on small business Web sites. eBay used its products to create a new service for sellers that debuted in summer of 2005: ProStores. This extra-fee service allows sellers to set up an outside-of-eBay e-commerce Web site, complete with shopping cart and secure checkout through Pay-Pal. Time will tell if this takes off with sellers, but it is a great addition to their already-burgeoning lineup of products and services.

The second edition

The first edition of *eBay Income: How ANYONE of Any Age, Location, and/ or Background Can Build a Highly Profitable Online Business with eBay* was an award-winning success, and thousands of people used its wisdom and have created lucrative small eBay businesses and been wildly successful. E-commerce has changed vastly over the last six years, so this edition offers the most up-to-date information about eBay.

This edition starts you off with setting up your account and getting right into selling your first item. The rest of the book will give you the nuts and bolts to build your financially sound eBay business.

Many people may be shy about starting a new business during a recession, but there is no better time. People are more careful about how they are shopping and more than ever are looking for deals and discounts on items they might normally have paid retail for. eBay fills in this niche; people are still spending money, only more conservatively.

Chapter One

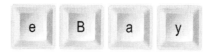

Think Before You Click

Planning Your Auctions

If you have not ever set up an auction, you will probably benefit from do-ing some pre-planning on paper. For example, follow the example of Willy and his neighbor, Suzy. Suzy has decided to start an eBay business and has written her business plan, set herself up as a sole proprietor, and obtained her reseller's license. She also registered with her state and local authori-ties, received permission from her local zoning board to run a business out of her home, and had Willy help her set up a basic recordkeeping system similar to his.

Suzy has decided she does not want to sell the same products over and over again like Willy does, so she has spent the past month attending every estate auction and garage sale she can to accumulate some inventory. She has some very nice items, some antiques, and many miscellaneous items that she got for next to nothing or in boxes of items for one low price. She feels that this will help her learn what the demand and resell value of many items are; as she learns which merchandise sells best or has the most demand, she can then start to specialize and search for only certain types of items to resell.

For her first auction, Suzy will sell a Wagner Ware waffle iron made in 1910. She obtained this item at an estate sale. She assigns it an inventory number, sits down to work out the details on paper, and signs into her eBay account to do some preliminary searches for other auctions of this item.

Note to the Reader

Unless noted specifically, such as in the case studies, you should assume the people and companies mentioned in this book are hypothetical and are included in order to help illustrate points and provide examples.

Determine your pricing strategy

One of the first details she wants to determine is what type of pricing strategy she should take with this item. She searches using the words "Wagner" and "waffle" to locate all waffle irons made by this same company. If it is an extremely rare specimen in perfect or like-new condition, she may find others in the current or completed listings that have sold for considerable amounts of money.

In that case, she may want to consider a starting-bid price that would be a reasonable amount for her to accept but still be a good deal for the bidder. Or she may wish to consider a reserve auction, where she sets a minimum price that is not disclosed to her bidders. If the reserve price is not met by the bidding, she is not required to sell the product.

However, Suzy has heard the reserve price feature actually turns away some bidders. Because this waffle iron is a bit rusty, the heat ring has a small piece missing from it, and there is some wood missing from the end of one of the handles, she does not believe it is a prime specimen of Wagner waffle irons.

By searching on eBay, Suzy has been able to determine that similar waffle irons with similar defects have sold for $6.50 to $20, depending on the year, how well one can see the details (the date made, patent number), and how rusty the item is. This also takes into consideration how many buyers are utilizing eBay during the listings; there may be many buyers wanting that item on any given day, or only a few.

She searched both active and completed listings. When she takes these factors into account and compares the prices for other similar items made by the same company in the same time frame, she aims for a closing bid of $9.99 or more.

TIP

To search completed listings, go to Advanced Search (the link under the search box that is at the top right of every eBay page) and click the box that reads "Search completed listings only." The results will show you all completed auctions in the past 15 days matching your search criteria.

Even though Suzy was very excited when she got this waffle iron at the estate sale for $2, she realizes now that while it seemed to be a valuable item to her at that moment, there are actually a fair number of these items available. This drove down the prices as supply has met the demand. This is all part of the learning curve for Suzy, and she takes it in stride. Next time she sees an antique waffle iron, she will have some idea of their value and rarity and only buy one in mint condition if the price is right. Or, she may turn this product into one of her specialties, continue to buy them in average condition, and be content to make a few dollars in net profit on each. But because she has just this one waffle iron, she will use this auction to feel out the market and learn a little bit.

Now that Suzy has determined what the approximate value is, she begins to think about how to price her item. There are numerous options and even different twists on ways to save a few pennies on a fee: By using a starting bid of $0.99 rather than $1, you will save $0.10 in listing fees.

One fee-saving strategy that you might see used by other sellers can lead to serious trouble with eBay. Read this PowerSeller's story of an innocent mistake that could have been disastrous:

CASE STUDY: EBAY VIOLATION

Brooke

Brooke in Virginia (eBay user "bbaysellers") recently owned a very hot item: a children's Old Navy monkey costume for Halloween. These are no longer available at Old Navy stores, and they were very much in demand one autumn. Brooke did a search to see how many of these were available and what their pricing and other options were. She found one seller who sold the identical costume for just $5. She could not believe it, so she read the listing and discovered that while the seller did indeed sell the *item* for only $5, she was also charged $35 for shipping it within the United States.

Brooke was aghast, or maybe intrigued. She knew that the costume should bring in about $40, but was surprised at the method this seller used to get that amount. She noted (from looking at the counter) that the low Buy It Now price had indeed attracted many lookers to the auction, but only one had been willing to pay that shipping fee. But because *getting a buyer* is the whole point, she thought maybe she would try the pricing strategy this one time.

She discussed it with her husband, Kurt, who did not think the other seller's method was very good business practice. To him, it seemed like trickery to advertise such a low price, when indeed the price technically was much higher. Brooke decided to list the costume anyway, just to see what happened, and did so for a Buy It Now price of $2.99. She was very clear in the auction listing that the shipping would be $35, so there would be no confusion or risk of a non-paying bidder to deal with.

She had plenty of lookers, but that was not all. Within days, she had received two rather unpleasant e-mails from potential buyers, blasting her methods. One person even noted that "eBay wouldn't be happy with what you're doing" but did not elaborate further.

Fearing any more negative e-mails and criticism, Brooke decided to revise the auction, raise the asking price, and lower the shipping to reflect the actual postage, plus her standard $1.50 handling fee.

Unbelievably, when she went to make the change, she found the auction had indeed sold — and had already been paid for as well. There was nothing to do but to complete the transaction and ship the item.

Shortly after this, she learned what one of her angry e-mailers had been hinting at: **fee circumvention**.

What Brooke did not know when she posted her listing is that it is against eBay's policy to price your item extremely low (such as the desirable costume for $2.99) and then charge an exorbitant amount of shipping (such as the $35 Brooke was charging). Even if the item is worth every penny of the $37.99 total paid, that is not the point.

The point is that Brooke's final value fee (the commission she paid to eBay based on the amount of the winning bid) amounted to only $0.16 because it is based on the winning bid amount (5.25 percent of the $2.99). Yet Brooke collected $37.99 for the item. If she had priced the auction competitively, she may have had a final bid of $35, and her final value fee would have been $1.59.

It strictly prohibited by eBay's policies to utilize this type of pricing strategy, for obvious reason: it robs eBay of fees that are rightly theirs. Most people have seen auctions like this; even Brooke had seen the one that gave her the idea to do an auction that way.

But despite years as an eBay seller, she had never heard of fee circumvention. Being an honest person, it would never occur to her to try something like this for *that* reason. She thought of it more as a slick marketing technique: a way to entice lookers into checking out *her* auction as opposed to someone else's.

Once she learned her auction had been a violation of eBay policy, she was quick to swear off that method of pricing. Not only does it cheat eBay of their well-earned fees, but also she feels that it does not lend itself well to her focus on good customer service. If you receive nasty e-mails from lookers, you are probably doing something wrong.

She learned her lesson and was grateful the e-mailer did not notify eBay of her violation. It was an honest mistake on her part, but the embarrassment of having eBay yank her listing or suspend her account could have been a costly blot on her otherwise clean and polished sales record.

Approved pricing strategies

Luckily, even though Suzy is new to selling on eBay, she has the benefit of knowing about this policy, and she will be careful to always price her items properly. She now turns her thoughts to some of the acceptable pricing strategies she might choose in conjunction with a reasonable shipping fee policy. She might choose to:

- Start the auction at $0.01, as this can spark mere curiosity on the part of lookers and qualifies her for the cheapest listing fee of $0.25.

- Start the bidding at $0.99, as that, too, seems to attract buyers and lookers who think, "Gee, maybe I can get that item for less than a buck." This starting price also qualifies for the $0.25 listing fee.

- Start the auction for a minimum price she feels she needs to cover her outlay, which includes her $2 acquisition fee, the listing fees, Final Value Fees, and PayPal fees that she may encounter. A starting bid of $3.99 would let her break even, even if the bids do not go higher.

- Try a Buy It Now in addition to a minimum starting bid. She might offer a Buy It Now for $9.99 or more, as her research indicates that sometimes these items do go for up to $20. Someone who wants it now may be willing to pay a bit more than the bidder who is not as earnest.

- Consider a reserve auction, but because Suzy has already determined there is nothing spectacular or rare about this waffle iron, she is not going to choose that option this time.

When you are a new seller, you cannot offer Buy It Now until you have a feedback score of 10 or greater, or unless you are ID Verified. *See Chapter 8, Section "Moving from a Looker or Buyer to a Seller," on becoming ID Verified.*

When deciding on a pricing strategy for your auctions, you will find there are as many ways to price an item as there are people with different opinions. Sellers who have a gambling spirit might start all their auctions with an opening bid of $0.01 to $0.99. Some believe this is the only way to go. They swear by it, and even if they do occasionally have to lose money on an item by selling for $0.99 or less, it is more than balanced out by the auctions that do earn them a tidy profit. Some PowerSellers of the highest echelon utilize this strategy.

On the opposite end of the spectrum are the sellers who are aghast at the thought of losing money on an auction or only breaking even. They absolutely will not sell any item unless they can get a comfortable profit from it, and preferably the maximum profit. They will not spend an extra penny on their listing that is not completely necessary (no frills here), and they set their minimum prices to give them a reasonable profit so they are assured of at least that amount. They do not feel the need to pique a looker's interest. Their attitude is: If the looker wants it for this price, fine; if not, fine.

Though this may be something we would all love — to get the maximum profit for every single item — it is not very realistic when you are talking about auctions. Items in your eBay Store are fixed-price and have a 30-day listing period for a small fee. Those are the items you can aim to get maximum profit from, but an auction format is geared toward the highest bid at the time your auction is running. The sellers who do not understand this can become bitter and give up on their business if they find they are constantly re-listing items because they do not sell. *Learn more information on re-listing in Chapter 9.*

Somewhere in the middle are the sellers who try a combination of all acceptable tactics. They may have some items they feel they can afford to just break even on, or maybe even lose a small amount on, because that gives them the opportunity to cross-promote their other items or their eBay Store. For that exposure, they are willing to risk doing the penny auctions on certain items, and they consider it almost as an advertising cost. If they make money, great; if not, that is fine, too.

However, there are some items they simply cannot afford to lose money on, so they employ minimum starting bids that will allow them to break even if the price does not go higher than that. They can add a Buy It Now for maximum profit, but this gives lookers the chance to try to get the item at rock-bottom pricing.

And for the items that they do not want to settle for breaking even on, they can either set a higher minimum starting bid (or a reserve price, if appropriate) or do a fixed-price auction (no negotiations or bidding). If they have a store, they could also choose to add it to their store inventory utilizing Buy It Now only.

There are a couple of other details to consider when planning a pricing strategy:

- You can always revise your listing to lower or raise your price if you feel that you are not attracting enough lookers. You must do so before at least 12 hours before the listing is set to end, and there must not be any bids on it yet. Potential buyers who have your item on their watch list may be enticed to take the next step when they see a price reduction.

- You can opt to have a link on your listing that reads "Submit a Best Offer." If a buyer wants to purchase the item outright, they can make their best offer instead of waiting for the bidding to get that high. Sellers can accept or decline any offers. Be sure to read about this topic (by searching that term on eBay's Help pages) before offering this option.

- If you see there are plenty of items identical, or similar, to yours available for auction, you can hold off on your particular item (as long as it is not seasonally in demand) and consider listing it again in a week or two. Perhaps there will not be as much competition at that time.

- If you have several items that go together, such as a group of collectible figurines, consider selling together for one price (this is called a "lot"), rather than trying to sell them individually. This will save on listing fees and, for the buyer, save on shipping as opposed to paying several shipping charges.

- Joining some of eBay's discussion boards is a good way to learn about different pricing philosophies and strategies from those who have been doing this a while. You may get some good ideas, or learn what truly does not work for certain merchandise types.

Buy It Now feature

The Buy It Now (BIN) feature also is looked at differently by various sellers. Some believe that if you list a BIN price, you are stating the maximum value of the item, which can translate into bidders not going above that point. Others feel that it is an excellent tool for speeding up transactions for those who do not want to bid it out and are willing to pay the asked price. And because that option disappears once the first bid is made, future bidders may not even know what the BIN price had been.

Fixed-price auctions are basically a BIN without the bidding, so the stated price is the only price the buyer must accept. This gives some sellers a better sense of security over their listings. Some buyers like this option, for the same reasons they like the BIN. All listings in your eBay Store inventory are fixed-price listings, but many people do not realize this because your current auctions are also displayed in your store.

Buyers may or may not warm up to a fixed-price auction, as that goes against their desire to "get a good deal" by shopping on eBay. Remember, they pay shipping and handling as well, so if they can get it for the same price locally, they might. Always keep in mind what even the largest retailers in the nation advertise: lowest prices.

Dutch auctions

Dutch auctions are probably not something the new eBay seller is going to jump into right away unless he or she is purchasing bulk wholesale lots for resale. When you sell items at a Dutch auction, every single bidder ultimately pays the same price: the amount of the lowest bid. Yes, the lowest bid.

For example, Willy decides to list ten of his gidgets at a Dutch auction. When someone places a bid, they specify how many of those ten gidgets they want to purchase, and a price they are willing to pay for each.

At the end of the auction, here are the bids that have come in:

Bidder number	Quantity desired	Price willing to pay for each
1	1	$1.99
2	1	$5.99
3	2	$6.24
4	1	$6.59
5	3	$6.99
6	1	$7.49
7	2	$7.99
8	1	$8.24
9	1	$8.55
10	4	$9.01
11	1	$9.40
12	3	$9.89
13	1	$10.09
14	3	$10.50
15	1	$10.99

By the end of the auction, Willy has 15 bidders wanting 26 gidgets. However, the auction was for only ten of them. So here is how it is decided who gets them and who does not. The highest bidders get them, of course. Bidder No. 15 will get quantity of 1. No. 14 will get 3 of them. No. 13 will get 1, No. 12 will get 3, and No. 11 will get 1. That leaves bidder No. 10. He wanted four, but there is only one left. So he gets only one, or he can choose to pass on the offer, and then the last one would be offered to bidder No. 9.

And the price they will all pay is $9.01 each: the same as the lowest bidder who will get a gidget. If bidder No. 10 passes on the offer to purchase only 1, then bidder No. 9 will be offered the final one for his bid price of $8.55.

Like with other auction styles, opinions vary on the effectiveness of Dutch auctions. Some believe that by having a Dutch auction, the seller is admitting to having an overstock of the item, and that can drive down the price. Or it may appear there is a large market for the item, as so many people are bidding on it. This may invite competition in its own way.

If you are considering a Dutch auction because you will be able to list it with just one listing fee, think again. The fee for these auctions is based on the quantity you fill in during the listing process and your opening bid price (the same way an ordinary auction would be charged), so doing a Dutch auction is not a big money saver.

There are other rules involved in Dutch auctions you need to be aware of. For one, proxy bidding is not allowed, and you can only place your auction in one category. If you have a large enough quantity, you can split into two groups and place each group in a separate category for more exposure. Dutch auctions can be good for the right seller with the right merchandise, but do some investigating and research before considering them to market your product.

Generally, no pricing strategy is always right every time, and there is always a risk that your auction will not sell. In fact, statistics show that only approximately 41 percent of auctions sell the first time around. Your best strategy is a combination of knowing the appropriate asking price, knowing when to take a bit of a gamble, and knowing how best to utilize all the options and tools available to you on eBay.

If the waffle iron that Suzy is now preparing to sell had been in her family for three generations; she may have had an emotional attachment to it that, in her own opinion, elevated its worth. It is very important you do not overestimate the true value of the items you sell, especially if they originated as your own possessions.

Bargain hunters

The reality is that people come to eBay, among other reasons, for bargains. If they can spend a few dollars more and get a brand-new equivalent of what you are selling by driving to their nearest mall, they might very well do that. Just because you paid $50 for an new item does not mean that you will get anywhere near $50 for it used (even if it is in like-new condition).

What you get at auction is based on the amount that the *current* lookers are willing to pay. You never know if the current lookers will be experienced buyers who are willing to wait it out for a better deal, or new eBay members who may overpay during the thrill of the auction. You may get lucky and, while your auction is running, someone who desperately wants just what you have will go hog-wild bidding on it.

Or, the auction gods may not smile on you, and your item will go unsold despite your attractive starting price and other good auction qualities. While that can be one frustrating thing about selling on eBay, it also is one of the most thrilling things: you never know just how much money you *might* make.

This brings up something sellers may not understand unless they also have some buying experience on eBay: how bidders bid. Suzy may watch her auction like a hawk the first few days, checking it frequently to see how many times her auction has been viewed (we have all done it, even if we do not want to admit it sometimes), and agonizing over the fees she will have to pay even if her waffle iron does not sell.

If Suzy has done any bidding herself, she may recall that when buyers search on eBay, the listings that are ending first are the ones that are shown first by default. Lookers can change the order to show items newly listed, items with the current lowest or highest prices, or other options. However, that choice cannot be made until after the default view pops up. Thus, she may not get a lot of searchers or bids on her listing until the final days or hours.

Searchers also include their interests on their "Items I'm Watching" list and wait until the last minutes to place a bid, hoping to be the first or only bidder to nab the item at the opening bid price. But anyone who has been outbid in the final seconds knows that is not a surefire technique for winning the item. Many buyers have been bested by other unseen lookers who had the exact same thing in mind.

Bidders can place bids on items hours or days before the auction ends through eBay's proxy bidding system. When they place an initial bid, they must do so at the current price (if they are the first bidder) or raise the current bid by a small amount. They also enter an amount that will be kept secret from the seller and other bidders: what their maximum bid amount is.

When the next looker comes along and thinks, "I'd be willing to pay a dollar more than that guy bid…" and puts in his bid, he may be outbid instantly by the proxy bid that had been previously set by the previous bidder. The computer will keep raising the bid up to the previous bidder's maximum.

Once any bidder has been outbid, he must enter a larger maximum bid, watch the auction himself, and try to sneak in a bid at the end — or give up.

How Bidders Think

It can be a dizzying spectacle to keep track of who is winning and who is losing when the bidding gets fierce; it is a seller's dream to have an auction that ends in a bidding war. The bidder who has just been bested keeps upping her bid amount a little bit more and more, thinking she will get the final bid in. Sometimes it works out in her favor, sometimes in the other seller's favor. And sometimes there are multiple sellers upping the bid, entering higher bids and proxy amounts, furiously hoping to be the highest bidder when the seconds tick down.

Bidding in the final seconds to win the auction is known as "sniping." Although it may seem unfair to the bidder who missed a great deal in the final ten seconds, it is completely allowed in eBay's rules. Many a seller has been pleasantly surprised to see an auction's final bid go up higher than they were anticipating because of sniping.

If you are really interested in getting the best deal but do not want to stay up all night trying to snipe, there are online sniping services available. You may be able to get a free trial, but after that time frame, you will have to determine if the fees will be worth the deals you will get.

Many people have studied another aspect of bidding: *when* bidders bid. eBay has done a lot of research to determine the buying patterns of the public and thus could be translated into the best time to start (and end) your listings. If you can time your auctions to end at the same time as a lot of buyers are online, then you may have an advantage over the seller whose listing is ending at 3 a.m. on a slow day of the week.

According to eBay's "Seller Central Report: How Buyers Use eBay" (located at **http://pages.eBay.com/sellercentral/buyers.pdf**), "just over one-third of all Internet users in the United States visit eBay each month." The majority of visitors to eBay surf during the weekdays, while Sundays and Mondays are the traffic-jam days.

When to start the auction

You might also want to consider other factors, such as time zones across the country, people who work second or third shift, or parents of small children who may not be able to access eBay except at naptimes and after the kids are in bed for the night.

One thought about listing ending times: Try not to compete with major events, such as the President's State of the Union speech or the Super Bowl. They may or may not play a part in how many people are online, but if you can avoid them, you might as well.

When she sets her auction, Suzy will be given a choice to schedule the listing to start at a specific time. If she were putting her listing on at 1:44 a.m., she knows that her listing will end at 1:44 a.m. as well. That might not entice the bidders who like to snipe, so in that case, she could have scheduled the listing to start the next evening, for an additional fee. When she downloads and uses Turbo Lister, Suzy can plan out her auction completely and then simply not upload it until a better time of day.

Duration of the auction

Once Suzy has decided when to start her auction (based on when she wishes to have it end), she also needs to consider how long to run the auction. She can choose to do a one-, three-, five-, seven- or ten-day listing. There is no difference in the fees for any of these listings (except for an additional $0.40 fee for a ten-day listing), so the choice between a five-day and seven-day listing is purely for strategy.

One thing that may help Suzy decide on duration is this: She has noticed someone has already posted a seven-day listing of a nearly identical waffle iron. She also sees that this competitor has a starting price of $12.99 and a Buy It Now of $24.99. Sally feels that, based on her research, this seller is expecting too much, and is not surprised that after two days, the listing has only been viewed twice (yes, she peeked at her competitor's counter).

If Suzy chooses to run a five-day listing starting immediately, her item will be ending at approximately the same time as the competitor's item. At the very least, when lookers search, both of their listings will come up in very close proximity to each other.

So Suzy decides, based purely on strategy, to do a five-day listing this time. And because it is currently a Wednesday, she will not miss any of the weekend viewing, as the auction will run until Monday evening.

Sometimes it may not be a good idea to time your auctions to end close to your competitor's listings. If you are a new seller, bidders might be wary of buying from you when they could just as easily buy from someone with experience. There are many unknowns about new sellers, and bidders may be worried that you will not provide timely shipping or have any customer service skills.

Entice a hesitant bidder with a better deal on shipping by comparing your competitor's costs and yours. If you can offer cheaper shipping with no handling fee, you may be able to beat out your competitor on overall price. If your shipping is cheaper than others, try to work that into your title (such as "Low Ship," "Free Ship," or "Cheap Ship"). Comparing shipping rates is one way bidders save money.

Other reasons for choosing the listing durations might be:

- If you have 15 identical items to sell, you might not want them all ending at the same exact time because bidders will soon clue in that if they did not win the first one for the minimum bid, they can wait five minutes for the second one and try again. To avoid this, you might list one or two at a time, a day or more apart.

- Or, if you want to list them all at once, then you would do several three-, five- and seven-day listings. In this case, notify the non-winning bidders in the first auctions that there are others available so they can bid on the next group.

- Just before a holiday, you might want to offer shorter auction times with speedy shipping (even if you have to take special trips to the post office twice a day). Buyers will appreciate your efforts during rush times.

- A one-day listing also might be necessary for items that are tied to an upcoming event, like tickets or during a special one-day-only sale on special items.

- A three-day listing that starts on a Friday evening will run all the way through Monday evening. Because the prime time is commonly believed to be during this time frame, you might want to consider a three-day listing.

- If your item is steadily a good seller (you know this from research), then five days might be enough time to attract the attention it needs. Remember, these auctions will get to the top of the list (when listings ending first are shown by default in search results) — two whole days faster than the same items on a seven-day listing.

- However, because you cannot control who is online at any given time or day, you will get the most exposure out of a seven-day listing. It might be considered the most bang-for-your-buck duration, but the drawback is that it takes six and a half days (or longer) to reach that all-important first page of search results.

- Ten-day listings have their place, too. If you want to start an auction on a Thursday and want it to be active through two complete weekends, then you can do that with the ten-day listing. The downside of this is that for the extra $0.40 you will spend, you could have done a seven-day listing and (if it did not sell in seven days) re-listed it immediately for 14-day exposure. If it sold the second time around, you will even get some credit of the second listing fee from eBay.

After Suzy has worked out her pricing strategy and decided on her five-day auction, she begins to hammer out a title and a description for her waffle iron. After numerous auctions, she may find that titles and descriptions come easier to her. She will find what works and what does not, and she will develop a flow in the way she words her auctions. She will begin to write auctions in a similar tone of voice, just as if she were giving the same sales pitch over and over again. While the product might change from auction to auction, she will utilize the same techniques or pattern and flow repeatedly.

Writing an Effective Title

Writing an effective title has become its own art form. The following are some tips to think about while you contemplate every one of your 55 available characters (including spaces and punctuation).

The point of the title is not just to entice the looker to click on your auction and view the description. The title is how buyers (for the most part) *find* your auction. The title points the search engine to your item through proper phrasing and use of keywords. While it is possible to search the title and the description for keywords and specific information, sellers often type their search criteria in the box and hit the "enter" key. In order to search the description as well, they have to move a hand over to the mouse and click on the box indicating they want to search title and description.

Not to imply that searchers are lazy, but the title should contain the words they are looking for, unless they are not searching properly. And many lookers are confident enough in eBay's search results that they do not go out of their way to search both title and description unless they are looking for a rare or unusual item.

So think of your title as the way *you* will locate the searchers and buyers. Think in terms of, "What words will they use to look for my item?" and act accordingly. The following are some tips about what to put in your titles:

- Use keywords, not full sentences. It does not have to be grammatically correct to be useful to the search engine. No one ever searched for "look at this cute sweater," but they will search for a "Ralph Lauren blue wool cardigan ladies size 8."

- Add the size, color, fabric/material used (tin, wood, resin), model number, and other important features.

- Specify if it is New or Used if you have room and it is not obvious by other items (such as acronyms).

- Use appropriate acronyms to save space, such as NIP (New In Package) and NWT (New With Tags), but consider typing these phrases out in the actual description.

- Your title must make it clear *what* your item is, and it cannot be misleading.

- Avoid gimmicks and catch phrases such as "L@@K," "Must See," and words that are subjective: "very pretty," "cute," "desirable," and "awesome."

- Just as in chat rooms or message boards, using ALL CAPS is considered screaming. Choose just *one* word you can scream, perhaps, and leave it at that.

- Go easy on terms that can seem fad-like, such as "Vintage," "Rare," or "Hard to Find," unless you have enough experience with the item type to say that definitively.

- Avoid punctuation in titles, as it can sometimes confuse the search engine (even if you have a few characters to spare, leave it blank, as too much punctuation can be..**annoying**..).

- No Web addresses, phone numbers, e-mail addresses, or personal information are allowed in titles.

- Do not use words that suggest an item is contraband, even if it is not (for example, "banned" or "illegal").

The entire 55 characters may make or break an auction (whether or not lookers can find it), and that added pressure can make new sellers anxious to create the perfect title. Suzy paid close attention to the titles in the current and completed auctions she searched when determining her pricing strategy. She found numerous words that were very common, such as Wagner or Wagner Ware, the name of the company that made this waffle iron. She decides that her title will also feature the company's name, to distinguish her waffle iron from those made by another common company at that time, Griswold.

Because the item more than qualifies for "antique" status (it is clearly marked with the patent date 1910), she will likely use that word as well as the year marked on the item, although some might call that redundant. Some of the waffle irons she saw did not come with the heat ring, which keeps the iron from sitting directly on the stove. Hers has that feature, so she may mention that.

Another phrase she saw in many of the auctions she looked at was "cast iron." Her own personal experience tells her this is cast iron, too, so she adds that to her list of possible words to go in the title. It has other markings such as the word "Sidney," "-0-," and "9." While she does not know the significance of these things, she may use them if she has space.

Suzy works out a few possibilities for her waffle iron; she will make the final decision when she is posting the auction online. Her possibilities:

- Antique Wagner Ware cast iron waffle maker 1910 NR
- 1910 Wagner Ware stove top waffle iron heat ring Sidney

 *Warning:* eBay has a very strong policy against keyword spamming, which is using keywords in your title or item description that do not specifically relate to your item. Read eBay's policy on this at **http://pages.eBay.com/help/policies/ search-manipulation.html.**

Writing a strong description

With a couple of titles in hand, Suzy now turns her attention to drafting a description.

Writing good descriptions is also important; just because you got the looker to click on your listing and read (at least some of) your description does not mean you will make the sale. Your own writing talent, attention to detail, and enthusiasm for your product all need to be utilized in order to sell an item. You may only get a searcher to read your description once before he or she decides whether he or she will become a watcher or bidder, or move on to the next search result.

The following are some suggestions to consider when writing your description. Much more help and information can be found in the Seller Central section of eBay, so do not hesitate to look there for good tips, too.

A nice descriptive tone is good for some items, but others will be better served by a bulleted list of features. You might want to consider what type of person will likely buy your item. If you are selling office supplies, you may be dealing with busy secretaries and businesspeople who do not have time to read a long, rambling tale of how you want to sell these items to them.

Write a simple and clear description of the item, adding sufficient detail for the bidder to have a full understanding, but not overloading the bidder with needless information or details. This can be a tough balance to find. Though you should always offer to answer questions about the item (or furnish additional photos), some buyers will not bother to take that extra step, or perhaps there is not time to do so (at the end of the auction), so make sure you are sufficiently thorough.

Keep your opinions objective; otherwise, it might seem as if you are guaranteeing that the buyer will be just as thrilled with the item as you are (and if they are not, you may have an unhappy buyer).

Be sure to check your spelling; the buyer will think you are not knowledge-able about your product if you spell the manufacturer's name wrong. Use spell check in eBay when you fill out your description online.

Include all relevant details: size, color, materials, year made, manufacturer/brand name, and condition. If an item is used, realize that what you might call "good" used condition will be called "fair" by another person. Rather than give it a personal rating, describe the qualities that make it "good" (no rips, tears, worn spots, or fading).

TIP   Search eBay's Help files for information about grading and authentication services. If you are new to selling any type of collectible, get help determining the difference between "mint condition" and "excellent condition" before you put it up for auction.

Provide suggestions for your potential buyer

Suggest new uses for your item, or point out cross-sell items that are part of a matching set. Suggest they buy a second of the same item (if you have additional quantities for auction) to give to a friend or to keep as a spare. Word your description as if you were selling the item face-to-face. If you are selling curtains, indicate how nicely they drape and that they will look stunning in the buyer's living room or den. Do not lie, but word things so the buyer takes that leap from looking at your item to imagining them-selves owning and using it.

End your listing description with a motivator, like "Place a bid today," as well as a "Thank you for looking" message and a brief statement about combined shipping (if you offer it, which you would be almost foolish not to offer), such as "Happy to combine shipping on all auctions won within a five-day period." Maybe top it off with one more invitation to check out your other items (because you just pitched your combined shipping offer).

And, finally, back up all claims about faults and condition with plenty of photos taken by you (not stock photos from the manufacturer, unless your items are new in the factory-sealed packaging).

After reading the other descriptions of waffle irons, Suzy feels she wants to be brief and to the point. There is no sense in trying to make this waffle iron out to be some rare treasure, as anyone who searches will know better, and she does not want to sound like she is clueless. But she thinks she has an angle that might lure in just the right buyer. Here is her rough draft:

Take a look at this 1910 model Wagner Ware waffle iron. This item has served many a family in the past century and shows wear and tear that would be expected. The heat ring has a chip in it, and the wood handles have no cracks but are missing a small piece at the end. See photos for close-ups of these noted items.

Wagner Ware waffle irons were made of heavy-cast iron for years of faithful use. This one has rusted somewhat after years of non-use after it was likely replaced by an electric model.

The fine details of early 20th-century cast iron pieces can be seen in the name and other markings on the top and bottom. Even the patent date is easily read.

With a good cleaning and some preservation, it will make a nice display piece in your country kitchen.

Bring this lovely piece into your home and give it the place of honor it deserves, just like all the hard-working cooks and parents who used it to feed their families in generations past.

Suzy may decide to change a word here or there, but she is satisfied with the approach that she took: appealing to the searchers' appreciation of old items and their sense of nostalgia. Notice how she invited the searcher to imagine the item displayed in his or her kitchen (giving a use for the old, rusted item), and how she tied the display to a sense of honoring family values.

There is no guarantee Suzy's description will make her waffle iron sell, because lookers are a fickle lot. They could enjoy her description but bid on a similar item with a smaller price instead, and still envision the same end result with a different item. But hopefully Suzy's description will entice them enough to hook them into bidding.

Policies

In addition to writing your title and description, you should decide what policies you will put in your auction listings every time. These can include your shipping policy, your return policy, or a listing of what payment types you accept.

Because these policies will likely be the same for every auction she posts, Suzy is going to type them up in a word processing document. She can use Microsoft Word, and later she will save them in a template in Turbo Lister. After the documents are in Turbo Lister, Suzy can copy and paste the text into her auctions without having to re-type it.

But first she has to spend some time reviewing all the items she may want to cover in her policies and decide what she will require of, and guarantee to, her customers.

The two most important policies for bidders to know up-front are your payment policy and your shipping policy, although all should be clearly laid out in every auction.

Payment policy

Your payment policy simply states what payment types you accept. Remember that if you have the PayPal logo in your listing and you state that you accept PayPal, then you cannot also state that you cannot accept debit and credit card payments through PayPal. *See Chapter 6 for more on payment policies.*

List what payments you will accept and any conditions that go along with any payment type (such as "personal check accepted but merchandise held for ten days while check clears" or "cash at your own risk"). If you receive payments via PayPal, eBay will automatically direct the buyer to your PayPal user ID, but some sellers still state it in the payment policy.

Also make sure you specify the time frame in which you expect payment to be received, and any consequences for not following the policy: "Payment expected within ten days of auction closing, or buyer will be reported and negative feedback will be given to buyer" is one example. Some buyers take exception to the implied threat, so you may want to craft a warmer way to say the same thing.

Shipping policy

Your shipping policy will generally be the same for all auctions and sales. You might revise this as time passes, and you learn how to balance serving your customers without overloading yourself. You might start out saying, "I ship the same day as your payment — five days a week." You will soon find that even if the PayPal payment comes in at 4 p.m., your buyers may expect you to still ship that same day. And even if they are paying for Media Mail, they might expect the same speediness as if they were paying Express.

Over time, you will know what you are capable of. Your Priority Mail☐ shipping policy might state, "If your PayPal payment for Priority Mail arrives by 9 a.m. (Central Time Zone M-F), your item will ship the same day. After 9 a.m., it ships the next business day. For Parcel Post®, Media Mail, and First-Class Mail, UPS or FedEx, shipping will be within two business days."

Combined shipping policy

Your shipping policy should also touch on your combined shipping policy. If you are willing to combine shipping costs and mail multiple auctions in one package, say so up-front and give a timeline ("all auctions won in a three-day period") and any other restrictions "Items must be paid for at one time to qualify for the discount"). *More about combined shipping will be discussed in Chapter 9.*

Most buyers are happy with their item being shipped in any reasonable time frame, so long as they know *when* it is going to be shipped. Consider sending a follow-up e-mail to your customer the same day the item ships to let them know that it is on its way. Give some thought to making a policy on optional services, such as Delivery Confirmation and insurance. Some sellers have made these items a requirement because they have lost money on packages that never arrived (or they could never prove they arrived) or that arrived damaged and the buyer demanded a refund. *There are differing opinions about how to handle a situation like this; learn more in Chapter 9.*

Policy on optional services

Your policy should be clearly stated as to what you require and what services are optional. Delivery Confirmation is not expensive and — as will be explained in Chapter 6 — when you purchase Priority Mail postage online, Delivery Confirmation is automatically included on all packages, regardless of their class. There is no additional cost for Priority packages, but there is a $0.13 charge for other mail classes.

Because of the free Delivery Confirmation (and the fact the buyers get Priority shipping supplies for free), some sellers have chosen to *only* ship via Priority Mail. However, do not limit yourself to one shipping provider or one class of shipping. Customers appreciate flexibility and cheaper shipping options if they are not in a hurry.

Merchandise return policy

You will also need to develop a merchandise-return policy. Whether you accept returns is entirely up to you. Return policies come in all shapes and sizes, from the extreme "All merchandise is as-is, no returns, no exceptions" to the less demanding "Returns only accepted if I made a gross error in listing the item or misrepresented it in some way." Some merchants (especially those who list brand-new items) state they will "accept returns only if the item is returned in the same condition as when shipped," unless it was damaged in transit.

A seller does not want buyers who return an item just because they have changed their minds or are not as thrilled with it as they thought. Impulse shoppers often have these second thoughts and can actually dislike an item they bought impetuously, even though it is exactly what they wanted at that moment.

Shipping fees are generally one item sellers do not refund. Make sure you specify the conditions under which you will accept a return, such as:

1. Buyer pays to ship it back to the seller.
2. Buyer must return it via the same shipping service and class of shipment as sent.
3. Item must be in an acceptable shipping container with appropriate protection (preferably the same box and packing material that you used).
4. The refund amount will be less any shipping and handling originally paid.

Sometimes having a policy like this will deter the buyer who wants to return an item for the wrong reasons.

International and local pickup shipping policies

International buyers will want to know right away if you have a policy about international shipping. Be sure to state your willingness (or not) to deal with international bidders after examining all the issues and particulars. *More information about international shipping is covered in Chapter9.*

You may also need to specify a policy on local pickups. If your buyer lives within reasonable driving distance, he or she may want to pick up the item rather than have it shipped. The choice is up to you, but it is nice to state up-front if this is an acceptable option to you. If you work from home, you may consider this a security risk, in which case you may choose to drop the item off or meet in a public location.

Make sure you specify if the item must be paid in full prior to the pickup (or meeting), or if it can be paid for at the time of the pickup/meeting. Expecting payment prior to arranging a date will assure you that the buyer will not try to pay with an unacceptable payment type (such as a personal check) at the last moment.

Another possible speed bump with local pickup is the lack of any Delivery Confirmation. If you frequently have local pickups, make a generic "Pick-Up Receipt" in your word processing software with spaces to fill in all the pertinent information: auction date, title, item description, date paid and payment type, and other pick-up information. Then, have the buyer sign and date the receipt for your records, verifying he or she did receive the package.

A word of caution: Present a clear picture to your buyers of all the aspects of the transaction so they can make an informed decision on whether to do business with you. Some sellers who have had bad experiences or been burned in the past use their list of policies to express their anger and frustration.

There is a fine line between laying out all your terms in full and appearing to be a cold-hearted seller with no customer-service skills. The difference is in your wording. Keep your policies brief and polite, and let the customer know you care about his experience and satisfaction as well.

After researching these topics in eBay's Help pages, Suzy has developed an initial policy statement that she is comfortable with. She decides to insert this statement after the item description (in case the searcher is not seriously interested, she does not have to be bothered with this information), in a font one size smaller than the item's description. This is so it does not appear that she is more interested in her policy than in the item she is selling.

I want every customer to be happy, and I have worded my descriptions and supplied photos with the intent that you will have a clear and full understanding of the item you're purchasing. If you'd like additional photos or details, feel free to contact me; I'm happy to help.

Please review these policies for conducting business together:

Payment: *I accept PayPal, money orders, or cashier's checks. Please pay within ten days, or communicate with me if there's a problem in doing so.*

Shipping: *I ship USPS (unless you have a special request) ASAP after payment is received — two business days or less. All shipping quotes include Delivery Confirmation. Insurance is at your option (unless otherwise noted in listing) but strongly suggested.*

Returns: *If you feel the item was significantly misrepresented by me (per eBay's policies), I will offer a return/refund, minus shipping costs (return shipping at your expense). Please contact me immediately if there is a concern, as I strive for 100 percent customer satisfaction.*

International bidders: *At this time, I am not offering international shipping, but thank you for looking.*

Local pickup: *If you live within 25 miles of my town, I will arrange to meet you halfway for a fee equal to half of the shipping cost. This fee must be paid, along with the item, prior to arranging a meeting (payment via mail or PayPal).*

One last thing Suzy needs before she begins the auction set up: take and prepare photos of the item.

Posting Photos on Your Auction

It is almost hard to overdo it when it comes to posting photos on your auction. They can pose downloading-time issues with Internet users who have a dial-up connection, but high-speed Internet access is becoming so common and affordable that this should not be a problem for many.

Photos are an integral part of every auction. Very few people will purchase an item without a photo displayed, and most people will not even look at an auction with no photo. There is simply no excuse for not having photos with today's technology.

If you are creative and have the software to do it, you can superimpose your company's name onto each of your photos. Not only does this put your company name into the mind of every searcher, but it will help prevent other sellers from using your photos as their own.

The quickest way to get photos of your items is by using a digital camera. The price of digital cameras has decreased significantly in the past few years; now, you can purchase a camera for less than $100. Digital cameras are fairly easy to use, and you can take as many shots as necessary to get just the right angle and lighting without wasting film, processing costs, or time.

Photo tips

- You should always have one straight-on shot of the entire item. Preferably, this would be the first photo the searcher sees when she clicks on your title. To be sure this is the case, use this photo for your "free" first photo from eBay, or as the first photo you place in Turbo Lister. *Learn more about photos in the next chapter.*

- Use a contrasting background for your item. If your item is dark in color, set it on a tabletop or couch that is covered with a white sheet.

- Set your camera on a fixed object, such as a stool or a tripod, at the same height as your item.

- To avoid light coming in from windows, try to lay your item on the floor, holding the camera directly above it.

- If your item gets a bright spot on it because of the flash, try turning the flash off and using other indirect lighting to diffuse the light.

- Get several different angles or close-ups of defects and special features, such as serial numbers.

- Do not get too close — the item may blur. Or, use the camera's built-in zoom, if it is available. Remember, you can always crop the photo and cut out everything but your item, which makes it appear closer.

- Reference the size of item by laying a yardstick, ruler, pencil, coin, or other common object next to it.

- A craft store can sell you a display stand used to hold a plate or photo frame at an angle. Drape a black cloth over a piece of wood in the stand and lay jewelry on the cloth. Drape the cloth over a piece of wood dowel (or a pen, even) to hold a ring for photographing.

You can purchase camera accessories to assist in getting the best lighting situations. Depending on what you sell (if you sell brand-new items and can utilize stock photos from your supplier, this is not an issue), you may want to put the following items on your business's "wish list:"

- **Cloud dome:** This is a white bowl or cone-shaped device that spreads out the light from your camera's flash, reducing the white spot on your item and evening out other light in the room. These are good for smaller items and close-ups.

- **Lighting tents:** These are nylon or other white fabric tents with an opening in the front for you to insert your item inside of it. You then take your photo through the front opening. Some kits come with fabric backdrops for contrasting colors.

- **Stands and other portable platforms that have a solid-colored background:** These give you a consistent background color for easier cropping.

- **Reflectors (like special umbrellas):** These are used to spread the light from your flash evenly around your object.

Much like other items that cost money up-front, having the nicest photo equipment right away is not a true necessity. Use your wish list to purchase items for your business that can be used as a tax deduction (thereby reducing your business's income). Your accountant will let you know when you have excess income that would be better used by making a needed purchase than paying taxes on it.

Hopefully you have a computer dedicated to your business, but if not, consider making a unique folder where you will store your eBay item photos. Pre-crop and rotate photos, as you can probably do this right in your photo editing software quicker than you can do it online (especially if you have dial-up Internet service). Consider renaming your photo to something easily identifiable, or better yet, give it the same name or number as the inventory number of the item it represents. If you are selling a book, you can often get a "stock photo" of the book right through eBay, but you also may want to take a photo of the actual book and include it in the listing, so people can see any damage, worn covers, dog-eared pages, or other details. Sometimes people are disappointed in books that are not as new-looking as the stock photo the seller used. Stock photos are nice to have in the photo preview, as they may be crisper and have better lighting conditions than your photo. However, make it clear that the preview photo is a stock photo.

If you have not yet located an online hosting site for your photos, there are many to choose from. Set up an account and upload your photos for your first batch of auctions. You can easily find these online hosting sites by searching the Internet for "image hosting" or "free image hosting" (there are some good free services to use). Registration is generally quick and simple. With the free services, you might have to tolerate banner ads, pop-ups, and other marketing, but to start with, at least try the free services if your business budget is tight. *Steps to inserting the photos into the auction will be covered in Chapter 2.*

Here is the overall photo of the entire item. This is the photo Suzy will submit for the preview picture that will appear on the search results page, and the photo that will be "free." Suzy will upload the other photos to her image hosting service online and later insert them into her listing information using HTML tags. This will save her fees because she will not use eBay's services to host them.

These photos are close-up views of both sides of the iron; one side obviously has more rust than the other. It is important for Suzy to show all defects, even rust that would be anticipated with an item like this.

These photos show the other defects that Suzy will note in her description: The chip out of the heat ring and the gouge out of the wood handle.

It is important for Suzy to also show the inside because of rust, and to show that all the other parts are intact.

Suzy's title, description, and photos are all ready to go; she has boxed up the waffle iron (but not taped the box, in case a bidder wants some other information), and weighed it so she can fill out the online postage calculator during the auction setup process. She has made decisions about duration and her pricing strategy. She has as many details written down or decided as she possibly can at this point. In the next chapter, Suzy will set up her first auction on eBay.

	Checklist of Tasks When Planning Auctions
✓	I have researched current and previous listings for comparison.
✓	I have chosen an appropriate pricing strategy: • *Auction without a Buy It Now* • *Fixed price (Buy It Now without an auction)* • *Auction with Buy It Now* • *Reserve-price auctions* And I understand the pros, cons, and right time to use each one.
✓	I understand eBay's policy against fee circumvention (low price, high shipping to avoid paying Final Value Fees) and agree not to use that technique.
✓	I have chosen a good time to start my auction, knowing I can schedule it to start at another time for an additional fee. Otherwise, it ends at the same time of day I posted it.
✓	I have chosen a duration for my listing, based on strategy or to get exposure: • *One-day listing* • *Three-day listing* • *Five-day listing* • *Seven-day listing* • *Ten-day listing (for additional fee)*
✓	I have written an effective title of 55 characters or fewer.
✓	I understand eBay's policy against keyword spamming in the title or description and agree not to use that technique.
✓	I have written a rough draft of a description, including information about any defects. I have checked my copy for spelling and grammatical errors.
✓	I have drafted a simple statement that covers my policy on these issues: • **Payments:** *what I accept and time frame* • **Shipping:** *how and when I generally ship* • **Optional services:** *whether I make options such as Delivery Confirmation and insurance optional* • **Returns:** *whether I will accept a return and under what conditions* • **International bidders:** *whether I am open to international bidders* • **Local pickups:** *if I will arrange a local pickup and under what conditions*

✓	I have a digital camera (and know how to use it) for taking photos of my items, or I have access to adequate stock photos (if selling new merchandise) from my supplier.
✓	I have my photos prepared for inserting in the auction listing: • *Downloaded from computer* • *Named them appropriately for ease of locating* • *Cropped away any unnecessary background and reduced the image size to a manageable level (400x600 pixels or 600x400 pixels or smaller is best)* • *Have several angles or close-ups ready and uploaded to my image hosting service* • *One photo designated to be the "preview" photo, which I will upload directly to eBay (free photo); note that if you use Turbo Lister, it is better to have them all uploaded*
✓	I have done these shipping tasks: • *Boxed up the item (but not taped in case bidders want more info)* • *Weighed it on an accurate scale (purchased digital postal scale is best) after packed* • *Added a couple of ounces to the weight, which I will use for the shipping calculator in my listings* • *Decided if I will add a "handling" fee to my listings, which covers my cost for shipping supplies (tape, packing peanuts, or other stuffing materials)*

Chapter Two

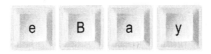

On Your Mark... Get Set... Auction

It is important to get your feet wet if you are a first-time eBay user. If you have already set up an account, you may wish to skip the beginning section in this chapter. However, you may want to read the section at the end of this chapter. Even if you have posted an item before, it is worth reading through the step-by-step instructions, as there may be areas that you were not aware of, and eBay's format changes time to time, so if it has been a while since you have posted an item, you may find some areas have changed.

Setting up an Account

Before Suzy logs on to sell an item, she must first register with eBay. The first step is to go to **www.ebay.com**. Once there, you will see toward the top left of the page an option to log on or to register. Click on the "Register" icon.

- Fill the personal information and select a user ID and password. At the bottom of the page, read the user agreement and privacy policy and then choose the box "I agree that..." Once you have completed all of the sections, click "continue."

- eBay will send verification to the e-mail account you entered on the form. Open your e-mail from eBay. Click on the link back to eBay.

- You will be led to a page in which you will need to enter your e-mail address again, along with the confirmation code that was contained in the e-mail that was sent to you.

- Once you reach the page, enter your e-mail address and the confirmation code that was part of the e-mail generated by eBay. That is it — you are confirmed and ready to begin selling.

Your First Auction

Suzy is ready to log into her eBay account. She will click the Sell button on her top toolbar for the very first time. It is an exciting moment, and it will be the start of what she hopes will be a long-term business for her.

Timing

In the world of eBay, timing is crucial. There are good times and bad times to sell, as well as good auction lengths and bad auction lengths. Ask any PowerSeller when the price goes up on an item, and she will tell you that this happens during the last half-hour of an auction.

Why people have auctions that are drawn out for weeks depends on the item. Hot items will have bids coming in during the entire duration, while items that are flooding the eBay market will sit quietly until the end.

If you have a hot item that is going fast, you can set your bidding for one day. People will bid fast and hard to get the item. The good thing is that if you are using just a one-day auction, your listing goes to the top of the results list. If you choose the one-day format, consider having your Buy It Now price at least 50 cents below your competition's, and consider making your starting bid a few dollars below your Buy It Now price.

If you are looking for a slightly longer auction, consider the three-day format. This works well with items that will shoot up in price quickly after posting. Three-day formats work well during the holidays for last-minute shoppers. If you see that a week-long auction is going well, consider putting up a three-day auction during the last few days with a similar item. Your buyers will jump over to the new item and immediately begin bidding on that one because the price will be lower.

The next duration is a five-day auction. These will work well during holiday rush time or if you want an extended weekend.

The seven-day auction allows more time for people to notice your auction. This gives people more time to find and bid on your item. These auctions work well for bulk sellers. This gives you at least one weekend, which is a good shopping time, but is not so long to the point where people are not interested anymore.

The ten-day auction costs an extra $0.40 for auction-type listings but is free for fixed-price auctions. This length of auction can give you two weekends if you time it right. Ten-day auctions are good for rare and expensive items.

The ending time is important for an auction. The timing of the auction is exactly one, three, five, seven, or ten days to the minute of when you place the listing. Late at night is not the best time to post a listing, as it could end at 2 a.m. The best bids are during the last part of most auctions. You can set a specific time for the listing to post as an additional option.

The best time for ending auctions is something you can research. Look at your past auctions and see what your best-selling times are. This depends on what you are selling and who is buying many of your items. Selling many items overseas can have an impact on the ideal time and date of your listings. Here are the best days, in rank order, for ending auctions:

1. Sunday
2. Monday
3. Thursday
4. Tuesday
5. Wednesday
6. Saturday
7. Friday

This is based upon PowerSellers' input and can be different for your individual business, but this is a good place to start. There are days that you should not have items end on, as they are the days when prices drop the most; these include the Fourth of July, Memorial Day, Labor Day, and Veterans Day.

Step By Step

The step-by-step Sell pages (referred to as the "SYI" or "Sell Your Item" form) are simple; you must complete all the required information before you can move to the next step. However, all that planning will make the process quicker and smoother for Suzy. She will not have to make hasty decisions on details that she will have to revise later (such as misinformation in her description) or areas that she will regret later (such as putting in the wrong shipping weight and having her shipping quotes be all wrong).

From the tab under "Sell," Suzy will choose "Sell an Item," and a page will come that will allow her to see what her item may be worth or to proceed with selling her item.

The "What it's worth" link will allow the user to compare their item to other items up for auction that are the same or similar. This can give a good idea of what price to list.

After she looks up the potential price of her item, she will choose the "Start Selling" button.

Step 1: Category

The first official step in setting up Suzy's auction is to choose a category for the waffle iron. This can be a confusing task — there are so many categories to choose from. This is something that can be done before starting your auction process online, but the search and browse features built in at this point in the setup are as good a way to locate a category as any.

Suzy has some ideas already, as she made note of what categories the other waffle irons were listed in. She wants to be sure she is in the same place as the competition. While she knows she can list her item in two categories that also doubles all the fees, so Suzy will not utilize that option this time. However, there are some times when this really is a very good marketing technique.

Following the same path that her competitors took, Suzy begins by choosing the category "Collectibles," as this item is not likely to be put to actual use; its primary purpose is for collecting and displaying. Suzy chooses Kitchen & Home > Kitchenware > Cookware > Cast Iron, because that is the most applicable from that box.

Second categories

This is not the only choice she could have made, and in the next box down, the computer has compiled a list of possible choices for her if she wishes to list in a second category as well. Knowing that this will double her listing fees, Suzy passes on the option but takes a moment to review the suggested choices in case the computer located a series of categories that made more sense than her choices.

There are a few good suggestions, but Suzy feels confident in her choice and clicks the "Continue" button to move ahead. There are a couple of other details to mention about categories Suzy may find useful for future auctions. When Suzy is confident she has chosen the correct category, she then goes to the bottom of this page and selects "Continue."

It is not just important for you to choose the right category — it is imperative. It is against eBay's policy to place items in a category they obviously do not belong in, just hoping they will be noticed and purchased by someone browsing in that category.

Step 2: Create your listing

Now that Suzy's category choices are in place, the next page begins with choosing the title. Having already worked this out ahead of time, Suzy makes a final decision between her two suggested titles and types it in: Antique Wagner Ware cast iron waffle maker 1910 NR. Suzy considers putting a hyphen between "cast" and "iron" because she has seen the word hyphenated, but then recalls that the purpose of keywords is to assist the search engine in locating her item. If a potential buyer were to type in "cast iron" in the search field as two separate words, and she had put "cast-iron" in her title, with hyphens, her listing might not come up in the search results. So she resists the urge to be grammatical and technical in these matters.

Like the second category, Suzy is not choosing to use a subtitle at this time. She feels she covered the keywords sufficiently enough in the title that most lookers will have ample information to decide if they will read further.

Next, she fills in the next few boxes as follows. These are boxes to describe the waffle iron. If you want to add descriptions that are different from what comes up in the drop down box, eBay gives you that option.

The next section of the form is the place you can add pictures. You can add up to 12 pictures for free. Select the "Add Pictures" button and select the pictures, then upload them from your hard drive. The item description is also worked out already and typed into a simple word processing program such as Notepad or Microsoft Word. Suzy opens her saved Notepad file, highlights and copies the text, then comes back to her browser window.

Using the mouse, she right-clicks in the description box and clicks "paste" to insert her text into eBay's description box. Simple as that. Now, however, she needs to spice up the text. She chooses a few items that she would like the searchers to zoom in on, such as the date, 1910. Highlighting those characters, she uses the drop-down menu just right of the font-size menu and chooses from among the colors available. She chooses to make the date red.

Next, she decides she would like the font to look less rigid, so she highlights the entire text and makes it italicized by clicking the box with the capital "I" on it. Suzy is pleased to see most of these items are familiar to her because they utilize the same icons as her word processor and other software programs.

At the end of the description, she starts a new paragraph and clicks on the drop-down menu called Inserts. Here, she highlights the "Seller's other items" phrase and, instantly, a link that reads "Check out my other items" is inserted. When customers see this, they can view her other auctions by using this link. After that, she types in the message, "Happy to combine shipping when possible."

Starting yet another new paragraph, Suzy minimizes her browser and opens up the Notepad file in which she has stored her statement about policies. After copying and pasting that item in at the end of the auction, she highlights the text, sets the font to one size lower than the description, and makes it italic.

To wrap up the entire description, she sets the font back to the original size and types in a brief closing message, "Thank you again for looking at my auction; please..." and again inserts the "Check out my other items" link.

She then clicks the link (at the bottom of the description box) that reads "Preview" and is able to see her auction for the first time. This is fun and exciting, especially when you are able to see the extra photos that you have added using the HTML coding.

You can also click the tab that reads "HTML," just to see what HTML coding looks like. eBay will automatically translate all the formatting you have done into HTML. It is quite interesting to look at.

There are some instances when you are wise to do your own HTML writing, such as when you insert items like tables and other graphics that are not able to be saved as a .jpg format, but most beginners will be pretty pleased with the choices that are available to them at this point.

If you are like me, you have been using computers for most of your adult life and do not work as well writing things out by hand. You may think better at the computer and prefer to write descriptions on the fly once you get to this page. That is fine, too — just remember that anything you put in your listing can be revised so long as there are no bids yet *and* the auction has at least 12 hours left.

In the last part of the section Suzy could choose a theme, which produces a background picture and design and creates a color scheme for the text. This costs only a little extra, but Suzy decides to pass this time. She does, however, choose the free Andale counter, which will give her an idea of how many people are coming to see her listing.

Andale counters allow you to count how many people visit your page. You can view the total number of bids broken down by day or week. You can add this application anywhere on your site, listings, or even your storefront. There are more than 100 counter styles, or you can choose a hidden counter.

Step 3: Price, preview picture, duration, and extras

She chooses online auction rather than fixed-price, because she can always offer the Buy It Now feature along with the auction.

This third step is where you will name your price, set the quantity, set up the duration, and schedule a start time (if desired, for an extra fee).

Setting your price and duration are as simple as filling in the blanks and choosing from a drop-down menu. Suzy has decided that she will start her auction at $4.99, which is a good deal for anybody and allows Suzy to make nearly double what she paid for the item after eBay expenses (listing fee and Final Value Fee). If she has a buyer who pays with PayPal, she will incur expenses there as well, which will eat away some of her profit, but she has decided a higher opening bid price might push away potential bidders in favor of other items, so she is willing to take the chance and hope she will sell for higher than the opening bid.

She has also chosen to set up a Buy It Now for $14.99. In this case, she will sell to the first bidder who is willing to meet her BIN price. This option, however, will disappear once someone places an opening bid on the item. Because this happens, many bidders who are certain they would be willing to pay up to the Buy It Now price and definitely want that item will opt to purchase using the BIN. Suzy would really like to see this happen, as would any seller. Not only does the transaction close quicker, but also you make a profit that is pleasing to you, rather than acceptable or merely palatable.

Of course, Suzy realizes that in order to turn this into a full-time business, she will need to do better than turning a $2 profit every auction, or sell hundreds of items every week. But she has set up her business so she can work at this during evenings and weekends for at least six months while she learns, hones her technique, and zeroes in on a strategy for obtaining merchandise and selling it in the most efficient manner possible.

She has already determined she will run five-day listings and will place it in proximity to the competitor's listing of a similar item for a higher price. Take note of the Start Time option: If you wish to schedule your listing to start at a different time, this is the place to make that choice.

At the bottom of the page is a new part of the listing. This allows you to contribute to the charities of your choice with a percentage of the purchase price. This is not necessary to fill out, but it is available if you are in the giving mood.

Step 4: Payment & shipping details

If you have already set up (or have) a PayPal Premiere account (so you can readily accept all payment types), then the box for PayPal should already be checked with your e-mail address (the same business e-mail address that your eBay account should be linked to) pre-filled in.

Notice that there is a checkbox that reads "Require immediate payment." If you check this box, then people who wish to buy a Buy It Now of yours will be notified they will be required to pay immediately upon bidding for the BIN price. This may or not be a good option to have.

Sure, it is nice to seal the deal quickly, but what if your buyer wants to be sure he gets your item — but it is Wednesday, and he does not get paid until Friday? If your payment policy states that they need to pay within a certain number of days, go back and revise it to state that the Buy It Now must pay immediately, if you utilize this option, to avoid confusion.

Below, check the other payment types you will accept. Even though you will have specified all these details in your policies statement that you will put in your listing descriptions, you should have all acceptable payment types showing as checked here.

In the next section, you can specify which foreign countries you will ship to, or worldwide, by simply checking the boxes. Make sure this, too, matches the information in your policies statement in the description.

Next, you will specify your shipping prices, or set up the shipping calculator to let prospective buyers know what the cost will be based on their ZIP code.

Flat shipping rates

First, consider flat shipping rates. This tab will let you set a flat fee for all buyers, regardless of their ZIP code (within the continental United States;

Alaska and Hawaii may be higher due to the sheer distances the item must travel to get there).

Suzy has not decided if she will use a flat rate or calculated rate, so she will calculate it both ways. To decide on a flat shipping rate, she must have the exact weight of her box and, if the box is irregular or very large, the dimensions. She needs to go to the Web site of the shipper she plans to use, such as **www.usps.com**, the U.S. Postal Service.

She uses the USPS's Web site's postage rate calculator to determine that Priority shipping for the waffle iron would be $18.80, and Parcel Post® would be $15.62 if she sent it a long distance (across country). *She does this using the ZIP codes trick, which will be discussed in Chapter 6.*

Then, Suzy must decide if she will charge a handling fee. She has re-used a box and packing peanuts she had on hand, so tape and labor are her only shipping investments so far. She decides to add a handling fee of $1. This would give a total flat-rate shipping charge of $19.80 for Priority Mail or $16.62 for Parcel Post.

When you purchase postage through PayPal (if the buyer pays via PayPal), then you will get Delivery Confirmation free for a Priority Mail package or for only $0.13 for the Parcel Post. But you cannot assume your buyer will pay with PayPal, so plan accordingly when using flat fee shipping.

There is one other thing Suzy must consider before choosing a flat fee: What if a potential bidder lives only two counties away from her? The shipping would not be anywhere near that much, and Suzy's high shipping charge (based on being sent a long distance) might scare closer buyers away.

Suzy re-enters the information into the Postage Rate Calculator using a ZIP code near her and discovers there is a rather large difference. To avoid scaring off any potential customers, Suzy decides to let potential buyers calculate their own postage based on their ZIP code.

There are times when a flat fee is appropriate, but that would be on items that are going to cost approximately the same postage regardless of where they are mailed. This would include all items less than 1 pound that are being sent Priority Mail. The cost is the same for any item 16 ounces and under for Priority Mail.

Calculated shipping

Most people know that U.S. Postal Service rates are based on zones, and the longer the distance between the "TO" zone and the "FROM" zone, the greater the postage. Thus, buyers appreciate getting a little break on shipping if they are closer to the seller than someone on the other coast. eBay has made their calculated shipping tool very simple to use, and the buyers can even calculate their shipping right from the search results page now. This is a very good reason to use the calculated shipping method when setting up your auction.

Buyers like to know the shipping up-front. Years ago, it was not uncommon for buyers to not get a shipping quote until they had won the auction. You had to contact the seller (or vice versa) and give him or her your ZIP code or shipping information. The seller would then take the package to the post office and get a quote for you, then come back and e-mail you, and so on.

It took forever to get a package sent from sellers who were not large companies with shipping departments. But that was the norm; there was no other way for the average home-based eBay seller to do it. Another situation that happened more frequently was that buyers backed out of the transaction if they found (after they had won the auction) that shipping was either more expensive than expected, or more than they were willing to pay. Shipping costs became a very significant detail for buyers to know up-front. With technology being what it is today, there is no reason why buyers cannot know that even before they bid.

If a buyer thinks the shipping and handling is too pricey, he can keep looking without having to actually open your auction and read your wonderful description and see all your extra photos. With an outrageously high shipping fee listed right in the search results column (or the calculation link that they can use without opening your listing), you can turn away good buyers who may feel you are being dishonest.

Because Suzy realizes the weight of her package may make some shipping quotes large (even though potential buyers should realize cast iron is heavy, some may not realize how heavy), she revised her description to put in this information:

> *This item weighs nearly 12 pounds packaged up. The shipping quotes from the calculator reflect only actual shipping costs — no handling fees are being charged.*

Because Suzy's only cost is packing tape, she feels that having a statement like the one above is more important to buyers. They love to know that they will pay only exact postage costs.

To set up the calculated shipping tab, simply enter the weight of your package by using the drop-down menu on the left. If the item is heavier than the highest weight on the list, use the custom weight option, which will bring up boxes for you to enter the exact number of pounds and ounces.

Suzy's packaged waffle iron weighs 11 pounds, 9 ounces with no tape, receipt, or thank-you note in it, so Suzy has guessed a little high and entered a weight of 11 pounds, 12 ounces into the calculator.

She chooses to offer two shipping services — Parcel Post and Priority Mail — as buyers who live farther away might want the cheapest option available if they are not in a hurry for the item. If a buyer requests a third service, such as Express Mail, she can calculate it and revise the information in an invoice after the auction closes.

On the calculated shipping page, you will see there is a box where you can enter your handling fee, which will then be added to every quote that a searcher requests, without her knowing how much it is (although, as noted, if your item is not heavy, experienced lookers will be able to spot a heavily padded shipping charge any day).

> If you have not yet set up a shipping discount program but want to set up parameters for shipping discounts, click on the link that says "My Preferences," and you will be taken to the page to set these up. Buyers like to have shipping discounts, such as paying full-price for the first item and a small flat fee (such as $1 or $1.95) for each additional item, as long as they can go in the same box. *This topic is covered in more detail in Chapter 9.*

Further down the page, Suzy's sales tax information is displayed. She has set up her PayPal account to automatically charge sales tax to customers living in her own state. If the eBay page is not updated with that same information automatically, she can do so here.

Next on the page is a box devoted to the Suzy's return policy. Because she stated it in her auction description, she can merely put "See Item Description" in the page provided, or repeat the information. The same holds true for the "Payment Instructions box;" she can repeat, or refer the buyer to the auction description.

The "Buyer Requirements" section is a way for you to prevent certain classes of buyers from bidding on your auctions, such as those with little or no feedback, those with a high percentage of negative feedback, or those who have been reported as non-paying bidders.

Suzy is now almost done setting up her first auction. She is ready for the last step. Select "Continue."

Step 5: Review & Submit

Here, eBay offers a plethora of options for extra fees, and photos are no exception. You can super-size your photos or have them placed in a slideshow format that will scroll at the top of your page. Want all the options? Get the "Picture Pack," which includes Gallery, Supersize, Picture Show, and additional pictures, all for one discounted price.

But you are not done with extras yet. The next section shows what your current listing will look like in a sample search result. This is an interactive display that will change with each feature you click on to show how your listing will stand out more with the various features. It does not cost anything to click on the boxes to see the results, but just make sure you un-click them all if you do not wish to utilize these features at this time.

If you choose to use one of these options on a regular basis, you can click a box at the bottom of the list and eBay will save your settings. The Gallery photo option is highly utilized.

If you do not pay the fee for the Gallery photo, you may find that all you will be showing is the little green camera icon; do not be fooled into thinking that uploading your free photo to eBay will give you the photo in the search results as well.

That does not mean that skipping the Gallery photo is a mistake, because the camera icon does let others know there are pictures in the auction. You may just want to give Gallery a second thought and see if you can work it into your budget of extra features.

Every person is different, and for others, they might want to look at every auction, even if he or she cannot initially see a photo. One way you can compensate is to make the title catchy enough to entice the looker to look closer. If you can build shipping costs into your actual item price, then advertise "FREE SHIPPING" in the title; that may help generate some numbers on the counter.

Next is a section of extra features that are not likely to be utilized by a new seller, unless your merchandise is pricey. However, if you are selling a high-end product you want maximum visibility for, check into the Featured Plus (for $19.95), Gallery Featured ($19.95), and Home Page Featured ($39.95+) promotions. If you click on the links that read "See example" after the brief description, you can see your listing in these settings.

Have you ever noticed what appears to be a graphic of a small gift in a search results page? That little gift icon means that the seller has paid an extra $0.25 to label this item as being "good for gift-giving." If you utilize this icon, make sure you talk about it in your item's description, noting what extra services you will perform so the item is ready for giving when it is received. That can include pre-wrapping the item, packaging with a gift card, or shipping directly to the recipient. Sign up for this feature on this page.

Just make sure none of the extra-fee features is checked when you click Continue, or you will have to go back and revise it before you submit your listing or you will be charged.

If Suzy has thoughtfully prepared her title, description, and all the details, she should be able to get through this step quickly. However, this is a good opportunity to re-read the title and description, checking for typos or incorrect information. Easily revise anything by clicking the "Edit" link at the right-hand side of that section.

At the top of the page, eBay provides recommendations on details that may or may not increase your listing's viewing and price. It does not hurt to read these items, in case you have missed something you actually did intend to do or offer.

If everything appears as you wished it to, then you need to make sure to double-check the box at the bottom of the page that reads, "Review the fees and submit your listing." Do just that; make sure all the fees are what you anticipated and that you are not paying for an extra feature you may have accidentally clicked on. If so, go back and revise everything necessary. Your auction will not appear if you do not click the Submit Listing button at the very bottom of the page, so you can revise and not have to worry about paying fees for services you did not wish to utilize.

When everything is acceptable, just do it: click the button and join the ranks of millions out there — become an eBay seller.

When your listing is submitted and accepted by eBay's servers, your computer screen will show a congratulatory message and your "item number." It is a good idea to have a column (either in your spreadsheet or log sheets) to track these numbers. This provides a reference point so you do not accidentally ship the wrong item to the wrong customer, per chance they are both named John Smith. Your eBay invoices will also reference this number as well as the title, but if you are selling several of the same item, titles are not much help. Having an individual number for each auction is helpful for inventory reasons.

If you forget to write down the auction number at this point, you can find it on the "My eBay" page. Click on the auction title and locate it on the auction page, or better yet, click "Customize Display" on the My eBay page and add "Item ID" to your list of columns displayed. *See Chapter 1 for information on customizing your My eBay pages.*

It is exciting to post your first auction, and while you have done a lot of work to get to this point, it is not necessarily downhill from here. There are some steps you will have to take while your auction is running.

Customers contact you to ask a question

Even though you have been thorough in your description and list of policies, it is not uncommon to have potential customers contact you to ask a question about something they are not clear about or simply want more information about.

Do not look at this as a failure on your part; it is not. There is just no way you can think of every possible angle that others will. Try to think of it as an opportunity to provide some excellent customer service by replying with a helpful, polite, and professional e-mail. Be sure to thank the customer for their questions and give as much detailed and correct information as you can (even if it means doing a little research or legwork). And, of course, be speedy in your reply.

When you reply to inquiries, you have a few options, such as sending a copy of your reply to your e-mail (in case you need to refer to it later), hiding your e-mail address from the sender, and posting the question and your response in the listing for other lookers to refer to. This last option is a good idea to utilize, especially if the question is one that others might ask as well, or in case there are bids on your item and you cannot revise something pertaining to the question.

If you do your eBay business on nights and weekends, you may not receive a question until after an auction has ended (if it was sent during the day). Even in these cases, reply to the sender and apologize for not receiving the question beforehand. You just never know who will be your customer tomorrow, or whom this person might refer to your merchandise because of your quality communication with them.

You may also get questions from international members who wish to bid or buy your item. If you have already specified that you are not willing or able to ship internationally (in your policies, and by not checking any international boxes during the auction setup), you still should reply to international requests in a professional and polite manner. Someday you might want to consider international shipping, and you do not wish to offend your future customer base by being rude now.

> **TIP** If you find that an international buyer has bid on your item despite your stated policies, you can cancel his or her bid (Note: Be certain the bidder is an international buyer first). Fill out a brief form with your auction number, the ID of the person whose bid you wish to cancel, and a brief statement as to why you wish to cancel the bid.

Revisions

During the time your auction is running, you also can make revisions to your listing. eBay allows you to revise your listing as long as it meets these conditions: There are no bids placed on the item, and there are at least 12 hours left before it expires. There are a number of reasons why you might make a revision, including the following:

- To change your price. Perhaps you have done additional research and now feel your opening bid is too high.

- To change your pricing strategy — you did not offer Buy It Now at first, but now wish you had.

- To add information to your description, fix a typo, or clear up something that seems confusing.

- To place your item in a second category for more exposure.

When you make revisions, such as adding Buy It Now or placing it in an additional category, you will incur fees. At the very bottom of the review page, before you click the "Submit Changes" button, there is a statement of what new fees you will be charged, or a statement stating that your changes do not require any additional fees.

Your listing will state that it has been revised, for lookers who may have looked at it previously.

Other than those two tasks, you are off the hook until your listing is complete. *The next steps are covered in Chapter 9.*

Repeat Business

Repeat business is like money in the bank. If you have regular customers, you will be able to spend less time and money attracting new ones. Making a buyer happy also increases your feedback scores, which helps you gain and maintain your PowerSeller status. Word-of-mouth advertising is golden. Below is a list of tips to show that you will go the extra mile to gain and maintain a customer. Anyone can sell a doll on eBay, but only a PowerSeller who is on top of customer service can grow a company. eBay is not just a fancy flea market online.

- If you are selling used equipment, take the time to clean it up. Make sure it is as clean and new-looking as possible. It is important for the merchandise to look its best when it arrives with the customer.

- Entice a buyer to look at your other items if you have them clearly listed and connected to your auctions. You will get quicker results. Make sure you have a number of Buy It Now items to choose from.

- Include buyers' positive feedback when listing similar items for future auctions.

- If there are any kind of flaws or damages on an item, make sure that you not only list it on your auction, but that you provide close-up shots of it for the buyers to view. That way, when they receive the item, there are no surprises.

- When selling items like cars, make sure you list everything you can about them, including flaws or scratches. Customers are relying on your honesty to buy an item sight unseen, so do not hide anything. It will only hurt your reputation.

- Make sure that your buyers can contact you. If they see your contract information available, even if it is just an e-mail address, they will be more confident buying from you, and they can contact you after the sale if they need to. You may even find that buyers will contact with praise or questions about other items you have for sale.

- When you mail the item, include a sales slip, invoice, and copy of the listing. You may even put a small note or a catalog in if you like. Never send the item without documentation included.

- Provide as many payment options as possible. Not everyone is computer savvy, so be patient when they want to send a check. Wait until the check is cleared before sending an item.

- You can learn from the mistakes of your competition. Look at their negative feedback to find out ways to improve your customer service and avoid pitfalls.

- Never delay shipping an item, if possible. Make sure it arrives while they are still excited about the item.

- Try to send a little extra. It can be a document explaining the item, or some other similar object of small value. Even small extras will get your buyers to notice and remember you. It costs little to make people happy. Consider sending older inventory that has not sold.

- If you have similar items, consider offering a "Second Chance Offer" to the losing bidder. It will save you on the costs of creating a new auction.

- Offer a return policy for items at the seller's shipping expense. Allow customers to change details like size or color. You might make an extra sale in the process.

- When creating a listing, create bullet-point summaries of items that have a large description. Make the summary highlight the main exciting points.

- Create a scale to describe items' condition, and post this with your auctions. Rate each item's condition on that scale so that the buyers know exactly what they are buying.

- When posting new items, consider posting them at the same time every week. That way, your buyers will know when to look for your new merchandise.

- Create a frequently asked questions (FAQ) link on your auctions and Web site. Include all of your policies, such as shipping costs and returns.

- When you get a used item, look for descriptions, and keep a database of what the item looks like and what it functions like when it is brand-new. This way, when you post an auction, you will be able to compare your item to the new item.

- Offer your buyers discounts on future items or same-day purchase items through your store.

- Do not forget that the worth of an item is only as high as a bidder is willing to pay for it.

- Do not use cute listing titles. All titles should include the description of what you are selling.

- Always strive to look and act professional. When you use several exclamation points or try other tactics of making the words look unusual, you will look like an amateur. Use the tools at your disposal to increase your sales — not gimmicks.

Chapter Three

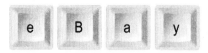

Plan Ahead for Success

Now that you have set up an account and posted your first auction, let us get into the nuts and bolts of eBay. We will begin with the essence of eBay, which is e-commerce. E-commerce in part hinges on one's ability to pay for the goods and services purchased online. Without these integral components such as PayPal, e-commerce would not have become what it is today.

Embracing E-Commerce

Although eBay cannot claim to have spawned e-commerce by itself, anyone who was aware of the Internet in the mid-1990s will tell you that for many Americans at that time, eBay was synonymous with e-commerce. For many, eBay was their first try at buying anything online.

E-commerce, short for electronic commerce, has been around since the 1970s, when technology became available for sending documents over local and private networks. However, in a broader sense, it refers to anything done electronically that moves businesses along. This can include tracking inventory and the supply chain for a wholesaler, making an electronic funds transfer (ETF) for a customer at a bank, or buying and selling through the Internet, a private network, or even a mobile phone.

For many non-techies of the world, e-commerce is more or less Web commerce: the buying and selling of products and services via the Internet. This is the type of commerce that sites like eBay are created to perform.

The amazing thing about e-commerce is that it makes distances, even those spanning the globe, irrelevant. Imagine finding the means to open your own store in the heart of New York City — more than 8 million people strong and millions of tourists annually. No matter how many years you were in business, it is simply not feasible to expect all those people to visit your store. However, thanks to e-commerce, your market includes not just New Yorkers and its tourists, but every one of those 135 million people who have already become buyers, sellers, and lookers. And that is not to mention the people who will join tomorrow, and next week.

Web sites are the portals that make e-commerce as successful as it is. Many new business owners go overboard in buying all the gizmos and gadgets they think they will need right away, and this is especially true when it comes to Web sites. They are so necessary to e-commerce that people often run headlong into getting one before they really have any business, per se, on which to do it.

Obviously, Web sites are crucial for e-commerce, but in this case, the Web site is already up and running for you: eBay. Having the tools already built into this amazing site is the time- and money-saver that every new businessperson needs. Like the old adage cautions: Do not reinvent the wheel.

Having your own personal domain and Web site might be slick and impressive, but it is not a true necessity at the starting gate — and slick and impressive can be costly. Spend some time building your presence on eBay, and when you are turning a real profit (after expenses) on a monthly basis, then look into it. *Web sites are covered in Chapter 7 as well.*

The e-commerce tools that you will primarily use to start an eBay business are e-mail (and other Internet messaging, such as instant messaging or text messaging on a mobile phone) and e-banking, such as a PayPal account, for sending payments to your suppliers or receiving payments from buyers. *PayPal is covered in more depth in Chapter 6.*

E-mail is generally available through your ISP (Internet service provider), but if you do not want to use your personal e-mail address for your eBay business (which is a wise move), you can easily obtain another free e-mail address at a number of providers such as Hotmail, Gmail, and Yahoo!. The competition in these sectors has become so fierce in recent years that the amount of storage space and additional features are quite nice compared to even a few years ago.

E-mail pointers

However, merely having an e-mail address is not enough. To really make your business profitable, know how to get the most from your e-mail.

Professionalism

While you might really love your bulldog, you are not going to impress business clients, suppliers, and lenders if your e-mail address is ILoveMySlobberingDog@FakeE-mailProvider.com — unless, that is, you are selling dog-related products. However, even in that case, consider something a bit less dramatic. Poochproducts@e-mailprovider.com is more memorable and is not likely to turn anyone's stomach.

Signatures

Nearly every e-mail program today has an option for you to create a custom signature, which is a sentence or two containing virtually any information you want. Your signature will automatically be inserted at the end of every e-mail you send. It is yet another simple way to get the e-commerce components to work for you.

Use your signature line to promote your tagline for your business, such as "Selling the best in grooming and health products for your dog for ten years." Get creative, but remember to be professional at the same time. Do not forget to include links to your eBay Store or company's Web site when you move up to those levels.

Templates

This trick is one of the most valuable in terms of time saved versus time spent creating them. A template is a pre-fabricated letter for a specific situation. When an auction is complete, open your pre-fabricated end-of-auction letter (made and stored in a word processing software such as Microsoft Word), copy and paste the contents into your e-mail program, add the auction number and title, and voilá. You can move on to your next task. Using templates greatly reduces your spelling and grammar mistakes, adding to the professional image you want to achieve.

Grammar

Yes, your high school English teacher was right. Someday, she predicted, your lessons in conjugation and spelling would come in handy. If you were one of those students who snoozed through English composition class, find yourself a good reference book on usage and style. To those customers whose grammar and spelling is above average and polished, nothing will make you look unprofessional faster than an e-mail full of errors.

Anonymity

The beauty of e-mail is that you can do it in your pajamas while sipping your morning coffee. Even when you are having a bad day, you do not have to speak to a customer face-to-face or via telephone. E-mail can give you a cheerful demeanor regardless of your mood at any given moment. Let e-mail be your poker face. As you advance in your e-mail business, you may want to purchase a Web cam in order to do more personalized business, but for now, you can keep wearing those fuzzy bunny slippers.

Opt-out

E-mail is one of the slickest, and most annoying, marketing techniques there is. By law, if you are using e-mail for marketing, as opposed to auction-specific communications, you must include directions for opting out. You may as well include this important information in your template or signature so that you are not in violation of the law.

A simple opt-out message can be something like this: *Unsubscribe: By unsubscribing, you are authorizing [your name/business] to discontinue all e-mail correspondence with you. You will not receive any information from [your name/business] via e-mail. Please send an e-mail to [your e-mail address] and type "unsubscribe" in the subject box.*

Be very careful to follow through and remove the people who request an opt-out from your databases and address books. Keep a list of all persons who request this so you do not accidentally contact them again.

Speed

E-mail is lightning-fast, and as such, people have come to expect speedy replies to their e-mails. Nothing annoys a potential buyer more than sending an inquiry for more details about your auction item and not receiving a reply until after the auction has ended. Answer all e-mails in a timely manner; the sooner the better. Even if the buyer does not buy your product, you will have left a good impression with a speedy and professional e-mail.

Alerts

One way to stay on top of incoming e-mail is to be alerted by your e-mail provider. Sign up for your provider's instant messaging program and set it up to automatically sign in when you connect to the Internet.

File

Organizing your stored e-mails is critical. You can create folders to save e-mails, keeping your inbox clutter-free. Spend some time thinking about the best way to organize your folders for your use. Perhaps you could use a different folder for every month or a different folder for each activity (shipping quotes, invoices, post-payment note, and thank-you notes).

You can set many e-mail systems to automatically file items for you based on key words. Look into this, because the amount of e-mail that is exchanged can become overwhelming if you are not organized.

Clean house

You do not have to keep every e-mail for all eternity, either. Set a pattern of cleaning out e-mails related to an auction once feedback has been completed, unless there is some unusual reason to keep it.

Lists

E-mailing is a convenient way to announce a new product to your lineup or a sale on seasonal goods. Once you have completed a sale, you are privy to the buyer's e-mail address, even if not so beforehand. Set up a system *(such as a separate group in your e-mail address book or a database; see Chapter 7)* to record these addresses before you delete the e-mails, perhaps with a notation about what they purchased or about other correspondence you had with this customer.

For instance, if you note which customers purchased flea-and-tick shampoo from you last summer, then the following spring, you can e-mail them (by sending a message to all contacts in a specific address book or group) and announce that you are giving a discount on flea-and-tick products to repeat customers for one week only. Many people will be appreciative that you remembered them. Those who are no longer in the market or not appreciative of your efforts will use your "opt out" information, mentioned previously.

 Do not forget your manners. Always begin and end a business e-mail with a note of thanks or appreciation for being a customer, a past customer, or with hopes for their future business. Although business e-mail should be more formal than e-mail you send to your friends, people also like warmth and personalized service. The Internet can be impersonal and cold, so do your part to give it some heart.

You will find that your business communications will be simple and efficient if you take the time to use the built-in features offered by your e-mail provider and follow these guidelines to more professional business e-mailing.

Web safety

This is also a good time to discuss some basics of Web safety. The Internet has its seedy side, too, and it can be used for a tool to harm others as well as help them. Internet scams abound, and it seems that new ones pop up every day. Finding the perpetrators of these scams can be nearly impossible, so the best thing to do is to try to avoid them. The following is a brief list of security concerns and precautions to take.

Phishing/e-mail scams

This is a term that refers to unscrupulous persons who are "fishing" for your personal information in order to commit identity theft and fraud. They often use e-mail as their way to get to unsuspecting users by creating what appears to be a legitimate e-mail from someone you trust online, such as eBay, PayPal, and even your personal bank. This is called "phishing."

The e-mail urgently requests your attention and, ironically, they often claim "someone has tried to access your account illegally" and that they are "warning" you of this. To protect yourself, the e-mail explains, just click the following link and enter your user ID and password to verify you are indeed the correct user, or your account may be suspended altogether (for "your own protection," of course). It all seems so friendly and wonderful that your online business acquaintances are looking out for you.

But look out. Do not ever click the links in an e-mail like this. In fact, most places you do business with online will state right in their policies that they will never send you an e-mail asking for your password. That alone should send up a serious red flag.

eBay recently started posting all e-mails they send to you in your eBay inbox as well. So if you ever get an e-mail from eBay that does not quite seem right, open a new browser window and log into your eBay account. If the identical message does not appear in your eBay inbox, then delete it or report it to eBay by forwarding the suspicious e-mail to spoof@eBay. com. You can also report suspicious e-mails that claim to be from PayPal by forwarding to spoof@paypal.com.

To learn more about how to combat suspicious e-mails, go to eBay's "Help" button on the navigation bar and type "Suspicious E-mail" in the search field. Among the helpful information is a tutorial that will teach you how to spot "spoof" e-mails, and in-depth discussions on protecting your identity online.

Anti-virus software and firewalls

Despite growing concerns about online fraud and identity theft, many people let their anti-virus and firewall subscriptions expire or do not use them to their fullest potential. If you are going to be a serious business-person online, you must stay on top of these issues. Merely having these protections is not enough; you must update them regularly. You can pro-gram any anti-virus software to update automatically while you are con-nected to the Internet. Take advantage of this automation. Having your system wiped out by a virus or having a hacker access your accounting, customer database, and personal financial information is devastating and could wreak havoc for your customers as well.

Operating system and Web browser updates

Another oft-forgotten item is the regular updating of your operating system and Web browser. These items can also be set to update on a schedule, either at specified intervals or as updates become available. This is done differently based on your operating system and browser, but it is not hard to find out how to do this. Simply search the Help files of your own computer or the Web sites of your software providers. Many times these updates are security updates that help protect the integrity of your system and personal information.

Passwords and user IDs

While it may seem like common sense to you to create passwords that are difficult to guess and unique for each Web site you log in to, it is probably not for most people. Unfortunately, many use the same password for multiple sites to avoid having to remember or write down all the various user IDs and passwords.

If you must, keep a log sheet of all your names and passwords, and keep it in a secure place that you can quickly access if you have a memory lapse.

EBay's "Help" sections can give you excellent suggestions on creating a good password. Although eBay does not prompt you to change your password periodically, it is a good idea to do so (and do not forget to update your log sheet.). When you change your eBay password, there is a password meter available that helps gauge the strength of your new password, so you can improve it before finalizing it.

System backup

Newer versions of Windows operating systems will assist you in creating a set of "recovery disks" in case your computer is hacked or attacked by a virus, or in case of a crash due to mechanical failure of your machine. Even things like smoke during a house fire can damage your computer, even if it does not burn it.

All your hard work, customer databases, and stored e-mails are at risk if you do not have your system backed up regularly. Your local computer dealers and repair shops can assist you in setting up an appropriate backup system.

A number of different sites also allow you to back up your system online. In the case your entire system crashes or is destroyed, you can reconstruct it using this online service. Some Web sites to consider include **www.idrive. com**, **www.datadepositbox.com**, and **www.mozy.com**. Be aware that some of these sites require you to purchase software or pay a monthly storage fee. But it is usually minimal compared to what it will cost you if you lost all of your data.

The Better Business Bureau is committed to keeping e-commerce safe and combating scam artists. Their excellent Web site (**www.bbb.org**) can help broaden your knowledge base about safety and e-commerce. The BBB is also one of many information sources that you will use when setting up your business.

If one man can start so small and grow a multibillion-dollar business, what is stopping you? The founder of eBay started from scratch without the guidance you now possess in this book. Remember, you do not have to reinvent the wheel; you just need to get on board, learn the ropes, and grow business. With the skills you will acquire in the next chapters, you will be well above the learning curve of many people trying to start their own eBay business.

CASE STUDY:
WHERE'S WALDO?: WISCONSIN

Patrick Walden (eBay user **"waldo53)"** is not really a geeky-looking kid with round glasses and a red-and-white-striped shirt. Neither is this Wisconsin man trying to hide; in fact, he wants users to *find* him and *buy* from him.

A longstanding member of eBay (since 1998), Walden started selling for a specific reason: extra income to increase his collection of New York Yankees memorabilia and sports cards. It did not take much for him to "get hooked" on eBay; his very first auctions were the stuff that makes new sellers foam at the mouth with jealousy. "I bought some toys at an auction cheap one day, brought them home, and made $175 on my first listings," Walden said. In the years since, he has gathered a feedback rating over 1,500 with over 99 percent customer satisfaction.

"I will sell anything I can make money on," he said, rattling off a list of items that includes new computers, collectible toys, and clothing. Additionally, he will ship an item wherever it is desired (as long as it is legal) with a customer list from countries like Poland, Russia, Israel, England, Germany, France, Singapore, Australia and… Pennsylvania?

One memorable item, an empty 55-gallon Amoco Corporation oil drum, went all the way to Pennsylvania. "I sold this to a frat house; they used it as their garbage can," he said, noting that the shipping charge was "ten times what they paid for the item." As long as the customer was happy, which they apparently were, Walden will do his part to help the transaction along.

Selling on eBay is more fun than a garage sale, he noted, and nets him more money in the long run. He is glad not everybody feels this way, because much of his inventory is gleaned from local garage sales, estate sales, auctions, and thrift stores. He even occasionally lands a good deal from an antique dealer who might not know the true value of an item. As a part-time business, he averages net earnings of $5,000 a year, though one spectacular year he earned close to $15,000.

To make sure he stays on the good side of Uncle Sam, Walden reports all his income with a federal tax ID number, which then qualifies him to take the appropriate deductions for things like eBay and PayPal fees, mileage, and shipping costs. He uses QuickBooks to track all this information. This makes his tax-time paperwork much easier. His education in accounting also helps a little, too, he admitted.

Overall, he has one bit of advice for those who are getting into the business: "Make sure you find items you can make money on," he said. "Too many people I know have lost money because they didn't do their research. If you are going to buy and resell, then know the value."

To illustrate this point, he recalls an estate auction he attended with his mother. One item up for grabs was a plastic bag with several small, old, plastic-type toys in them. It contained cowboys, Indians, horses, and such. He knew nothing about the toys but was willing to give them a shot. The auctioneer got a bid of $3 out of him. Someone else bid more. Did that other person know something about the real value of these items that he did not? Although you cannot always be knowledgeable about every little thing, he wished he had known to do some research on this type of product beforehand. He could lose money if he overbid and could not resell them on eBay for any profit.

At the urging of his mother, he outbid the other person, and so it went until the little bag of items reached $6. Walden won and hoped to make back his $6 on eBay, maybe even a few bucks more.

That small bag of early plastic horses, cowboys, and Indians turned out to be rare and highly collectible Stuart Toys that were marketed in dime stores in the 1950s and '60s. Patrick listed them and was amazed at the results. "They went like crazy on eBay," he said, adding that he "could not believe it." That single $6 investment netted him about $674. Although he wishes he could find such a great deal every day, he realizes these finds are few and far between.

Still, every penny made on an auction gets him that much closer to his next acquisition of sports cards. Thanks to his eBay income, his collection of 10,000 cards in 1998 now numbers roughly 400,000 cards — and is still growing.

If you have already made a decision to start a business on eBay, then you probably want to get to the good stuff already: the auctions, the sales, and the income. However, you will do yourself an injustice if you skip all the proper preparations and move right to the selling. In fact, you may even be doing damage to your business by not following all the rules of setting up a business. Pleading ignorance in the future is not likely going to win you any sympathy with the IRS or potential investors or lenders.

This chapter covers such tasks as writing a business plan, becoming an official business (as far as the government is concerned), accounting and inventory basics, and tax liabilities. It sounds worse than it really is, and because you are just beginning to plan and set up your business, it is much easier to do these tasks now than after the fact.

But wait — tons of people out there have set up shop on eBay and have not ever filed any paperwork or paid any taxes on their earnings, right? Well, yes. But the purpose of this book is to assist you in setting up a *business*. Those who sell without the proper setup are more like an online garage sale than a real business. If it works for them, that is fine. But if you seriously want to become a high-volume eBay seller with clout and credibility, you would be foolish not to invest some time into the proper setup.

That being said, let us move to the most basic item: the business plan.

Writing a Business Plan

Think of your business plan as your company's résumé. As your company grows, so will the items that it covers. Initially, however, your business plan can be as simple as a bulleted list of objectives (goals) and strategies (how you will accomplish the goals). If you are not planning to seek any financing for start-up costs or initial inventory, then you may be the only one reading your plan for some time. You can always polish and expand it if the time comes when you seek financing or investors to grow your business.

If you are seeking financing or investors right away, then you need to write a polished and professional plan with proper grammar, punctuation, and terminology. There are numerous ways you can accomplish the task of writing such a specific plan, including online sources such as the Web sites below.

A business plan is specific and unique to one individual business. The plan contains information about operational and financial goals and explains how those goals will be achieved. The essence of a business plan contains the following elements:

- Begin with a simple statement of what you hope to accomplish with your business. Define what products or services your business will provide and to whom they will be provided. Include any supporting evidence you have for the need or desire for your product or service.

- Outline a plan of action for getting your products or services to your customers, including marketing tools.

- List the personality traits or strengths you have that will carry this project through, and identify those traits or weaknesses that may hinder you. Be honest; admitting your weaknesses is not a sign of failure. Just the opposite is true in business.

- Set a timeline for you to accomplish certain goals, in reasonable increments, to achieve that ultimate definition from your first paragraph.

- Project a statement of your financial situation at present and financial goals (future forecast of sales and expenses).

- Tie it all together with a brief recap or summary, using a positive tone that brings confidence to your endeavor. When things seem bleak in the future, you can pull out your plan and read it for a quick, inspirational pick-me-up.

There are just about as many different ways to write a business plan as there are types of businesses. Realize that if you are just starting out, you may not have a great deal to say in each of those categories. Just do your best for now, and keep working on it as your business grows and expands. Also, if this suggested layout does not seem very interesting, or if you want to be more detailed and specific, check out the ideas about writing business plans at these sites:

- **The Small Business Administration:** Created by the U.S. Congress in 1953, this agency provides assistance in just about every aspect of starting and growing your small business. Their Web site, **www.sba.gov**, contains a wealth of information.

- **SCORE:** Originally, this acronym stood for the Service Corps of Retired Executives, but as this non-profit organization has grown and expanded since its inception in 1964, so has its name. Now, the group refers to themselves as "SCORE: Counselors to America's Small Business." In 2009, SCORE has assisted more than 8 million clients with its advice and direction for small-business needs. Check out their templates and sample business plans in the "Business Tools" section of **www.score.org**.

- **Bplans:** Located at **www.bplans.com**, this site offers more than 500 different sample business plan samples to choose from. They offer free suggestions and step-by-step instructions, and offer the software Business Plan Pro for about $100.

- **My Own Business:** Located at **www.myownbusiness.org**, this is a non-profit that offers online courses on starting your business and creating business plans. The course is free; however, the textbook is $39.50 plus $5.50 S&H. If you choose to take the certificate program, it costs $79.50.

A Web search will turn up dozens of sites dedicated to helping small businesses. Peruse them, but be cautious: Do not sign up for anything, nor give out any private information without investigating first. Some sites claim to help small businesses but are only interested in selling you things perhaps you do not really need. Be sure to investigate, and if you have any questions about a site, contact the Better Business Bureau (**www.bbb.org**) for advice on determining legitimacy.

As for the actual writing of a business plan, if you are able to verbalize your ideas and concepts but just do not have a flair for words, you can always hire someone to write it for you. Possible places to locate a writer include Elance or Guru, located at **www.elance.com** and **www.guru.com**, which may be the way to go for economical reasons. These sites allow providers to bid for services, not unlike eBay.

There are many software bundles full of tools for starting a business, such as Palo Alto's Business Plan Pro, MYOB BusinessEssentials, and Quicken Legal Business Pro by Nolo Press. These software titles range in price from $100 to $300, but in addition to business planning assistance, they also contain many standard forms, accounting and legal advice, assistance, and other great features.

eBay Tools

Other programs are specifically designed to work with eBay and can help you manage and keep up with your business.

Seller tools

Many tools can be found under **http://pages.ebay.com/sell/tools.html** on eBay. Some of these tools are free, and some cost a few dollars. Many new sellers do not know they exist, while others are using them every day. You may not want to buy or use all these applications, but they are worth looking at and considering. As they are specifically created for eBay sellers, they are user-friendly and are easily integrated into the eBay system.

Let us look at a few of the seller tools available to you through eBay.

Sell Your Item (SYI)

The Sell Your Item (SYI) is a tool that allows you to list your items quickly. You can create customized listings and tool guides easily through the listing process. The SYI form offers you timesaving features and allows you to keep a draft of the form you did not finish creating; you can go back and work on it later. The form allows you to remove steps and customize your form with colors, fonts, and reusable templates. SYI also allows you to receive more categories to look over for your items.

Turbo Lister

One of the best things about this tool is that it is free. This tool can help you create professional listings and allows you to upload them in bulk sets. It has search tools that allow you to find items quickly. It also boasts a dynamic toolbar that allows you to control your listings more efficiently.

You can create your listing offline and then upload multiple listings all at once, which saves time and aggravation. You can also duplicate and copy existing listings to create new listings of your inventory.

My eBay

This tool is already integrated and free. You should look over this tool carefully and see whether you are using it to its maximum potential. "My eBay" allows you to view all your selling activity in one place. You can see active listings and their starting dates. You can also easily view what the current prices and bids are on your items and manage cross promotions from this area.

You can add notes to help you keep track of items you are selling; here, you can also use the picture manager under this tool to manage and view all the pictures on your listings. There are status icons with the listings that allow you to keep track of which items have been paid for and shipped, and you can manage your feedback on your items. This area allows you to view your selling reminders. These are important to keep track of so you do not miss an auction that has ended or needs attention.

Selling Manager

If you want to go to the next level of managing your listings, you might want to consider trying this utility. This tool is free to use. Selling Manager works with Turbo Lister and allows you to monitor multiple listings and give bulk feedback, which can save you time and money. You can also print invoices and labels in bulk for your shipping needs, and it will automatically relist items as you sell them. There are e-mail templates and feedback responses stored in this tool.

 Detailed seller rating (DSR) is an indicator of customer satisfaction. A recent addition to eBay is the ability for buyers to leave an anonymous rating of your business's performance in four different areas: item as described, communication, shipping time, and shipping charges. A buyer can anonymously leave these ratings. The ratings use stars on a scale of 1 through 5. DSR will not affect your ratings, but it can affect your eBay reputation and is essential if you ever want to pursue being a PowerSeller. A rating is an overall feeling your customer has about their experience with you. DSR includes more specific areas that can give you an idea of where you need improvement. *See Chapter 10 for new policy updates given to the weight of these ratings in 2009.*

Seller Dashboard

Another free feature sellers sometimes neglect to use and monitor is the seller dashboard. It is available to view after you have ten or more DSRs. On this board, you can view your most recent 30-day DSR scores. You should use this feedback to improve and tweak your eBay business. Keep in mind that it is repeat customers and word of mouth that create true Power-Sellers. You can easily compare your scores with the average eBay seller. You can also review what the minimum requirements are for rewards.

On this dashboard, you can see your current standing in search results. This can help you maximize the visibility of your listings when the "Best Match" feature sorts them. This tool also shows you how eBay views your ability to deliver your items and connects this to your eligibility for incentives or risk of penalties. You can see whether you have violations and learn how to avoid restrictions.

Finally, you can view your balance, payment status, and other related alerts. Look at this dashboard daily, as it can help you increase your sales and status, and can even save you money in discounts.

Selling Manager Pro

As you business grows, you may want to consider the Selling Manager Pro, as it is geared for more advanced PowerSellers. You can try it out free for 30 days. After that, it could cost you $15.99 a month, or is free if you have a subscription to Premium or Anchor Store memberships.

This tool helps by having a full sales-management function. This allows you to create and even schedule your listings in bulk batches. This way, the listings are placed on eBay at certain times without your having to do anything further. It contains a designer utility that allows you to create more professional listings. As listings are posted, it automatically decreases or increases your inventory.

Selling Manager Pro can save you time by automatically sending feedback when you receive a payment from a buyer. It sends the buyer an e-mail when the item is shipped. A more advanced feature you might be interested in is the ability to create monthly profit and loss reports. These can work easily into the business plan you are creating. To determine whether you have the right price set on a recurring item, you can see a particular product's success ratio and the average price it is selling for. A nice function of this utility is that you can export your sales data to QuickBooks using Accounting Assistant.

Blackthorne Basic

This tool, free for the first 30 days and $9.99 a month thereafter, allows you to create and edit bulk listings. It contains a number of easy-to-use templates. This tool will insert payment terms, shipping information, and other items automatically into your listings. There are a few bulk-listing utilities, such as sending bulk e-mails and feedback to buyers, and it will also mark the status of payment and shipping in bulk batches.

Blackthorne Basic saves sales and customer information for later retrieval. It also has a number of different invoice templates.

Blackthorne Pro

This utility, free for 30 days and $24.99 a month thereafter, was created for high-volume sellers or those sellers who meet the criteria of PowerSellers. It contains the features of Blackthorne Basic with a few more exciting tools.

This Pro version contains free listing templates and client-controlled listing schedules, and it will increase or decrease your inventory automatically. It can also create listings that are linked to other items you are selling.

The more advanced features include bulk printing of labels and invoices, the ability to create monthly profit and loss reports, support for multiple user profiles so that different people within your company can access information, and the ability to manage your suppliers and consignment clients.

File Exchange

This tool is available for free to qualified sellers. You must have been on eBay for 90 days and averaged 50 or more listings a month for the past two months.

This utility allows you to edit a listing or update the status of a listing and leave feedback all in one file. You can download your active listings and sales reports in a flat file format. You can then import this file into your own offline software so you can make changes. This utility can create a template for any category you wish.

The nice component of this utility is that it allows you to create listings from any software application you choose. It even supports Web page posts.

If all these different options are confusing, eBay has two ways to help you choose.

You can go to **http://pages.ebay.com/sell/toolrecommendations.html**. On this page, just choose how large your company is and what types of features you want, and this utility will make recommendations for you.

Or, you can compare the different tools side by side at the same site. This shows the different features available with each tool to help you make a decision. You should try some of these tools; you will be amazed how much easier some functions, such as mass listings, can be.

Becoming an Official Business

The eBay seller who has an official, legitimate business has both benefits and expectations above the seller who merely sells for a hobby. And unfortunately, merely writing your business plan is not going to be the end of the paperwork. The good news is you will save yourself a serious headache later if you do things right from the start.

You need to also consider what type of business structure you have. If you are starting a business with you as the sole owner, you would file a "doing business as" (DBA). This is the process of securing the name of your business. Most new eBay businesses begin as a sole proprietor, which means you are the only owner and operator of your business. You must understand that if you file as a sole proprietor, you are liable for losses, bankruptcy claims, legal actions, and more. As you are personally liable for these things, you could lose personal and business assets.

Business Name

You cannot just use any name; some names are trademarked. There may also be some state regulations that may prohibit some specific words from being used in your company name. You should check for state regulations concerning naming a business. You can go to the U.S. Patent and Trademark Office Web site at **www.uspto.gov** to see whether your name has been trademarked. You can also conduct a Google search of the name. This will especially be important when choosing a domain name for a Web site.

When you choose a name, you may want to register and trademark it. You will register it as a DBA, which will allow your company to exist as a separate entity from you. If you choose a limited liability company (LLC) structure, the process of naming your business will be a much more official process. It is necessary for an LLC to come up with a unique name that is not currently being used by any other LLC, and it must include the letters "LLC" or its equivalent at the end of the company name. Owners of an LLC will then reserve their company's name at the secretary of state's office in the state in which the business is run.

If a corporation has been chosen as a preferred business structure, the process of naming the business comes with even more formalities. Like LLCs, corporations must reserve their preferred business name with the secretary of state's office in the state in which their corporation is run. They must also include "corporation," "incorporated," "Corp," or "Inc." somewhere in the business name at the end so the public will know the business is a corporation.

Another aspect to consider is whether you will need to trademark your business name. The definition given to a trademark by the U.S. Patent and Trademark Office is any smell, sound, noise, "word, name, symbol, or device, or any combination used, or intended to be used, in commerce to identify and distinguish the goods of one manufacturer or seller from goods manufactured or sold by others, and to indicate the source of the goods." Although you do not have to register to trademark a business, there are a number of benefits if you do, including easier registration for dealing with foreign countries, nationwide recognition of your company, and ownership of a trademarked name. To register for a trademark, you will need to contact the Trademark Electronic Application System (TEAS), which can be found online at **www.uspto.gov/teas/index.html**. The form can be filed at the secretary of state's office or through the U.S. Patent and Trademark Office for more protection.

Although there are many benefits to trademarking, a smaller business not planning to work with foreign countries, or on a large scale, will have less need for a trademark.

Because the business is conducted solely online under eBay, the Small Business Administration (SBA) suggests registering a business name as a domain name. Unlike business names and trademarks, domain names are registered online under various online businesses.

These businesses will require a search to make sure a name is not taken, which will require a small fee. If you choose this option, you will have the advantage of having your business more publicly recognized because it is both a dot-com and an actual business.

You must still make sure your business name is not taken on the domain level, as it cannot be used twice. It is important for you to put plenty of thought into your business's name. A name that is too clichéd or too serious will give customers the wrong impression. A business's name should convey, or at least hint, at what type of services the business will provide to the public. A business will be looked at more quickly if the name offers what customers need. A business's name should be straightforward; too many clever names just get lost in the shuffle. After you come up with a good name and go through the proper steps of acquiring that name, you are ready to begin forming your chosen business structure. Some structures are easier to form than others — namely, sole proprietorships, partnerships, and LLCs — but it is still important to go through every motion, no matter the size, to ensure a successful formation. Corporations require significantly more paperwork and licenses. *See Appendix A for a sample DBA statement.*

In addition to a DBA, you may choose to trademark your name. It is up to you whether this is necessary for your particular business. If you are interesting in trademarking your name, you can find the necessary forms and information at **www.uspto.gov.**

Determine the Legal Structure of Your Business

Deciding which legal structure you would like to build your business under will be the backbone of your operation. The legal structure of your business will set the platform for your everyday operations, as it will influence the way you proceed with financial, tax, and legal issues — just to name a few. It will even play a part in how you name your company, as you will be adding Inc., Co., LLC, and such at the end of the name to specify what type of company you are. It will dictate what type of documents need to filed with the different governmental agencies, and how much and what type of documentation you will need to make accessible for public scrutiny, as well as how you will actually operate your business. To assist you in determining how you want to operate your business, a description of the different legal structures is provided as follows, along with a sample of documents that you may need to file with state and federal agencies, depending on where you live.

Legal entity	Costs involved	Number of owners	Paperwork	Tax implications	Liability issues
Sole proprietorship	Local fees assessed for registering business; generally between $25 and $100	One	Local licenses and registrations; assumed name registration	Owner is responsible for all personal and business taxes	Owner is personally liable for all financial and legal transactions
Partnership	Local fees assessed for registering business; generally between $25 and $100	Two or more	Partnership agreement	Business income passes through to partners and is taxed at the individual level only	Partners are personally liable for all financial and legal transactions, including those of the other partners
LLC	Filing fees for articles of incorporation; generally between $100 and $800, depending on the state	One or more	Articles of organization; operating agreement	Business income passes through to owners and is taxed at the individual level only	Owners are protected from liability; company carries all liability regarding financial and legal transactions
Corporation	Varies with each state; can range from $100 to $500	One or more; must designate directors and officers	Articles of incorporation to be filed with state; quarterly and annual report requirements; annual meeting reports	Corporation is taxed as a legal entity; income earned from business is taxed at individual level	Owners are protected from liability; company carries all liability regarding financial and legal transactions

Becoming a Small Business

A small business is a company with fewer than 500 employees. You will be joining more than 29.6 million other small businesses in the United States, according to the Small Business Administration. Small companies represent 99.7 percent of all employer firms in the country and contribute more than 45 percent of the total U.S. private payroll. More than half are home-based. Franchises make up 2 percent.

Of those 29.6 million small U.S. businesses, the SBA states that 627,200 new companies first opened for business in 2008. During the same period, 595,600 of the 29.6 million total closed shop. However, two-thirds of newly opened companies remain in business after two years, and 44 percent after four years. The odds are with start-ups. Just keep in mind that virtually every company that survives does so because the owners are working hard and care about their company.

Sole Proprietorship

Sole proprietorship is the most prevalent type of legal structure adopted by start-up or small businesses, and it is the easiest to put into operation. It is a type of business that is owned and operated by one owner and is not set up as any kind of corporation. Therefore, you will have absolute control of all operations. Under a sole proprietorship, you own 100 percent of the business, its assets, and its liabilities. Some of the disadvantages are that you are wholly responsible for securing any and all monetary backing, and you are ultimately responsible for any legal actions against your business. However, it has some great advantages, such as being relatively inexpensive to set up, and with the exception of a couple of extra tax forms, there is no requirement to file complicated tax returns in addition to your own. Also, as a sole proprietor, you can operate under your own name, or you can choose to conduct business under a fictitious name. Most business owners who start small begin their operations as sole proprietors.

General Partnership

A partnership is almost as easy to establish as a sole proprietorship, with a few exceptions. In a partnership, all profits and losses are shared among the partners. In a partnership, not all partners necessarily have equal ownership of the business. Normally, the extent of financial contributions toward the business will determine the percentage of each partner's ownership. This percentage relates to sharing the organization's revenues as well as its financial and legal liabilities. One key difference between a partnership and a sole proprietorship is that the business does not cease to exist with the death of a partner. Under such circumstances, the deceased partner's share can be taken over by a new partner, or the partnership can be reorganized to accommodate the change. In either case, the business is able to continue without much disruption.

Although not all entrepreneurs benefit from turning their sole proprietorship businesses to partnerships, some thrive when incorporating partners into the business. In such instances, the business benefits significantly from the knowledge and expertise each partner contributes toward the overall operation of the business. As your business grows, it may be advantageous for you to come together in a partnership with someone who is knowledgeable about international trade and will be able to contribute toward the expansion of the operation. Sometimes, as a sole proprietorship grows, the needs of the company outgrow the knowledge and capabilities of the single owner, requiring the input of someone who has the knowledge and experience necessary to take the company to its next level.

When establishing a partnership, it is in the best interest of all partners involved to have an attorney develop a partnership agreement. Partnership agreements are simple legal documents that normally include information such as the name and purpose of the partnership, its legal address, how long the partnership is intended to last, and the names of the partners. It also addresses each partner's contribution both professionally and financially, and how profits and losses will be distributed. A partnership agreement also needs to disclose how changes in the organization will be addressed, such as death of a partner, the addition of a new partner, or the selling of one partner's interest to another individual. The agreement must ultimately address how the assets and liabilities will be distributed, should the partnership dissolve.

Limited Liability Company

A limited liability company (LLC), often wrongly referred to as limited liability corporation, is not quite a corporation, yet is much more than a partnership. An LLC encompasses features found in the legal structure of corporations and partnerships, which allows the owners — called members in the case of an LLC — to enjoy the same liability protection of a corporation and the recordkeeping flexibility of a partnership, like not having to keep meeting minutes or records. In an LLC, the members are not personally liable for the debts incurred for and by the company, and profits can be distributed as deemed appropriate by its members. In addition, all expenses, losses, and profits of the company flow through the business to each member, who would ultimately pay either business taxes or personal taxes — and not both on the same income.

LLCs are a comparatively recent type of legal structure, with the first one being established in Wyoming in 1977. It was not until 1988, when the IRS ruled that the LLC business structure would be treated as a partnership for tax purposes, that other states followed by enacting their own statutes establishing the LLC form of business. These companies are now allowed in all 50 states and, although they are easier to establish than a corporation, they require a little more legal paperwork than a sole proprietorship.

An LLC type of business organization would be most appropriate for a business that is not quite large enough to warrant assuming the expenses incurred in becoming a corporation or being responsible for the record keeping involved in operating as such. Yet, the extent of its operations requires a better legal and financial shelter for its members.

Regulations and procedures affecting the formation of LLCs differ from state to state, and they can be found on the Internet in your state's "corporations" section of the secretary of state office Web site. A list of the states and the corresponding section of the secretary of state's office that handles LLCs, corporations, and such is included in the next section of this book. There are two main documents that are normally filed when establishing an LLC. One is an operating agreement, which addresses issues such as the management and structure of the business, the distribution of profit and loss, the method of how members will vote, and how changes in the organizational structure will be handled. The operating agreement is not required by every state.

Articles of organization, however, are required by every state, and the required form is generally available for download from your state's Web site. The purpose of the articles of organization is to legally establish your business by registering with your state. It must contain, at a minimum, the following information:

- The limited liability company's name and the address of the principal place of business
- The purpose of the LLC
- The name and address of the LLC's registered agent (the person who is authorized to physically accept delivery of legal documents for the company)
- The name of the manager or managing members of the company
- An effective date for the company and signature

Corporation

Corporations are the most formal type of all the legal business structures discussed so far. A corporation can be established as a public or a private corporation. A public corporation, with which most of us are familiar, is owned by its shareholders (also known as stockholders) and is public because anyone can buy stocks in the company through public stock exchanges. Shareholders are owners of the corporation through the ownership of shares or stocks, which represent a financial interest in the company. Not all corporations start up as corporations, selling shares in the open market. They may actually start up as individually owned businesses that grow to the point where selling its stocks in the open market is the most financially feasible business move for the organization. However, openly trading your company's shares diminishes your control over it by spreading the decision-making to stockholders or shareholders and a board of directors. Some of the most familiar household names, like the Tupperware Corporation and The Sports Authority, Inc., are public corporations.

A private corporation is owned and managed by a few individuals who are normally involved in the day-to-day decision-making and operations of the company. If you own a relatively small business but still wish to run it as a corporation, a private corporation legal structure would be the most beneficial form for you as a business owner because it allows you to stay closely involved in the operation and management. Even as your business grows, you can continue to operate as a private corporation. There are no rules for having to change over to a public corporation once your business reaches a certain size. The key is in the retention of your ability to closely manage and operate the corporation. For instance, some of the large companies that we are familiar with, and tend to assume are public corporations, happen to be private corporations — companies such as Publix Super Markets, Inc., L.L. Bean, and Mary Kay cosmetics.

Whether private or public, a corporation is its own legal entity capable of entering into binding contracts and being held directly liable in any legal issues. Its finances are not directly tied to anyone's personal finances, and taxes are addressed completely separately from its owners. These are only some of the many advantages to operating your business in the form of a corporation. However, forming a corporation is no easy task, and not all business operations lend themselves to this type of set up. The process can be lengthy and put a strain on your budget due to all the legwork and legal paperwork involved. In addition to the start-up costs, there are additional on-going maintenance costs, as well as legal and financial reporting requirements not found in partnerships or sole proprietorships.

To legally establish your corporation, it must be registered with the state in which the business is created by filing articles of incorporation. Filing fees, information to be included, and its actual format vary from state to state. However, some of the information most commonly required by states is listed as follows:

- Name of the corporation
- Address of the registered office
- Purpose of the corporation
- Duration of the corporation
- Number of shares the corporation will issue
- Duties of the board of directors
- Status of the shareholders, such as quantity of shares and responsibilities
- Stipulation for the dissolution of the corporation
- Names of the incorporator(s) of the organization
- Statement attesting to the accuracy of the information contained therein
- Signature line and date

Sometimes, finding the correct office within the state government's structure that best applies to your needs can be a challenge. The same office may have a different name in different states. In this case, the name of the office that provides services to businesses and corporations may be called Division of Corporations in one state, Business Services in another, Business Formation and Registration in another, and so forth. Therefore, to save you time and frustration while trying to establish a business, the following is a shortcut so you can reach the appropriate office for filing articles of incorporation without having to search though the maze of governmental agencies in your state:

State	Secretary of State's Office (specific division within)
Alabama	Corporations Division
Alaska	Corporations, Businesses, and Professional Licensing
Arizona	Corporation Commission
Arkansas	Business / Commercial Services
California	Business Portal
Colorado	Business Center
Connecticut	Commercial Recording Division
Delaware	Division of Corporations
Florida	Division of Corporations
Georgia	Corporations Division
Hawaii	Business Registration Division
Idaho	Business Entities Division
Illinois	Business Services Department
Indiana	Corporations Division
Iowa	Business Services Division
Kansas	Business Entities
Kentucky	Corporations
Louisiana	Corporations Section
Maine	Division of Corporations
Maryland	Secretary of State
Massachusetts	Corporations Division
Michigan	Business Portal
Minnesota	Business Services
Mississippi	Business Services
Missouri	Business Portal
Montana	Business Services
Nebraska	Business Services
Nevada	Commercial Recordings Division
New Hampshire	Corporation Division
New Jersey	Business Formation and Registration
New Mexico	Corporations Bureau
New York	Division of Corporations
North Carolina	Corporate Filings
North Dakota	Business Registrations

Ohio	Business Services
Oklahoma	Business Filing Department
Oregon	Corporation Division
Pennsylvania	Corporation Bureau
Rhode Island	Corporations Division
South Carolina	Business Filings
South Dakota	Corporations
Tennessee	Division of Business Services
Texas	Corporations Section
Utah	Division of Corporations and Commercial Code
Vermont	Corporations
Virginia	Business Information Center
West Virginia	Business Organizations
Washington	Corporations
Washington, D.C.	Corporations Division
Wisconsin	Corporations
Wyoming	Corporations Division

S Corporation

An S corporation is a form of legal structure; under IRS regulations designed for the small businesses, S corporation means "small business corporation." Until the inception of the limited liability company form of business structure, forming S corporations was the only choice available to small business owners that offered some form of limited liability protection from creditors, yet afforded them with the many benefits that a partnership provides. Operating under S corporation status results in the company's being taxed close to how a partnership or sole proprietor would be taxed, rather than being taxed like a corporation.

Under the S corporation legal structure, the shareholders' taxes are directly impacted by the business's profit or loss. Any profits or losses the company may experience in any one year are passed through to the shareholders who in turn must report them as part of their own income tax returns. According to the IRS, shareholders must pay taxes on the profits the business realized for that year in proportion to the stock they own.

In order to organize as an S corporation and qualify as such under the Internal Revenue Service regulations, the following requirements must be met:

- It cannot have more than 100 shareholders
- Shareholders must be U.S. citizens or residents
- All shareholders must approve operating under the S corporation legal structure
- It must be able to meet the requirements for an S corporation the entire year

Additionally, Form 253, "Election of Small Business Corporation," must be filed with the IRS within the first 75 days of the corporation's fiscal year.

Electing to operate under S corporation status is not effective for every business; however, it has proved to be beneficial for a number of companies through many years of operation. Because of the significant role S corporations play in the U.S. economy, The S Corporation Association of America was established in 1996, serving as a lobbying force in Washington protecting the small and family-owned businesses from too much taxation and government mandates. Membership in the association comprises S corporations, both big and small, from throughout the nation. This includes companies such as the Barker Company, a family-owned business that manufactures custom refrigerated and hot display cases for supermarkets and convenience stores based in Keosauqua, Iowa. Another example is the Sumner Group, headquartered in St. Louis, Missouri. The Sumner Group is one of the largest independently owned office equipment dealerships in the nation.

Federal Requirements

After everything is finished on the state level, you are ready to file the necessary paperwork on the national level. Thankfully, the federal government requires much less paperwork than the state government, and much of the hard work has already been completed and must be transferred over to the national level. The IRS requires businesses to apply for an employer identification number (EIN) to be allowed to operate as legal businesses. All structures, with the exception of sole proprietorships, are required to apply for an EIN, even if the business does not have employees.

There are a number of ways to apply for an EIN, all of which can be found on the IRS's Web site, **www.irs.gov**. The easiest option is to apply online by filling out the Internet EIN application. The application only takes a few minutes, and EINs are issued as soon as the application is validated — minutes after completing the form. The only requirements for this method are for the owners to be legal residents of the United States and have a valid taxpayer identification number, which the IRS names as social security number; a different EIN; or an individual taxpayer identification number.

Your state's department of commerce is generally your best source for information on starting a business; however, do not forget to check with your county and local authorities, as well. You may need to register your business with the county clerk's office, and you may need to have approval from your local zoning board to run a business out of your home. Do not bypass these steps, as pleading ignorance later will not get you very far with the IRS.

Once your business setup is in place, you can do several easier tasks to legitimize your business. Setting up a business bank account is a necessity. Bookkeeping is time-consuming enough without trying to separate all the business transactions on your monthly statement from your personal transactions. The IRS also will frown upon your methods if you do not have a separate account. Dream big: Someday, your business might be large enough that you will need to rent office space and buy large inventories. When it comes time to seek financing or investors, you will look foolish if your business finances are mingled with your dry cleaning and doctor bills.

As a business, you have the opportunity to purchase your inventory or supplies to make inventory without paying sales tax on them. You do this by obtaining a seller's permit or resale license from your state. The rules vary greatly from state to state, but it is important to have. Your state's department of revenue will be able to assist you in obtaining what you need to get started.

Even though you will probably operate your eBay business from your home, you need to start thinking in terms of separation for more than just your business bank account. If you are already an eBay and PayPal user, you need to start separating your personal transactions from those your business does. This is important for a professional appearance online, but also will be much easier for your bookkeeping. Consider starting a second user ID for eBay and PayPal. Depending on the user ID, you may choose whether to keep your old eBay name for your business.

It is best to have your eBay name reflect your business name or focus. In your "About Me" page, you can mention the reason you started a second eBay name. Your feedback follows you if you change your ID on an existing account, so the good transactions you did prior to becoming a businessperson will still be with you. This is one reason for changing your ID name for your business (as opposed to starting an entirely new ID for your business, which will have zero feedback), as the feedback will do you more good for that than for personal buying.

Another way of providing a more professional appearance to your business is getting a separate business address. This generally will be a post office box as long as you are operating your business out of your home. Sure, it may be a bit of a hassle to go check your mail if you do not live near a post office, but realize that the vast majority of your transactions and correspondence are going to take place online. In addition to your U.S. Postal Service, there are independent sites where you can rent a mailbox, such as the UPS-owned store Mail Boxes Etc.®, and many other regional companies that provide these services. Having a separate address can also be a buffer zone in the rare case that a customer becomes angry enough to look you up online and, using your home address as a reference point, obtains your home phone number.

While you are at it, having a separate business phone number is also a good idea. Per chance your suppliers or shipping company need to contact you, it is probably wise that they call a number that will not be answered by your toddler or tied up by a chatty teenager. Both the fees for the post office box and a separate phone number may be deductible expenses, so make sure you keep all receipts and bills. Do not forget to pay for these items with your business account for easier bookkeeping.

Checklist of Tasks When When Setting Up Your eBay Business
✓   I have written my business plan.
✓   I have carefully decided on a business structure and have determined what resources are needed to set it up.
✓   I have chosen a catchy, appropriate, and memorable name for my company.
✓   I have located the proper entity to file a DBA (doing business as).
✓   I have set up a business bank account.
✓   I have contacted my state department of revenue for a seller's permit/ resale license.
✓   I have determined if I need to file for an EIN or will use my SSN as a tax ID.
✓   I have separated my personal life online from my business life online.   • *New e-mail address using my business name in it*   • *New eBay name or converting current one for business use*   • *New PayPal account or converting current one for business use*
✓   I have decided which address I will use for business (home or PO box).
✓   I have a separate business phone number.
✓   I have done what I can to make sure my business records will be safe.
✓   I have called my insurance agent for assistance in insuring my business.

It is important not to skip these steps. If you set up the business right from the beginning, then you will not have difficulties later on, and it makes you look much more like a professional and not a garage salesperson.

CASE STUDY: FROM HOBBY-SELLERS TO POWERSELLERS

Brooke and Kurt from Virginia are PowerSellers with a feedback rating of nearly 3,000 and rising, with 99.7 percent of their customers satisfied with their experiences. After registering with eBay in 2000, both used the site for purchases but did not consider selling until at least a year later.

The selling bug was planted in Brooke when Kurt was caught up in the frenzy of an auction for an out-of-print music CD that he really wanted. He won, to the tune of nearly $40. Brooke was shocked that her husband had paid so much, the rarity of the CD notwithstanding. However, when he told her about the excitement of the bidding and how he got "sucked into" the desire to win the auction, it made her wonder if she could sell items and get others excited about buying them. Shortly after that, she began dabbling in selling "mostly outgrown but still nice" clothing from her children and other quality used clothing she found at rummage sales and thrift stores.

She laughs, recalling that her desire to re-sell her children's clothing was so great that the children became almost "neurotic" about staining or damaging their clothing in any way. Her hobby also gave her the ability to spend a bit more on her children's clothing: Buying good quality items may cost a bit more to begin with, but when you re-sell it, you make back the difference on what you would have spent on lesser-quality goods. It is a system that works for Brooke.

As they sold more clothing, Kurt and Brooke began to get a feel for the market and trends. At some point, both Brooke and Kurt began picking up new clothing from clearance racks and other discount locations with the intent to resell them next time those items were in season. What followed was a flood of items in the next couple of years: up to 1,000 items would be stored in their home in clean, plastic storage bins, awaiting the following spring, summer, or winter. Huge closets were built and a home office set up to accommodate what had somehow become a serious selling endeavor.

They are a familiar sight at department stores and outlet malls, and they are looking for one thing: the "deepest markdowns of the season," said Brooke, who said that she rarely buys anything that is not marked down at least 80 percent off the original price. To get these great buys, she keeps a fairly constant watch on the prices and even has a few inside contacts at some of the stores. But it is mostly persistence and patience that gets her the best bargains. Waiting for that rock-bottom price is not always easy, but if you want to sell the item for a nice profit and still give the buyer a good deal, you must wait it out.

As their business evolved, so did their realization that they, too, must evolve along with it. A few costly errors — such as shipping the wrong merchandise to the wrong buyer — prompted a simple but effective inventory system. Every item that comes into their home is assigned a number, which is then recorded in a hand-written log. Identical items are all give the same inventory number, but the log will note how many and the specific sizes. Kurt then translates the log into a Microsoft Excel spreadsheet and enters all the other data from the sale. It is not a fancy system, said Brooke, but it works well for them.

In addition to keeping a proper inventory, Brooke and Kurt have also moved closer to all the aspects of setting up an official business in their state. Their continued success has shown them that they *are* a business, not just hobby-sellers anymore. With their good recordkeeping thus far, setting up shop should be a breeze.

A little technology has made setting up auctions a breeze as well. Kurt made a few basic templates with HTML coding so they add just item-specific information and copy and paste the works right into eBay. HTML has saved them loads of money on picture fees as well. They are fortunate to have an Internet service provider that allows them a certain amount of free Web storage space with their account. This lets them store store the photos online and use HTML programming to insert the photos into the auction, thus bypassing eBay's fees for multiple photos.

Not everything has been as easy to figure out, however. Along the way, Kurt and Brooke have encountered a few roadblocks that they quickly maneuvered around. They had a few sales where the buyer did not receive the item. Either it was lost, or perhaps there was a dishonest buyer.

Because they did not initially make Delivery Confirmation a requirement (in an effort to save on shipping costs), there was no way to track the package and they were left with no choice but to refund the buyer's money. This led to a firm policy of Delivery Confirmation being required on every sale.

What do you do for sales where no Delivery Confirmation is available though? That is a dilemma they face every time they ship to a foreign country. Many shippers have no way to track a package once it has left the United States. Many carriers also do not sell insurance for international shipping. It is a risky business, for sure, but Kurt and Brooke's customer base is growing internationally, so for the time being, offering shipping overseas is still an option for them.

Good customer service is important to Kurt and Brooke, but Brooke admits she is the stingier of the two. She has always had a disclaimer on their auctions that all sales are final unless a gross misrepresentation has been made on the seller's part. However, she felt that this was more to prevent buyers from asking for a refund just because the item did not fit them well or they did not like it as much once they saw it. Having to take returns and attempt to re-list the item was more hassle than she wanted.

Brooke now notes in her auctions that any dissatisfaction with the item should be brought to the seller's attention immediately so something can be done to make the transaction successful. This more "warm and fuzzy" refund policy is better for customers, which ultimately is better for business. "It's really important for customers to feel that customer service is there," she said.

Chapter Four

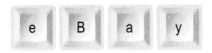

Keeping Track

Y ou may have noticed the word *bookkeeping* sprinkled throughout Chapter 3, and for those of you who are petrified by numbers, this is a most crucial topic to consider. Basic bookkeeping is not as complicated as corporate accounting, but its importance cannot be stressed enough. Most new businesses need assistance in filing their quarterly tax payments and annual tax forms, and your accountant will be forced to charge you substantially more in fees if your "books" (your recordkeeping) are not in order. As your business grows and changes, you may find that hiring an accountant for your ongoing bookkeeping is a wise choice. Not only can accountants do the tasks faster and with more accuracy, but they can help you stay abreast of changes in the laws and keep an eye out for tax deductions for you.

But as you are starting out and trying to keep expenses to a minimum, you probably cannot afford the services of a professional accountant immediately. Just set up a simple system right now and keep it updated with every transaction you make.

When the time comes to get an accountant involved, he or she will be able to take your basic setup and incorporate it into their accounting software with relative ease. They will thank you for keeping good records from the start.

Accounting and a Simple Recordkeeping System

Recordkeeping is important for many reasons, least of which is to back up your deductions and other data about your income or expenses. Having accurate records helps you get a sense of how your business is doing, whether your inventory is selling well, or whether you can afford to start expanding your business.

Having neat and efficient records will also assist your future accountant, which you might need as your company grows. You will also need to prepare financial statements (see the following list of accounting terms) about your company if you seek ever must seek financing for an expansion.

While you are starting your recordkeeping system, give some consideration to ensuring the safety of your business records. Even well-meaning spouses or family members may mess up a pile of receipts or accidentally throw away an important paper. If you have a completely dedicated room to set up shop, consider installing a new door handle with a lock, even if it is just a bedroom door. You do not have anything to hide, but you have plenty to protect. This will keep curious pets, kids, or visitors from inadvertently causing chaos.

If you invest in a filing cabinet, be sure to get one that locks. This extra layer of protection is wise for the few extra dollars you will pay for that feature. And, of course, keep it locked and keep the keys in a safe place.

In order to use your computer's depreciation as a tax deduction, you need to have a dedicated computer as well (meaning it is not used by other family members to surf the Internet or play games). Set up a password system so that nothing can be accessed without first logging in, then make sure you remember to log out every time you leave the computer.

If your computer has a CD or DVD-writer, take advantage of it. Buy a supply of rewritable CDs, and use them to back up your data regularly (weekly or daily, if you have a lot of new data daily).

Of course, none of this will do you any good if you do not protect your computer from viruses or power surges that can knock out your hard drive. Spend the extra money for high-end surge protectors and the best virus and firewall protection you can find.

Another hazard that can wipe you out in a big hurry is a home fire. While saving your inventory will may be low on your list of concerns in a fire, having your data all up-to-date and stored safely (in a fireproof safe or off-site) will give you what you need to file accurate insurance claims and start back up quickly. Good protection for your home, such as properly installed and serviced smoke detectors and a sprinkler system, are also good investments.

Check with your homeowner's/renter's insurance company about losses that would be covered by your policy in case of a house fire or other natural disaster, break-ins, or other malicious acts by others. If you are not covered, your agent will be happy to amend your policy or sell you a different policy designed to cover your business.

Protecting Your Business

Every day there are stories in the news about people being duped by con artists and crooks. Increasingly, there are stories about crooks on eBay and Craigslist who steal people's money and identity, and people who commit violent crimes.

These thieves can be anywhere. You can be operating your business out of a small town in Montana while someone in the Ukraine is trying to hack into your system to get at your PayPal and bank account password. There are a host of other frauds and scams that the online business owner must contend with.

This chapter is meant to help you deal with this reality of e-commerce. Even big companies understand there will be a certain amount of loss each year. Ask yourself how much loss is acceptable, and what steps should be taken to deal with this loss.

There are certain steps you can take to prevent it from happening, but you should expect a certain amount of a decreasing rate on your returns. Even most security experts will accept this as just a part of business.

Ways to Protect Yourself

Secure your passwords

Memorized passwords are one of the easiest ways hackers can get into your computer and cause real, lasting harm. If you use the same password for everything, or if you have an easy-to-recall password, it can be either guessed or, with patience on the part of the hacker, a brute-force program can try hundreds of different passwords in an instant, eventually unlocking bank accounts, PayPal accounts, or your eBay account.

With passwords, live by the following rules, or else you are leaving yourself wide-open to a possibly traumatic theft. This type of identity theft is becoming so common that most banks, credit cards, and other money-managing corporations will hold you responsible for fraudulent charges or deductions. They have reasoned that people leaving themselves open to hackers in this way is no longer an acceptable loss. Because the perpetrator can be anywhere in the world, these "identity thieves" are rarely caught.

Password security guidelines:

- Change your password regularly, for instance, about once a month. Some security experts will counsel you to change your password even more often — about once a week. As long as you are consistently changing your password, you should have no problems.

- Never leave your password in a place that is easily accessible, as you never know who might try to cause you harm. Do not trust anyone. Neighbors, friends, and others who traffic your house may snoop around in your stuff and steal your password. On hacker discussion boards, it is said that the most reliable, easy way of hacking a person's password is by gaining their trust and then stealing a password by either having the "victim" tell them the password or by looking into their records when they are not around. This is called "social hacking."

- Always use a mix of alpha and numeric characters. Some passwords have become so common that hackers use them first, like "password," "letmein," "123456," your name, the name of your spouse or other loved ones, or a pet's name.

- Your password should be at least eight characters or longer, because as you increase the number of characters in your passwords, the number of permutations a brute force program must perform to crack your password becomes almost infinite.

Get a good firewall

A firewall for your computer is something that protects your computer from the unwanted invasion of foreign parties. If your computer does not have a firewall, it is like a house without any walls — vulnerable to invaders who are then able to just walk right in and take whatever they want.

A firewall does not need to be the most expensive thing you buy for your online business. Computer companies specialize in making these firewalls effective and relatively inexpensive. It works like an invisible wall around your computer by keeping out unwanted intrusions into your computer that can either harm it or allow someone from outside access to sensitive areas.

Use a URL filter

Many Web pages contain "active code" in their Web addresses, or universal resource locators (URLs), which means that as soon a page is open, programs start running. Some of these are innocent, but many of these will try to install some type of "malware" (software that will harm your computer), such as spyware, adware, Trojan programs, and others that can do serious harm to your program by directly harming your computer or by stealing vital information stored in your computer.

Get a good URL filter and a good spyware blocker to help protect yourself from attacks against your computer.

Different security tools you need to have on your computer:

- Anti-virus service
- Anti-spyware
- Anti-spam
- Firewall
- URL filtering

Keep everything up-to-date. Pay attention to when subscriptions run out, and renew with the companies that provide the software as needed. Also, check often for updates that may be available for these programs. In most cases, you can set them up to automatically update so you do not have to do anything.

Protecting Yourself from Fraud

Scams from suppliers

As the owner of an eBay business, one of your chief concerns is finding products to sell. Thieves know this, and they will try to use it to their advantage. Most legitimate sellers know the reality of illegitimate suppliers' scams, and they will try everything to put potential customers at rest. Be on the lookout, use some common sense, think before you buy, and follow these basic guidelines:

- Do not believe the hype of "get-rich-quick" schemes or outrageous claims of high profits.

- Only buy from suppliers that have actual physical addresses.

- Do not buy supplier lists. More often than not, they are useless, and you can often get the same information online by doing a little research.

- Stay far away from multi-level or pyramid marketing schemes.

- Try to only buy from a supplier with a proven track record and a list of references.

- There should be a support call number or a help desk that answers all your questions in a helpful, respectful manner.

- If you are going to buy a large supply of these products, the supplier should be willing to send you a sample product for free or for a small fee.

There are many different scams related to eBay. eBay will never send you an e-mail that requests any identifying information, password, bank information, or any personal information. These are scams. Delete them, and do not go to any links provided. If you have any questions, go directly to the site and send an e-mail to customer service.

Delivery Confirmation

Many dishonest buyers will order products by standard USPS shipping because they know that USPS does not automatically track these packages, and the seller would have to pay extra for Delivery Confirmation. When the package arrives, he or she will file a complaint with eBay or PayPal that the item was not received. If you do not have proof that the item was received, you will have to send another one, or he or she can refuse to pay you. When they refuse payment, unless you have paid the extra $0.50 or so for the Delivery Confirmation — which is just a receipt saying that your package was indeed delivered — you are out of luck. Now that dishonest customer has a perfectly good item he or she can use or resell for an extremely marked-up price, as they did not pay anything for it at all. This is the online equivalent of shoplifting.

Many sellers calculate the extra $0.50 into their budgets for the added peace of mind, and if you are an online customer, you should receive an e-mail from the USPS when your parcel reaches its destination. Some sellers are so worried about this type of fraud that they refuse to ship via standard mail. The mistake is that many honest customers do not mind waiting the extra time it takes the item to travel to them via snail mail, as long as they are getting the lowest-possible shipping rates. Honest, good customers may not buy from you because you will not offer them the type of low shipping costs they want.

Phishing

You could be working on your computer, when suddenly a window pops up from PayPal, stating they need to make sure you are the real user of this account. There may be some official-sounding warning on the page about phishing scams, and the page may even look identical to the login screen that appears when you first sign into PayPal. They will likely ask you to verify your identity by inputting your user ID and password.

Do not click on any link in that window. Although the aforementioned Internet security programs minimize such intrusions, it is hard to stop all of them, and at some point in your life, you will encounter these; this recently happened with MySpace. A hacker or a group of hackers managed to replicate the MySpace sign-in page. After people sign in, they frequently surf other people's sites as well. At some point, they press the "Back" button on their browser, then they find themselves back at the sign-in page. Thinking that they must have accidentally signed out, they re-input their sign-in information, giving the hacker has all their account information. The hackers use these sites to advertise to everyone on their newly hijacked friend list by posting bulletins or leaving comments about special offers.

If you ever have any doubt about the integrity of the page, contact the page's owner immediately. Most services that require you to sign in state that no one from their company will ever ask you for your user ID and password.

Identity theft

If you find you are unable to log into your own account, you may be the victim of identity theft. Here, someone has gained access to your account and is pretending to be you. They may then run auctions as you or buy things with your money. Contact eBay and PayPal immediately to try to rectify the situation. Then, look around eBay to see whether you notice any activity bearing your name that you did not conduct. You can do this without having to log in.

Liability insurance

You may have grown accustomed to certain things, such as a house, a car, and savings. If so, you should be aware that you could lose it all because of a lawsuit against you and your company. You need liability insurance, which covers you and your business. The type of insurance you get and the type of business structure you are working under will determine how much personal liability you are covered for. You should ask an insurance agent. Try to find an agency that works specifically with online businesses or even eBay businesses; you can ask other eBay business owners whom they would recommend.

There are different types of liability insurance, depending on the types of products you are selling on eBay. Business liability insurance covers you in case of any lawsuits concerning property damage or personal injury. The products you sell on eBay could injure someone, and you could be responsible for any injury, not eBay. You could not only lose your business, but your personal property could also be in jeopardy. You may have asked yourself how you can afford insurance. But if you are moving to the level of PowerSeller, you will be moving with the big dogs. You cannot afford to not protect yourself, because you will have more to lose.

Types of Business Liability Insurance

- **General liability insurance:** This type of liability insurance is recommended for most PowerSellers. Its policy usually covers injury claims, property damages, and advertising claims. This type of insurance also is known as commercial general liability (CGL). For most PowerSellers, this is all the liability coverage they may need, so it is a good place to start.

- **Professional liability insurance:** As a PowerSeller, you should never need this type of coverage, because this usually applies to those professionals providing a service of some kind, like a doctor, lawyer, or counselor. This is listed here solely to inform you of its existence so you will be less confused when shopping for liability insurance.

- **Product liability insurance:** Because you are providing products, you may need this type of insurance. If you are creating a product, such as a dog treat, you are responsible for any damage or injury it could cause. There are different levels of this type of insurance, depending on the level of risk your product could pose to the general public.

When shopping for liability insurance, you can contact your local chamber of commerce or other similar trade organizations. Sometimes they offer good deals for their members and policies that are specific to the type of business you are running or for the type of products you are selling. You can find listings of different agencies that offer liability insurance on the Internet or in certain trade magazines. Look in the back of many of these types of magazines in the classified advertisement sections.

Take the time and compare the rates and coverage from a few different companies before settling on a particular policy. The research and time you invest could save you hundreds of dollars a year. When comparing coverage, look for details such as whether they cover legal fees and how much of those fees they will cover.

To gain a better perspective of the amount of coverage your eBay business needs, look at eBay company lawsuits online. See how much companies have had to pay out. Ask around and see what other companies are covered for.

Sometimes you can land a package deal with a company if you are buying more than one policy or if you already have other insurance policies in place. You can decide whether a package deal of policies is the best fit for your growing business. You do not need to be covered for everything under the sun, but you need a minimum amount of coverage for the more common situations you could find yourself in. It seems that everyone is suing everyone. You may not want to advertise that you do not have liability insurance, as some unsavory characters will target you as a company that they could potentially get a decent payout from.

There is simply no way this book can cover all the intricacies of record-keeping and accounting, so we will cover just a few things that you need to know or do in order to make sure you can accurately present your information come tax time. The recordkeeping and inventory-keeping systems shown here are likely different from what your accountant will set up for you someday, when your business grows, but they are sufficient for now.

The goal is not to show you how to do your accounting yourself, but rather to discuss *keeping* accurate records that will make it easy for your accountant to do the quarterly and end-of-year tasks for you, such as taxes. You will find that keeping accurate data will have advantages to you, the business owner, by offering a very clear picture of your daily affairs.

Go to the IRS Web site, located at **www.irs.gov**, and download Publication 583, "Starting a Business and Keeping Records." Print this 27-page document and refer to it often during the start-up phase of your recordkeeping.

One of the first things you need to commit to in your recordkeeping is to do it daily. Getting caught up in the listing and selling on eBay is easy to do, but a fresh memory is your best ally when it comes to documenting your finances.

There are two ways you can choose to set up a system of basic bookkeeping: on paper or on computer. Whichever method you choose, the basic premise is the same: You need to keep track of all money coming into your business and all money going out of it.

Regardless of whether you do this on paper, use a spreadsheet or formal accounting program on your computer; one way to start is to make a comprehensive list of all the possible sources of income you might receive and all the possible expenses you might incur.

Your sample list may look something like this:

Income

- Total eBay income (final bid amounts, Buy It Now amounts, and fixed-price auction amounts)
- Total eBay re-list refunds
- Actual shipping fees paid by seller
- Shipping and handling fees added (above actual shipping and handling)
- All sales tax collected
- Bank interest on your business account

Note that the "income" column lists *all* the money received, regardless of whether you get to keep it. In the "expenses" column, you will then list all the costs incurred and items you must pay out from the money you received.

It might seem strange to think of a re-list refund as income, but in accounting terms, it is, because it is a credit given to you. The same is true of the shipping fees paid by the buyer. They are income because they were paid to you.

Expenses

- eBay listing fees (basic fees and fees for additional options)
- eBay Final Value Fees
- Fees to PayPal (not including postage purchased through eBay)
- Losses from fees on auctions that did not sell
- Money paid to shipping companies (including actual postage purchased through PayPal. It is really sent to USPS, not kept by eBay)
- Cost of shipping materials
- Office supplies
- Larger purchases (equipment, upgrades)
- Accounting or attorney fees

- Sales tax forwarded to the state
- Cost of inventory (or raw materials to create inventory, if you make your product)
- Your time and labor to create inventory
- Your time and labor for other activities (packing shipments, doing paperwork, and running errands)
- Bank fees on your business account (service charges, if any)

Note to the Reader

Your list can get as detailed as you wish it to be. The best records reflect every aspect of the business, regardless of how small it seems. For instance, if you only record "expenses" in general and do not break them up into all the categories, how would you know if you are spending an excessive amount of money on office supplies every month? Wasteful spending is more easily identified once you can see in real numbers what you spend on each category in a month.

Additionally, under "eBay fees," you might want to track the different types of fees separately, such as how much of that amount was the actual listing fee and how much was for additional features — for example, bold, gallery, and extra photos. *Learn more about these fees by reviewing Chapter 2 and moving on to Chapter 7.* This level of detail may not be necessary for tax purposes, but keeping good records will help you judge the soundness of your business over time. You may find these extras are worth the money (the listings with extras sell the first time around and do not need to be re-listed), or you may find that they do not necessarily attract buyers any quicker than listings without those extras.

Keep all documentation related to anything in these two columns. Then you need to figure out how to sort, organize, and utilize this information. A basic filing cabinet is all you will need to store your paper trail, at least for now. Set up files in a manner that makes sense to you and is not too complicated so you can keep up with it. The following is a suggested list of files folders to start:

- eBay invoices, which are sent to you electronically every month, or you can print them out from the site

- PayPal statements, which you can print out from their site

- Individual summaries of each PayPal transaction (the monthly statements do not specify what each transaction was for) stapled to any other documentation for that particular auction, such as Delivery Confirmation receipt or tracking numbers

- Business bank account statements, with an envelope to put all deposit slips and other documentation for that month

- Receipts for all inventory purchases

- Receipts for all office or business supplies (such as shipping supplies and printer paper)

- Receipts for all shipping, including Delivery Confirmation receipts and insurance documents. If you purchase shipping via PayPal, much of this information can be accessed by printing the transaction record

At the end of every month, paper clip or envelope all the appropriate items from each folder together so they will not get mixed up with the next month's items. If you are careful to save and print supporting documentation, you should have the information you need for your tax filing.

TIP How long you need to keep records can vary from state to state, or by business type, so be sure to ask the accountant or attorney who is assisting you for this answer. One thing to note: You may have to keep records for your insurance company or your creditors *longer* than you have to keep them for tax purposes.

Make a point of reconciling your business bank account as soon as the statement arrives. Your bank statements and your checkbook log are good documentation, but you will need your receipts as back-up proof of your expenses. Another possibility is to gather all the receipts for the checks listed on your monthly statement and staple them to the statement. Other statements you should make a point of reconciling are your eBay and PayPal statements. Although eBay and PayPal both have accurate systems, comparing your invoices with your monthly spreadsheet, log sheet, or accounting program is a good way to make sure you did not overlook something. Be sure to mark invoices and bank statements as "reconciled" before filing so you do not later second-guess yourself. You can download eBay and PayPal statements and save them on your computer, or import them into software, including Microsoft Excel and most accounting systems.

If you plan to purchase a computer program to do your accounting for you, such as QuickBooks or Peachtree Accounting, then ask your accountant what types of records you should be keeping and how best to send them the information. This will ensure you are keeping all the right information and entering it in a logical fashion that will give the results you need.

An accountant can help you set up a chart of accounts, which is based on the list of Income and Expenses sections you made earlier, with category titles and/or a numbering system (for ease of entering transactions). Accounting software is more efficient when you input as much data as necessary for proper reporting and tracking of income and expenses. If you have the financial ability to do this right from the start, it is highly recommended.

Another way to track expenses is with a spreadsheet program such as Microsoft Excel. Basic spreadsheets are not difficult to set up if you have some knowledge of how they work. This is a valuable program to learn, so consider investing in a tutorial program on CD-ROM. Numerous companies have them available, but probably the best source is Microsoft itself. It makes a CD-ROM tutorial that sells for less than $15. Of course, you must have Excel initially, as the program is not included with the tutorial. Excel is standard in all versions of Microsoft Office, which is definitely a software package that any business needs today.

If you do not yet have Excel, accounting software, an accountant lined up yet, or the knowledge to put the software to work for you, do not delay in recording details of your auction transactions. Set up your file folders and keep every piece of documentation. For analyzing your daily expenses and income, you can always do it the old-fashioned way — the way many small businesses did it until approximately 15 years ago.

Go to an office supply store and ask for a ledger book. This book will save your skin until you pull your accounting practices into the 21st century. A ledger book is simply a bound set of blank sheets with a pre-printed grid on it in rows and columns.

There are a number of ways to set up a ledger, depending on what you wish to track. For tracking individual auctions and the costs involved, use a simple setup like the following example:

Willy's Widgets 'n Gidgets Sales Ledger   January 2010   page 1 of

Inventory Number	Auction Start/End	Re-list? y/n	A (acquisition)	Start bid/ Buy It Now Price	B (List fee)	C (upgrades)	D (final v. fee)	E (Ppal fee)	F (postage)	G Total Out (A to I)	H Gross Sold $	I Total S&H	J Relist refund	K Total In (J+K+L)	Profit (K - G)	S. tax
W001	1/1-1/2	n	2.00	.99/9.99	.25	bid/2.0 bin/.05	.52	.71	3.85	10.38	9.99	4.25	0	14.24	5.86	-
G011	1/1-1/3	n	1.00	.99/9.99	.25	bid/2.0 bin/.05	.52	.71	3.85	9.38	9.99	4.25	0	14.24	6.86	-
G012	1/1-1/8	n	1.00	.99/9.99	.25	bid/2.0 bin/.05	.21	.54	3.85	8.90	3.99	4.25	0	8.24	1.34	-
G013	1/1-1/8	n	1.00	.99/9.99	.25	bid/2.0 bin/.05	.47	.68	3.85	9.30	8.99	4.25	0	13.24	5.94	-
G014	1/1-1/8	n	1.00	.99/9.99	.25	bid/2.0 bin/.05	.44	.67	3.85	9.26	8.45	4.25	0	12.70	5.44	-
W002	1/1-1/8	n	2.00	.99/9.99	.25	bid/2.0 bin/.05	.52	.73	3.85	10.93	9.95	4.25	0	14.75	5.82	.55
W003	1/9-1/16	n	2.00	1.99/9.99	.35	Bin-.05	.42	.66	3.85	7.33	8.00	4.25	0	12.25	4.92	-
W004	1/9-1/12	n	2.00	1.99/9.99	.35	Bin-.05	.52	.71	3.85	7.48	9.99	4.25	0	14.24	6.76	-
G015	1/9-1/13	n	1.00	1.99/9.99	.35	Bin-.05	.52	.71	3.85	7.48	9.99	4.25	0	14.24	6.76	-
G016	1/9-1/16	n	1.00	1.99/9.99	.35	Bin-.05	.41	.65	3.85	6.31	7.85	4.25	0	12.10	5.79	-
W005	1/9-1/9	n	2.00	1.99/9.99	.35	Bin-.05	.52	.71	3.85	6.48	9.99	4.25	0	14.24	7.76	-
W006	1/9-1/16	n	2.00	1.99/9.99	.35	Bin-.05	.31	.60	3.85	7.16	5.95	4.25	0	10.20	3.04	-
W007	1/14-1/16	n	2.00	2.99/10.99	.35	$/.50 bin/.10	.52	.71	3.85	8.03	9.99	4.25	0	14.24	6.26	-
G017	1/14-1/15	n	1.00	2.99/10.99	.35	$/.50 bin/.10	.52	.71	3.85	7.03	9.99	4.25	0	14.24	7.26	-
G018	1/14-1/21	n	1.00	2.99/10.99	.35	$/.50 bin/.10	.36	.62	3.85	6.78	6.95	4.25	0	11.20	4.47	-
G019	1/14-1/21	n	1.00	2.99/10.99	.35	$/.50 bin/.10	.31	.60	3.85	6.71	5.95	4.25	0	10.20	3.54	-
W008	1/14-1/19	n	2.00	2.99/10.99	.35	$/.50 bin/.10	.52	.71	3.85	8.03	9.99	4.25	0	14.24	6.26	-
W009	1/20-1/22	n	2.00	3.99/9.99	.35	bin/.05	.52	0.00	0.00	2.92	9.99	0.00	0	12.99	10.07	-
G020	1/20-1/21	n	1.00	3.99/9.99	.35	bin/.05	.52	.71	3.85	6.48	9.99	4.25	0	14.24	7.76	-
G021	1/20-1/23	n	1.00	3.99/9.99	.35	bin/.05	.52	.71	3.85	6.48	9.99	4.25	0	14.24	7.76	-
W010	1/20-1/20	n	2.00	3.99/9.99	.35	bin/.05	.52	.73	3.85	8.03	9.99	4.25	0	14.79	6.76	.55
W022	1/20-1/27	n	2.00	4.99/9.99	.35	bin/.05	.47	.68	3.85	7.40	8.99	4.25	0	13.24	5.84	-
G023	1/20-1/27	n	1.00	4.99/9.99	.35	bin/.05	.45	.84	5.40	8.09	8.49	6.00	0	11.49	3.40	-
TOTALS:	**22**		**34.00**		**7.45**	**9.65**	**10.68**	**15.10**	**86.25**	**170.48**	**203.44**	**95.25**	**0.00**	**299.79**	**129.31**	**1.08**

Willy's Widget 'n' Gidgets - Ledge Categories		
Column	**Title**	**Explanation**
Re-list y/n	Re-listed Items	If this particular item had previously been listed and did not sell, then the loss would be on the ledger of the month it did not sell, but if I re-list within 90 days and it sells, I may receive a refund of some listing fees. I mark items that are re-listed with a "Y" in this column so that when it sells, I can be on the lookout for the refund amount to fill column J.
A	Acquisition Cost	This is the total cost that I incurred in obtaining or producing/making this product, including labor and materials if I made the item myself. I have kept all receipts & records to verify this number completely.
B	eBay Listing Fee	This is the basic flat fee that I paid to eBay to post this item for auction. It does not include any extra services or charges.
C	Listing Upgrade Fee	These are the fees for optional services I chose for this auction. See chart for list of upgrades and fees.
D	Final Value Fee	This is the incremental fee based on the sale price. Will be -0- if item not sold. See chart for structure.
E	PayPal Fee	This is the fee that PayPal charges to process the transaction between the buyer and me. This does not include any extra fees I incurred when buying postage through PayPal. See chart for fee per transaction based on monthly payments received.
F	Postage	This is the amount of actual postage I paid to ship the item, including insurance, Delivery Confirmation, or other options chosen by the buyer or required by me. This does not include any fees I incurred while buying postage through PayPal.

G	Total out	Because columns A through F are "expenses," they are in parentheses, which means they are "subtracted" from the income columns. Total these columns here (add all expenses together).
H	Gross sold price	This is the total amount the item sold for at auction, not including any shipping & handling fees/charges.
I	Total shipping & handling charged	This column is the total amount paid by the buyer for shipping & handling. It may be more than column F if I added a shipping and handling charge when I started the auction.
J	Re-list refund amount	If I had previously listed this and it did not sell, I am now eligible for re-list refund. I enter the amount of that refund (eBay will let me know when I have received a refund).
K	**Total in**	Add columns J, K, and L, which are my income columns. This gives me my *gross* income for this auction.
	Net profits	Subtract column J's total from column M's total. This is my *net* profit after auction-related expenses.
	Sales tax	Even though sales tax collected is an income and sales tax payable to the state is an expense, for this type of chart it is easier just to set it aside immediately.

eBay's Final Value Fees

Final Auction Price	Final Value Fee
unsold	No charge
$0.01-$50.00	8.75% of the final price
$50.01-$1,000.00	8.75% of the initial $50.00, plus 4.0% of the remaining final sale price balance ($50.01 to $1,000.00)
$1,000.01+	8.75% of the initial $50.00, plus 4.0% of the next $50.01 - $1,000.00, plus 2.0% of the remaining final sale price balance ($1,000.01 – final sale price)

Fee Structure for Reserve & Buy It Now Options

Reserve Price	Fee (refunded if item sells)
$0.01-$199.9	$2.00
$200.00+	1.0% of reserve price (up to $50.00)

Buy it Now Price	Fee
$0.01-$9.99	$0.05
$10.00-$24.99	$0.10
$25.00-$49.99	$0.20
$50.00 +	$0.25

Notes:
* **Fees were current as of 8/2010. eBay will notify all sellers before changes in fee structures.**
* **Fees are based on *Auctions*, the fees for *eBay Store* may be different**

eBay's Fee Structure

Starting or Reserve Price	Insertion Fee
$0.01 - $0.99	$0.10
$1.00 - $9.99	$0.25
$10.00 - $24.99	$0.50
$25.00 - $49.99	$0.75
$50.00 - $199.99	$1.00
$200.00 or more	$2.00

PayPal Fees

Monthly Payments Received	Fee Per Transaction
$0.00 - $3,000.00	2.9% + $0.30
$3,000.01 - $10,000.00	2.5% + $0.30
$10,000.01 - $100,000.00	2.2% + $0.30
> $100,000.01	1.9% + $0.30 *

If you receive more than $3,000.00 USD per month, you're eligible to apply for PayPal's Merchant Rate, see web site for details.

10-Day Duration

Listing format	Fee
Auction-style	$0.40
Fixed Price	Free

eBay Picture Hosting Fees

Feature	Fee
First picture	Free
Each additional picture	$0.15
Picture Pack (1-6 pictures)	$0.75
Picture Pack (7-12 pictures)	$1.00

Listing Upgrade Fees

Feature	Fee-Auction Style and Fixed Price Formats (3,5,7, 10 Days)	Fee-Fixed Price Formats (30 Days, Good 'Til Cancelled), Classified Ads
Value Pack	$0.65	$2.00
Gallery	Free	Free
Gallery Plus	$0.35	$1.00
Listing Designer	$0.10	$0.30
Subtitle	$0.50	$1.50
Bold	$2.00	$4.00
Scheduled Listings	$0.10	$0.10
AdCommerce	Pay only when buyers click your ad linking to your listing or Store	Pay only when buyers click your ad and linking to your listing or Store
List in Two Categories	Insertion and listing upgrade fees are doubled. Scheduled Listing and final value fees are charged once.	Insertion and listing upgrade fees are doubled. Scheduled Listing and final value fees are charged once.

A pre-printed ledger book is generally the same size as legal-sized paper — 8.5 by 14 inches — and will have many more boxes on it, so you can neatly print the numbers and decimals. The ledger used in this example is a table in Microsoft Publisher, but it can be done in Word and Works as well. Notice that in this example, the fictional Willy has set up a "legend" sheet, so he can refer to it if he forgets what goes in which column. Putting the wrong data in the wrong column pretty much negates whatever you were trying to accomplish. For further reference, Willy also made a few handy charts available to help him figure his fees quickly. Because of all the various details he wants to track on one ledger sheet, this would be printed on legal-sized paper. An office supply store can sell him a binder for this size, and he will have his own custom-made ledger book.

If Willy were to fill out this chart accurately for every auction (either on the computer, or printing it blank and filling in by hand as he goes through the month), he would know exactly how much money he spent on every auction-related fee or function that month. He may also be able to spot some trends, such as whether adding bold to his auctions really earns him that much more in final sales price — or just eats away at his profits. But mostly, he will know how much money he made this month after all auction-related expenses are deducted.

Realize, of course, this is not always money Willy can then pay to himself. His expenses are more than the actual auction expenses (refer to list of expenses, above). He may have a service fee at his bank; he may need to purchase another supply of shipping materials; and he might need to refresh his supply of widgets and gidgets. He also may have some sales tax he needs to earmark for the state and send to them on a schedule. Willy cannot just go spending his profits — at least, not until his business is strong enough that there are profits above all expenses. Then he can start utilizing another expense on his list: paying his own labor.

Here are some basic terms you need to become familiar with in order to work well with your accountant, attorney, or tax advisors.

Accounting period: For most small businesses, this is the same as the calendar year — January 1 through December 31 of every year.

Accounts payable: Expenses you have not yet paid out.

Accounts receivable: Income that has not yet arrived in your possession.

Assets: Every item of value that is owned by your company. Money in your business account, computers, office equipment, company vehicle, and accounts receivable are all assets.

Balance sheet: This format displays your company's assets, liabilities, and equity, usually calculated as of today's date.

Break-even: The point at which your income minus expenses is zero.

Expense: All outgoing money, also called a debit.

Income: Money coming in, also called a credit.

Income statement: This is a simple statement showing your business's income and expenses for a certain time period, usually from the start of the most current accounting period to the current time.

Inventory: The value of all merchandise in your possession that is currently unsold.

Liabilities: Every item that is "owed" by your company, including accounts payable, business loans, any bills from vendors or utilities, and funds in your possession that belong to others (like income tax due to the state).

Owner's equity: This is what is left when you take your assets and subtract your liabilities. Hopefully, this is a positive number.

Profit: The point at which all income minus all expenses is above zero.

In addition to all this organization of receipts, files, and sales data, you need to set up a system to easily identify and track your inventory. In the example, Willy sells only two products: widgets and gidgets. Because he has multiples of each identical item, he uses a combination of numbers and letters so he can track individual sales based on the inventory number of the item. He uses a W### for a widget, and G### for gidgets.

For those who sell a variety of items, new or used, assigning a number that stays with the item until it is shipped is a good system. You can use a two-stage system as well, if it does not confuse you and you want to track individual types of products. For instance, if you sell antiques, but your two main products are old dolls and old postcards, you can number your dolls D1, D2, and D3, and your postcards (or large lots of postcards) as P1, P2, P3, etc.

That way, you can see how many items (or lots) of each type of merchandise you have sold. If you occasionally have other items that are not either a doll or a postcard, you can assign them to yet another category, such as "miscellaneous," M1, M2, M3. As long as the system makes enough sense to you that you can explain it to your accountant, it should be good enough for a start.

Regardless of how you decide to set up your inventory system, odds are that over time, you will fine-tune it and find other ways to make the system work better for you. However, you should start another spreadsheet or ledger sheet for yet another cross-reference so you do not reuse any inventory numbers.

The following chart is a simple ledger for tracking inventory.

Willy's Widgets 'n Gidgets Inventory Log for January 2010   page 1 of ___

Date acquired	Description	Category	Inventory #	Date item sold	Sold amount	Buyer's Username	Auction #	Payment type, date	Date Shipped	Shipping method / confirmation-tracking #s	Feedback G/R
1/1	Widget	W	001	1/2	9.99	buyer1		Paypal 1/4	1/5	Priority	y/y
1/1	Widget	W	002	1/8	9.95	buyer2		M.O. 1/13	1/14	Priority	y/y
1/1	Widget	W	003	1/16	8.00	buyer3		Paypal 1/16	1/17	Priority	y/y
1/1	Widget	W	004	1/12	9.99	buyer4		Paypal 1/17	1/18	Priority	y/y
1/1	Widget	W	005	1/9	9.99	buyer5					
1/1	Widget	W	006	1/16	5.95	buyer6		Paypal 1/18	1/19	Priority	y/y
1/1	Widget	W	007	1/16	9.99	buyer7		M.O. 1/21	1/23	Priority	y/
1/1	Widget	W	008	1/19	9.99	buyer8		Paypal 1/21	1/23	Priority	y/
1/1	Widget	W	009	1/22	9.99	buyerA		Paypal 1/24	1/26	Priority	y/
1/1	Widget	W	010	1/20	9.99	buyerB		Paypal 1/20	1/21	Priority	y/y
1/1	Gidget	G	011	1/13	9.99	buyer9		M.O.			
1/1	Gidget	G	012	1/8	3.99	Buyer!		Paypal 1/10	1/12	Priority	y/y
1/1	Gidget	G	013	1/8	8.99	buyer1		Paypal 1/9	1/10	Priority Repeat cust!	y/y
1/1	Gidget	G	014	1/8	8.45	buyerC		Paypal 1/10	1/12	Priority	y/
1/1	Gidget	G	015	1/13	9.99	buyer@		Paypal 1/14	1/17	Priority	y/
1/1	Gidget	G	016	1/16	7.85	buyer10					
1/1	Gidget	G	017	1/15	9.99	buyerD		Paypal 1/16	1/17	Priority	y/y
1/1	Gidget	G	018	1/21	6.95	Buyer&		M.O.			
1/15	Gidget	G	019	1/21	5.95	Buyer*		Paypal 1/26	1/27	Priority	y/
1/15	Gidget	G	020	1/21	9.99	buyerE		Paypal 1/23	1/24	priority	y/
1/15	Gidget	G	021	1/23	9.99	buyer11		Paypal 1/23	1/24	Priority	y/
1/15	Widget	W	022	1/27	8.99	buyerF					
1/15	Gidget	G	023	1/23	8.49	buyerA		Paypal 1/24	1/26	Pri-combined	y
1/15	Gidget	G	024								

You may notice there is some duplicated information from Willy's sales ledger. What information you store on your various ledger sheets is entirely up to you, so long as all of it is available in one place. Because Willy is obtaining his merchandise from only one source, he does not have a column to list the source of merchandise, but if you have several sources, you may want to track where items came from. Additionally, in the "acquisition cost" column, be sure to factor in any shipping costs you incurred while obtaining your products.

You are already familiar with Willy's numbering system from viewing his sales ledger. However, you may choose not to have a numbering system at all, if your products are each unique enough to be identifiable by their description alone. Still, many sellers do eventually turn to a numbering system.

Labeling your inventory has at least one significant benefit: You are less likely to accidentally list or sell the same item twice. It may seem almost ridiculous at the outset to imagine that you would ever do anything like that, but sellers report that it has indeed happened to them before they got organized. Another benefit of having a cross-reference number is that you are less likely to ship the wrong item to the wrong person. While you need to accept that a mistake is possible at any time, you will be less likely to make silly mistakes like this if you are organized and efficient.

Sellers use a variety of methods to label their inventory. Some use adhesive notes to attach the assigned number to the item until it sells. Others place items in zippered storage bags and write the number on the bag with a permanent marker. If they are selling clothing that needs to remain hung, they may set aside closet space (this is handy if you are using a spare bedroom as an office) and wrap a piece of blue painter's tape around the hanger's neck with the pertinent information. There are as many ways to label your items as you can think of, but generally a simple system is best.

Willy has chosen to track the user IDs of his buyers in case they later have a question or complaint. He can easily scan this column for their ID and have all the pertinent information at hand, including the confirmation or tracking numbers in the next column (he will have stored all the actual Delivery Confirmation and tracking receipts in his postage file).

When you acquire inventory at estate sales, flea markets, or garage/yard sales, you likely will not be provided with a receipt for your records. When going to these types of sales, you should make it a habit to bring a notebook or a receipt book. Then, when you return home, you can accurately record your acquisition costs of the items. If you purchase numerous items at one sale, you will quickly forget how much you paid for each and could end up asking too little for an item later.

If you end up taking a loss on an item purchased secondhand, you will need some documentation of what you paid for it in order to have that loss decrease your income for the month. Of course, this system requires a fair amount of honesty, but being dishonest about your actual costs paid will not give you a true picture of your business. It will hurt you in the long run.

Many accounting software programs also will have a built-in inventory tracking system, such as Peachtree. If you are starting off with this advantage, be sure to have your accountant set up your inventory right away and teach you the proper way to input your merchandise. This will save you a lot of time in the future. For the rest of us, keeping accurate paper or spreadsheet logs is sufficient and could also be translated into data for a computerized inventory system at a later date.

Depending on your own personal interest in tracking things, you may want to set up ledgers or spreadsheets to track the business or office supplies you purchase. Set up one spreadsheet for those items you will have to pay use tax for and ones you bought in your own state. You could have a spreadsheet to list all your other deductibles: Internet service, post office box fees, storage, and rent, if you are working away from your home or renting space to store inventory). The more detailed you are in your records, the less time you (or your accountant) will have to spend sorting receipts and totaling them all up every spring.

If you are the type who does not care to see every detail laid out like a magnificent buffet, then you will probably be content to file receipts appropriately and bundle them monthly. In this case, keeping just two ledgers (inventory and sales) will be sufficient for you. Either way is fine, so long as you are prepared come April 15.

Investigating Your Tax Liabilities

In the same way this book presents accounting information as a reference with simple tools to help you along the way, it also approaches tax information with the same goals. The entirety of tax law is far beyond the scope of this publication, and because tax laws change regularly, an accountant or attorney is the most accurate source of assistance.

With that in mind, familiarize yourself with these basic ideas and lists of sources to check out before tax time.

Probably the best resource for learning about small business taxes is the Internal Revenue Service's own site, **www.irs.gov**. This one-stop site is filled with publications, forms, advice, educational opportunities, and more for the small business owner.

Whenever you are exploring the topics of importance to you, the new business owner, be sure to pay attention to the gray bar on the left of the screen, which will continue to direct you to other important items about the topic you have chosen. A good place to start, right from their home page, is the "Businesses" link under the header "Small Business/Self-Employed." From that link, you will come across these excellent publications, articles, and charts to read or download and print:

- **Publication 334, "The Tax Guide for Small Business (for Individuals Who Use Schedule C or Schedule C-EZ)":** Under the Small Business/Self-Employed Topics sidebar, click the "Forms & Pubs" link. Visit **www.irs.gov/pub/irs-pdf/p334.pdf**.

- **Husband and wife businesses:** This brief article highlights some of the nuances of husbands and wives both working in the same family-owned small business. Under the Small Business/Self-Employed Topics sidebar, click "Business With Employees" link. Visit **www.irs.gov/businesses/small/article/0,,id=97732,00.html**.

- **The forms you will need:** Based on your business structure, you will need the various forms listed on the Business Structure Chart. As with the informational publications, it would not hurt to download these forms for future reference, especially if you are a sole proprietor and will be filing your business information along with your regular income tax forms. Remember, forms change annually, so do not use a form unless it is labeled for the correct tax year.

Other useful information includes tips about getting an EIN — an employer identification number. An EIN is an identification that a business must use in their tax records. This becomes necessary in a business structure besides a sole proprietorship in which there are other employees involved. In a general sense, businesses should have one of these numbers, established by the federal government, if they are any business structure other than a sole proprietorship. Sole proprietorships can get them as well, but they are not as necessary because taxes can be reported under the owner's SSN. Search the **www.irs.gov** Web site on this topic for in-depth information about whether you need to have one of these, or call your tax professional.

Of course, every small business owner is concerned about taxes. There are three basic types of taxes you need to be concerned about at the federal level. The forms needed for each type of tax are listed on the Business Structure Chart, which is easily located by searching that phrase on **www.irs.gov**. These tax types are:

- **Income tax:** This is the same thing that is withheld from and sent to the IRS by your employer. Because you will be working for yourself, you must pay the taxes yourself. Quarterly tax payments are made using the appropriate form based on your business structure.

- **Self-employment tax:** This is how you contribute to social security and Medicare while self-employed. Like the income tax, the form you use for this differs based on your business structure.

You need to be sure you do the taxes right for any employees, or even freelance labor. You might want to consider what you will be financially and legally responsible for if you decide to hire employees. You may need to check with the laws concerning hiring in your area and state. Make sure you follow the guidelines of fair hiring practices. A good place to look for and request copies of this information is from the U.S. Office of Personnel Management. They have the current laws and practices of hiring and maintaining employees at **www.opm.gov**.

If you have employees, make sure you have a solid understanding of employee taxes, as these can be the trickiest taxes to deal with. If your company reaches a point where you feel you should hire more employees, you need to be prepared to commit 30 percent of your payroll to taxes and paperwork. It will be your responsibility to withhold all your full- or part-time employees' federal and state income tax, social security, and Medicare taxes from paychecks. At tax time, you will need to remit them with your overall tax bill. In addition, you will have to pay your company's portion of social security and Medicare benefit funds. You must consider that employee salaries of up to $87,922 will likely be taxed 6.2 percent for social security and 1.45 percent for Medicare.

Social security and Medicare are taxes that are used to provide financial assistance to workers and families under the Federal Insurance Contributions Act (FICA). Social security tax also provides financial assistance to those who fall under the old age, survivors, and disability insurance part of FICA. The taxes collected for Medicare are used to provide hospital insurance benefits under FICA. You have to pay your portion of your employees' taxes that matches what you have withheld from them. You should use Forms 941 to file the federal, social security, and Medicare taxes.

In addition to these taxes, you will also be responsible for Federal Unemployment Tax Act (FUTA) taxes. You have to pay this separately from other taxes. Your employees do not pay into this tax; you are totally responsible for it. This is another factor to consider before hiring others. You will need to file a form 940 to cover the FUTA taxes. Make sure that you deposit the taxes in a financial institution that is able to hold these types of funds.

Here is the calendar of when payroll taxes are due:

- April 30 for wages paid January — March
- July 31 for April — June
- October 31 for July — September
- January 31 for October — December

If you owe more taxes than $500, your due date changes to the 15th day of the next month.

There is another option you may want to consider instead of hiring employees, and that is hiring independent contractors. Hiring independent contractors can save you paperwork and expenses. If you hire seasonally, you will be more likely to hire these types of workers, as you need the extra help at certain times of the year. A list of independent contractors is a good thing to develop.

The definition of an independent worker applies to workers who are in business for themselves, and pay their own taxes and insurance. Independent workers use their own equipment or facilities. One of the benefits of hiring independent contractors is that they may require little or no supervision, and they are typically paid per day or for short periods of time. These are some things you must consider when determining whether a worker is an employee or an independent contractor. This assists you in avoiding the threat of tax fraud and liability charges. You must be sure the above factors apply to them and that these points are clear to the workers.

One of the best ways to ensure you do not make any errors in using independent contractors is to develop and use a written independent contractor's agreement. You can find a copy of it on the CD-ROM. Include the contractor's full name, address, and social security number or EIN.

A bonus of using an independent contractor is you do not have to withhold or pay any taxes on payment you make to them. They are responsible for their own taxes.

Deductions are the "good news" of taxes. When you pay taxes as a legitimate business, you get some benefits. Here are just some items that are likely deductible for your eBay business. Of course, double-check everything with appropriate tax professionals before taking a deduction.

Possible deductions

- Depreciation on your office equipment, or purchases of new/upgraded equipment
- eBay fees and PayPal fees paid
- Fees paid to your attorney or accountant regarding your business
- Home office space (though this is a tricky one; do so with professional advice only)
- Internet service
- Office supplies and shipping supplies
- Phone service (if you have a separate business line)
- Rent (if you rent storage space for inventory or rent an office)
- Traveling costs (mileage to and from your shipping point or for supplies and inventory)
- Utilities (if you rent space and pay for the heat and electricity, for example)

Keeping accurate records of deductible items is crucial, per chance you were to be audited by the IRS.

For mileage, keep a small spiral notebook and pencil in your car and log your mileage very carefully. Store this log in a small, weatherproof container, such as a child's plastic flip-lid pencil box. This will not only keep them from being separated in your car, but it gives you a place to stash your receipts from the gas station. Unless you are using a vehicle strictly for business, you need to be able to show exactly how many miles you drove for business versus personal use. There are two options on deductions for vehicle use: standard mileage rate or actual expenses. Each option has its own rules, benefits, and requirements, so be sure to learn about those before filling out your annual tax forms.

Keeping receipts, bills, bank statements, and monthly statements and invoices from eBay and PayPal will generally suffice for most other deductions. One issue that has come up in recent years is that receipts printed on the shiny rolls of thermal paper fade over time. In this case, photocopy or scan your receipts monthly and store those with the original receipts.

You bear the burden of proof in matters of deductions: You must be able to prove the expense in order to justify it. Here, again, you will be happy you separated your business and personal finances, especially when it comes to separating your personal eBay purchases from your business sales.

It cannot be stressed enough how important it is to get appropriate tax assistance. Although you can keep a majority of basic bookkeeping records yourself, interpreting the IRS's forms and instructions for businesses is not as simple as the ordinary tax forms the average American files annually. Not to say you cannot learn to file these items yourself, but hire a professional to guide and teach you to do them properly.

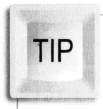

TIP

The IRS is concerned about small business owners' understanding of tax laws and requirements. They would much rather help you get it right the first time than audit you. To do their part in educating small business owners, they offer workshops in every state. To find out when the next workshops will be in your state, search the IRS's site for "small business tax workshop."

If you cannot attend a workshop near your home, or simply do not have time to dedicate in one lump sum, you can also take online versions with streaming video from an actual workshop. This is a great alternative for those whose busy lives force them to do a lot of work late at night.

To help you stay up-to-date with tax issues, the IRS also offers a free e-mail mailing list you can join. Once the IRS knows about your business, they take the initiative to send you the appropriate quarterly forms in advance.

This is just one way they try to make sure that business owners do not get behind or accidentally botch taxes.

Your own state also wants to do its part to make your business successful. To find information about how your state's taxation system works, search "state links" on the **www.irs.gov** home page. This page has a link for every state's basic information.

Do not neglect to register your business with your state and local authorities as well; you will find that they are just as anxious for your business endeavor to be a success as the IRS is. After all, you are helping your state's and country's economies grow.

One more topic that falls under "taxes" is that of sales tax and use tax. As a legitimate business, you are required to collect sales tax on all sales to buyers in your own state and forward them to your state's department of revenue. Your state's department of revenue will be happy to assist you by sending forms to use and reminders of the dates you must submit payment and verification. At this time, charging sales tax for sales in other states is not necessary, as your customers are required to report their purchases and pay the taxes themselves. This is called use tax.

You may have to pay use taxes to your state for all items, supplies, and other tangible goods that you purchase out of state (such as on eBay, or from the Web sites of suppliers) and are using for your own business use. This does not apply to inventory you purchase for resale, but for the items that you normally would pay sales tax if you had purchased them in your own state.

The companies that sold you these goods were not required to collect sales tax from you, but you may be required to pay it yourself. Keep a separate spreadsheet or ledger page listing the items you buy that are subject to use tax, and make copies of applicable receipts for verification. Your accounting professional, or your own state's department of revenue, can help you determine if you must pay use tax.

When you contact your state department of revenue, be sure to get the details on all of these topics:

- How often do I need to forward sales and use taxes?
- What specific items are or are not taxable?
- What is the tax rate?
- What is the process for forwarding taxes?
- What assistance is available to me by way of forms or advice?

If you collect payment for auctions through PayPal, you can program it to automatically collect sales tax within your state. Beware, though — PayPal's fees are based on the entire amount of money sent by the buyer, and they do not exclude sales tax in that figure. So, technically, you will be paying PayPal fees on the sales tax you collect. To make up for this, you may wish to add a few pennies more to your shipping and handling fee when you set an auction up to make up for that.

Taxes can be complicated matters that require professional assistance. The penalties, interest, and headaches incurred when mistakes are made are just far too costly for most small businesses. They can sink your ship before it sets sail, or leave you deserted on an island of debt. The information contained here is only of general nature and should not be considered the definitive answer to any of your tax questions.

Though it may seem overwhelming to consider all these issues (setting up an official business, recordkeeping, inventory, bookkeeping, and taxes), do not be discouraged. Everyone involved wants you to become a successful business, and even though there are many rules to follow and taxes to pay, they will do what they can to steer you away from pitfalls and failure. The rest is up to you: Do it right the first time, take the time to learn the rules and follow them, and be prepared to spend some money for the tasks you cannot do yourself.

Once you have your business structure set up, with your business plan down on paper and your recordkeeping and inventory systems set up, you are ready to nail down some important details. You will need to obtain a product to sell, choose how you will receive payments, ship items, and learn how to promote your business.

	Checklist of Tasks When Setting Up a Recordkeeping System and Learning About Tax Issues
✓	I have thought about and made a list of all the possible expenses and income sources I might have in this venture (my early chart of accounts).
✓	I have determined how I want to file receipts, invoices, and bank statements, and I made a list so I can set up my filing cabinet right away.
✓	I have decided how to track auctions, inventory, expenses, & income. • *By hand in a purchased ledger or computer-made ledger-type form* • *By spreadsheet program that I know how to use, or will get assistance in setting it up* • *By accounting software that I know how to use, or will get assistance in setting up*
✓	I have given some thought to how I will store and label my inventory.
✓	I have contacted an accountant or attorney for advice on how to deal with tax issues when starting a new business.
✓	I have become familiar with the various online resources at **www.irs.gov** and my home state's business start-up Web site and am comfortable with what is required of me. • *Quarterly income tax payments* • *Collection of sales tax for sales to others in my state* • *Documentation and payment of use tax for items I purchase online*

CASE STUDY: "LUV MAKES THE WORLD GO 'ROUND"

While her husband, Timothy, was stationed in Iraq, Tana just needed to keep busy. It eased the worries about his safety. What better way to keep busy than to start a home-based business? Tana did just that, though at the time she did not know it was what she was doing.

Her husband's parents, recently deceased, had 50 years' worth of collected and everyday items in their house. It all needed to be sold. By the time she was through with the project, Tana (eBay user "amommysluv") was pretty comfortable in her new role as an eBay seller. She decided she would like to keep at it and, in addition to cleaning out her own unused items, began to sell for other people. Consignments would soon become a large share of her business.

Timothy came home from Iraq and retired from the military after 27 years of total service. He went right to work helping Tana in their burgeoning business in the Spokane, Washington, area. They worked together as a team, posting auctions, answering questions from customers, and boxing and shipping the items in an efficient manner.

Soon, they had 15 consignment accounts that had helped them branch their selling into many new categories, such as eBay Motors and children's clothing. By this time, they were also selling brand-new retail items, such as clothing and home decor. Their eBay Store, A Mommy's Luv Embroidery, helped set them apart: They could personalize many items with embroidery for the customer.

The large variety displayed on their eBay Store changes frequently, and they often have entire collections of items to sell from their consignment clients. Their house has been swallowed up by their business, so they recently took the next step: moving to a retail location. They are proud of being able to get to this level. "We see this business becoming a full-time growth opportunity," Tana said. "We are adding to our consignment base while also looking at some wholesale opportunities."

Setting up their business efficiently was easy for Tana, who has more than 20 years of experience in the financial services industry. She has been an income tax preparer as well, so IRS rules or paperwork did not frighten or confuse her. Though they have managed to keep the business running with just their own manpower, Timothy and Tana's two daughters, Amanda and Sara, are utilized as seasonal employees when things get crazy. It gives the entire family a real sense of accomplishment to have their own business together.

Although running their business efficiently and profitably is important, Timothy and Tana also like to give back to the eBay community by helping train others in the art of selling online. With experience in both eBay and Half.com sales, they feel they have much to offer the new seller in way of encouragement and practical advice. Some advice they give new sellers:

- **Organize**. Find one system to do all the customer management for your business. A lot of money can be wasted in trying to piece a system together — we learned the hard way.

- **Purchase the right items for resale.** It is crucial, but it is also unpredictable. Be willing to purchase items out-of-season and hold inventory until it is back in season.

- **Get help.** Learn to rely on the information given to you via eBay and other market research companies.

- **Put the customer first.** Always try to treat others the way you yourself (as a consumer) would want to be treated.

Their feedback is a good testament to their customer-service focus. With their feedback steadily climbing toward the 2,000 mark with over 99 percent positive responses from their customers, these PowerSellers credit their "underlying character" for propelling them to this high status. "We want our customers to be happy," Tana said.

It is not just a matter of making your customers happy, however. Good customer service starts with the seller's own personal commitment to being an honest seller. "Never lose sight of your ethics," Tana said. "Don't play into the games that other less-ethical sellers may be playing. Keep your customer's interests at heart, and remember to cater to them."

One way to practice honest, ethical selling is in your product descriptions. "Always list your products with an honest, full description. If questions are asked that you can't answer, let the customer know," she said.

One final note of advice: Have fun. When you become burnt out to the point that you are no longer enjoying your eBay business, your attitude will carry over into every part of your experience. Customers will notice this change, and your business will suffer.

Finding support through other eBay sellers helps lessen the stress and frustration this type of business-venture can bring. If Timothy and Tana have their way, they will be doing just that type of education and support of sellers, both new and seasoned, for some years to come.

Chapter Five

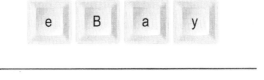

Stuff to Sell

You are getting closer to the reality of starting your own business; perhaps you even have a good start on the tasks in Chapters 2 and 3. If so, then you are on the right path to success.

Before you delve into setting up those auctions, let us explore some other things that are better to have figured out sooner than later. Though these tasks may not be as crucial as the legal issues and tax obligations discussed previously, they are all part of what will make or break your business. This includes topics such as obtaining merchandise, choosing your payment and shipping options, and advertising yourself. All these tasks are part of the strong foundation you are building for your business.

Obtaining Merchandise

This is one thing most people have some idea about when they first consider opening their own business on eBay. Part of it is pure logic: Sell what you like. If you are an avid collector of Hummel figurines, for example, then you will be a good seller because you know your merchandise well. If you worked throughout high school in a sporting goods store, then you may want to put that knowledge to work for you and sell sporting goods.

However, simply selling what you know is not the final word on what you should sell. You may have several specialties or interests, or you may have a product you want to make yourself. But the question is this: Are these things that people are actually buying on eBay?

Spend some time searching current and completed listings to see if the item or types of items you want to sell are currently being marketed. This will give you a good idea of whether your product will generate interest, and what sort of price you can expect to ask. *Tips on searching for products to sell are included in Chapter 1.*

Determining the price you will ask for your product is dependent on being able to obtain your product cheaply enough to make a profit for yourself and still give buyers a good price. If you cannot do that, you probably will not sell much. See what your competition is charging for the same, or similar, products on eBay.

Remember that you will have to acquire the product and maybe pay some shipping fees to receive it. Then, you will have to spend money on eBay fees (remember Willy's Widgets 'n' Gidgets Sales Ledger) and still turn a bit of profit in the end. Simply the price of the product does not give you a full sense of how much profit you will have in the end.

eBay is a highly fluid market, and what sells well one month may not sell well the next. Do not become too attached to any one category, and do not be afraid to branch out. Think beyond the ordinary. There is money to be made in selling day-to-day products, but it is a little different on eBay than it is anywhere else. If you do insist on trading in ordinary commodity goods, you have to realize you are selling something eBay shoppers can probably get at a store within a few miles of their home, and you have to give them some incentive to buy it from you instead.

The incentive is usually price. Take those compact fluorescent light (CFL) bulbs people have started using to replace their regular bulbs. They are energy-efficient, but you can also get them at any corner drugstore for about

$4 each. If you can somehow get your hands on a shipment of them that has been deeply discounted, and you can sell them for $2 apiece, you will make money. However, if you list them on eBay for the same price they can get them at their neighborhood store, you are out of luck. You also must figure in shipping costs. People will be more willing to pay for shipping if it is for an item they cannot find anywhere else.

Put items together

You can make your products seem like a better deal sometimes if you package products together that complement one another. The idea here is to take two or more products and, instead of selling them in separate auctions, sell them as a set. You will increase your odds of selling both products in one sale, as opposed to selling only one.

Retailers do this all the time. Look at computer advertisements. When you buy a computer, many times, you do not just buy the computer. Dealers sell a bundle that includes the computer, an inkjet printer, some software, and other assorted peripherals. Using a similar technique, you get more money from each customer, you have better odds of selling all the products, and you save on your eBay listing fees.

Consumable goods

Goods that get used up and must be purchased periodically are also a good type of item to sell. If you are offering a good deal, you can get repeat business using this approach. Take a product like inkjet cartridges. This market is highly competitive, and buyers are always looking for a deal. Granted, cartridges are a commodity item, and they can be found anywhere. From that perspective, it is a hard sell on eBay — but if you can make a good pitch and offer them at a competitive price, you can make a sale.

When you make a sale, you may not make much profit on that one sale, but you get a customer who is likely to return several times to your shop to buy more. They are buying your company's reputation. If you can sell them something simple in a way that meets their standards, customers are more likely to buy from your company again.

If you are dealing in this type of consumable product, be sure to build a mailing list so you can send out occasional reminders to your customers. They will remember to come back to you when they need more. Offer special incentives to keep them returning.

Your own backyard

Before you start looking for potential resources all over the world to find merchandise to sell, you should begin by searching around you. There are many different places you can go to find all sorts of stuff to turn a profit with on eBay. Your hometown has resources you may not realize exist. The advantage of local sourcing, too, is that you will save on shipping costs. eBay sellers who deal in collectibles, antiques, arts, and crafts are especially adept at finding things locally. Of course, you do not want to pay their retail price, but remember, these people do not have a huge market and are always looking for a sale. Tell them about your eBay business, and ask for a volume discount. It may well be that they have thought of selling on eBay but have not gotten around to it, do not have the time or inclination, or do not have a computer.

When you engage in local buying, you are bound to get people who hear about it and will constantly come around and offer you things. While you can occasionally get good deals this way, more often than not, these people have an inflated sense of what their item is really worth, so you will have to do some serious bargaining with them. On the other hand, they may just be looking for a few extra dollars, and you can get some good deals if you know what to look for and can separate the trash from the treasure.

There are eBay sellers who will go where no others like to go to find their treasures. They root through trash and pull out discarded odds and ends. They then take them to an acquaintance of theirs who deals on eBay and attempt to sell these discards. Surprisingly, they are often successful. Of course, not everyone wants to drive through alleys picking through people's trashcans, but the point is you can find saleable items almost anywhere.

Online bulletin boards

An online bulletin board is a locally or nationally recognized site where people post all types of information, such as apartments for rent, services offered, jobs available in the area, and things people are trying to sell. More often than not, there is some nominal fee charged for people to post something for a certain amount of time. You will be surprised at some of the deals you will come across if you keep an eye out for some items that people in and around your own neighborhood post on such sites. Two of the most nationally used online bulletin boards are **www.craigslist.org** and **www.sellstufflocal.com**. Both allow you to look at listings according to geographic location.

Be on the lookout for Web boards that are set up specifically for certain areas. For instance, if you live in Florida, **www.Ocala4Sale.com**, **www. Tampa4sale.com**, and **www.Gainesville4sale.com** are exceptional online bulletin boards you certainly do not want to ignore. Do some Internet research to see whether there are any popular Web boards in your area.

Local storage companies

Storage facilities are excellent places to pick up some items you will easily be able to turn a profit with. Most people use storage facilities to store things they do not want to part with, but that they have no room for in their home or apartment. They pay a fee for the storage facility to store it for them. Most of these places just offer a small, garage-like area, or a room where you can go to store your items yourself. Occasionally, the owner of the items in storage stops paying rent, and after a period of trying to get in touch with the owner of the items, the storage facility is free to dispose of them any way they see fit.

This is where you come in. Contact all your local storage facilities and find out when they hold their regular auctions to get rid of unclaimed items to make room for new renters. Sometimes, you may have to buy an entire set without ever getting to see what is in there. But chances are if they went through all the trouble in the first place to store it, there must be at least some items of value.

Even if most of the items have little or no resale value, you are likely going to find some gems that will make the whole purchase worth it. Donate the rest of the stuff that you are not going to be able to turn a profit on to a local charity, and get a receipt for a tax write-off.

Flea markets

Selling at a flea market can be a frustrating experience. If the weather is too good, people frequently have better things to do than browse a flea market, and if the weather is bad, then people do not want to be walking around. For vendors at flea markets, it is frustrating when people think of flea markets as giant yard sales, regardless of the quality of the merchandise. People are looking for a bargain, and they will not want to pay top-dollar for your items.

For you as a reseller, flea markets can be a gold mine. Find out when there are going to be flea markets in your area. If the weather is too good or too lousy, count your blessings and go anyway. Dress comfortably, and try to find those vendors who are so desperate to part with some of their goods that they are willing to bring down their prices to make a sale. You will be surprised at what people will overlook at a flea market that you can buy and resell for a large profit.

Try to make many contacts as well. Most veterans of flea markets are hoarders of treasures and junk. What they have brought that day most likely represents only a small portion of what they have at their homes. If you are looking for some particular products, mention them in passing as you are going about your day. You never know when someone may say, "Oh yeah, I have a box of that in my basement." Many resalable items can be obtained in this way.

Yard sales

Yard sales come in all shapes and sizes. You will have all different types of sellers at yard sales: people who are looking to get rid of what they consider junk, people who are looking to raise money, and people who have other motivations for putting some tables up and selling all sorts of things at cheap prices.

Your basic strategy for going to yard sales should be to identify all the ones happening in your area by checking out local listings on a weekly basis, and then plan to go as early as possible so you can snatch up any gems that may be there. Then, go back late just as they are cleaning up and see what you can snatch up. Offer to buy all of something or everything they have left for a price that will not offend them, but one that you are sure to be able to turn a profit on. For instance, let us say that you bought a vintage record player at 6 a.m. for $10 that you know you are going to get at least $100 for. You noticed that in the corner there were a couple of boxes of books. Books will regularly sell on eBay, and these are priced here with the vendor at $1 per book. You estimate there are about 100 titles. When you come back later, as they are beginning to pack up for the day, you notice that not many of the books have sold. You offer to take all of the books off their hands for about $25. They agree, eager to be rid of them. You later go on to sell each book for about $5 to $10 dollars, making a respectable profit.

Go to your local yard sales, snatch up the obvious moneymakers early, and then take notes about which sales you are going to come back to later when they are closing, because there are many items you may be able to buy all together for one low price.

At rummage sales, if possible, have someone you know available to do a quick Internet search for items while you are out rummaging or auctioning. You may have a hunch about an item, and finding out whether an item sells well on eBay is a smart move before buying.

Church bazaars

Church bazaars are excellent places to get potential merchandise. Frequently, they have higher-quality products than available at flea markets and garage sales. Church members may be trying to raise money for a specific cause, so they are not likely to bring out stuff they just want to get rid of.

It may still be worthwhile to show up early so you can see whether they are selling any valuable antiques or under-priced gems. What you are actually looking for are items you will come back for later. Arrive as they are packing away crates and offer to take a box of something off their hands. You might easily pick up that box of several hundred DVDs they were going to sell for $1 apiece for $20 to $40. After a day of serving the needs of their church, volunteers will be eager to be rid of as much as possible, rather than having to put everything away.

Newspapers

Your local newspapers can be a quality source of potential goods. Get into the habit of checking local newspaper classified listings every day as you sip your morning coffee. Many times, people will announce all sorts of events, like flea markets, yard sales, and church bazaars, but they will also post items they are trying to sell. You may see furniture that you can resell, cars that can be auctioned on eBay autos, or even houses and other forms of real estate that you can buy and resell for a nice profit.

Also, be on the lookout for "collections" that an heir or a divorced spouse may not appreciate" books, costume jewelry, computer parts, games, electronics, art, comic books, videos, coins, stamps, old photos, rare baseball cards, or anything else that has been inherited or is no longer wanted.

Auctions

Auctions can be excruciating to sit through, with the monotone voice of the auctioneer droning on, but they can be a significant source of products to sell. Do some research and find out what kinds of auctions are going on in your area. Distributors often hold public auctions to get rid of merchandise that has not sold. If you go to a live auction, stay to the absolute end — that is when they frequently bring out the good stuff. You may have to sit through hours of useless merchandise before one or two gems come onstage. If you are just barely keeping your eyes open, stick with it. Think of it as a part of your job. You will likely be grateful that you did.

Thrift stores

Many charity-run thrift stores are nationally distributed. Goodwill, The Salvation Army, and other local charities often resell donated items to help raise money for their organizations. You will meet many people looking for things to resell, just like you, and the community that can develop at these thrift stores can be a valuable source of insight and encouragement for your own business.

Big corporations know the value of hiring consultants, whose value to the company is the knowledge and experience they bring to the table. They often pay their consultants large fees to attend meetings. Because you are likely not a multi-billion dollar company and cannot offer large monetary incentives, you must find other ways to gain friends who have been doing this much longer than you. These are the "old-timers" who can look at a pile of "junk" and immediately see the treasure scattered here and there. These are the people you want to get to know.

You can easily be able to differentiate the professional like yourself from the run-of-the-mill junk collector. Offer to help them sift through the thrift store's collections in exchange for some free advice and friendship.

You might even want to look into getting to know the owners of the thrift stores. Offering them the opportunity to become a trade assistant is an excellent way to have them put high-quality items to the side for you to look at first in exchange for sharing some of your profits with them. They likely would rather help you and get part of the profits than let something they know the intrinsic value of sit on a shelf and collect dust.

As a seller who has established yourself as someone who can effectively market and sell things in the online world, you have a valuable skill that you can share with others to make not only yourself money, but others as well.

Again, large companies understand the value of this profit sharing. They have no problem letting different companies share in some of their profits if they can be sure the business venture is going to make more money for everyone than any single company could make on its own; learn from them. Especially if you can find a thrift store run by knowledgeable people, it pays to share a small percentage of your profits in exchange for friends who are going to call you first when that valuable crate of stuff gets dropped off at their front door.

Estate auctions

Sometimes when a person dies or a bank has seized the entire estate of an individual, there will be auctions where almost an entire lifetime of collected stuff will go on sale to the highest bidders. Check your local listings and Web boards; you will be surprised how many estate auctions go on in your area on a regular basis. Attending one a week can be a valuable source of items and income. You never know what types of treasures were left behind. Often, grieving relatives, who always will have first pick, will take items of sentimental, rather than monetary, value.

Attend all the estate auctions you can, and once again, make sure you stay until the absolute end. Keep your eye out for collections that you can easily sell to make a nice profit. Even if you do not have dreams of quitting your day job and doing eBay full-time, attending one estate auction a week can turn into a fun hobby — and an incredibly satisfying second income.

When attending these estate auctions, it is absolutely vital to do a complete walkthrough several times over. Have an idea of what you are willing to spend beforehand. Be willing to bid on the contents of an entire table — even though most of the items may be going to charity for a tax write-off, bid on tables where there are items of significant resale value to make the whole purchase worth it. If you live close enough to the auction location, go home and check out the value of some questionable items that caught your eye. A cell phone with Internet service is an exceptional resource to have on these little excursions. It will make your life much easier by allowing you to look up things right away without having to leave.

Occasionally, you will have the opportunity to bid on the contents of an entire estate. If you can afford it, do it. Especially if you have done a walkthrough and seen many items that can be resold, you will have significantly increased your amount of product, and will also have plenty of stuff to donate to lower your tax bracket.

Moving Beyond the Neighborhood

After establishing yourself in the local neighborhood, you may want to start branching out. As your business grows, your potential source of inventory must grow with it. This is especially true if you start getting some regular traffic on specific types of goods; you are going to want to start thinking more in terms of the bigger picture.

These are all excellent ways to get large quantities of merchandise in your own area. Yet, these are not good ways to get merchandise on a continual basis. The best types of items to sell are the type of products you have an interest in and of which you have a working knowledge. That does not mean you cannot make a profit off digital cameras when you do not have an interest in digital photography. But if you want staying power in this industry, you are going to want to deal with products in which you have some degree of special knowledge.

That is when you begin to expand. You will find plenty of reliable sources of high-quality goods with excellent prices if you take the time to find them. This section will give you the inside track to some of the secrets of finding sources for the best products that are out there.

After building small, establishing a product for the market, and building up positive feedback from established customers, start thinking bigger. Look into the following potential product sources. When thinking about buying large lots, ask for samples, or buy a couple first to sell on eBay to see the potential to generate sales.

Trade shows

Trade shows have suppliers, wholesalers, and manufacturers who will exhibit their products throughout the country and the world. The benefits of attending trade shows are many. Not only will you be able to network and gain key contacts from all over the country, you will also get to see and try out new products, all under the same roof.

Do not forget to register yourself as a legitimate business; your tax ID number will open the door for you to get into many trade shows that are closed to the public. A tax ID number is not hard to get from your local authorities, and if you do not have one already, you should get one as soon as possible. It gives you an edge over all those on eBay who have not gone through the trouble to register themselves as a business.

Do your research right and go to the trade shows that are going to be featuring a category of merchandise that you specialize in. You will get to see the latest up-and-coming trends in your niche market. Even if you can only afford to go to one of these shows a year, it would help you stay current on all the latest trends.

Find the next trade show you can attend at **www.biztradeshows.com.**

Note to the Reader
The Better Business Bureau

Look for the Better Business Bureau's (BBB) Online Reliability logo on Web sites of wholesalers, distributors, and drop-shippers. Clicking on the BBB's logo on these sites should take you to the BBB's Web site, where you will see a message stating the company's compliance. If the logo does not take you to the BBB's site, or it takes you to a site that does not begin with www.bbb.org, then report it immediately to the BBB.

Direct manufacturers

Frequently, direct manufacturers work with only large-scale wholesalers who can buy large quantities of their products at a reduced rate. Most of the time, they will not deal directly with someone like you, who will not buy anywhere near the amount of bulk items a large-sale wholesaler would. Nevertheless, many of the smaller manufacturers who are based in your area may be willing to deal directly with you. Be polite and professional with them. If you assure them they will be getting continual business with your company, you stand a good chance of their wanting your business. At worst, you will get a list of wholesalers, and at best, you will cut out the middleman and deal directly with the manufacturer.

If you find a company that makes what you want to sell, contact them and try to get a list of wholesalers who carry their products. Although you will not get as good a rate as the wholesalers are getting, you still should be able to get a quality deal on bulk orders.

Also, there are custom manufacturers who will regularly deal in almost any-sized order. They make custom products, like pens with your company name, graphic T-shirts, mugs, banners, and other such customizable items. You can run a T-shirt company online by having a custom manufacturer make them for you. For instance, you can have them make a bunch of T-shirts for you that say, "I bought this shirt on eBay" and sell them out of your eBay store. They will make them for you in a variety of sizes and colors. All you have to do is sell and ship them.

Do your homework. Most manufacturers will have no problem selling you a bunch of products they know no one is buying. In the end, they will be out to make a sale. Do some research on the marketability of the items you are looking to purchase.

Remanufacturers

Remanufactured products are not new, and they are not exactly used, either. They are products that have been returned to the manufacturer, repaired, cleaned, and put back into new packaging. Many consumers love them because they are getting a product that in most cases is like new, but at a better price. Many remanufactured goods even have some existing warranties attached to them.

You have an excellent advantage if you can buy these remanufactured goods from the manufacturers; this is especially true with electronics. Most manufacturers will jump at the chance to get the merchandise off their hands. They will be willing to sell the merchandise for a reduced price, which you can mark up, and it will still end up costing the consumer much less than buying the same product new.

Make sure you do your homework and check with the manufacturers who deal in products you like to sell to see whether they have any remanufactured merchandise they would like to part with.

 Deal directly with manufacturers. Do not use intermediaries, as you can get better deals when working directly with the manufacturer.

Distributors

There are thousands of distributors out there who offer large catalogs full of wholesale-priced goods to people like flea marketers, craft show folks, and, of course, eBay sellers. You can find many of these places on the Internet. Some of these distributors are merely companies that re-distribute items from other distributors, so you must proceed with caution.

Beware of advertisements that claim you can re-sell their product at an exceptionally high profit. If they are selling an item to you for $5 a dozen, and their ad says "retail price $19.99 each," then you may do best to move on to the next place. There are unrealistic claims out there.

Another area to look out for when dealing with these sorts of wholesale distributors, especially if they are not local, is if a picture on the Web site looks much better than the actual product. If you are interested in a particular item, find out whether you can buy just one as a sample to inspect before placing a larger order. If they are not willing to sell you a single piece, that is a big red flag.

Finally, although you may be able to find some good products at attractive wholesale prices from these distributors, there are still thousands of others who are doing the same thing. These are stock items, and if you try to re-sell them on eBay, you may be surprised to find there are 100 other people selling exactly the same thing.

Drop-shippers

Like the wholesale distributors, drop-shippers also offer goods to thousands of resellers, many of whom deal on eBay. The advantage of a drop-shipper, though, is that you do not have to buy large quantities of any one product, and you do not have to worry about shipping. The drop-shipper ships out the product on your behalf, using an address label that reflects the name of your own eBay shop.

Naturally, there are some inherent limitations with this approach. Countless others may be offering the same thing. Drop-shippers make their money by getting small merchants to offer their catalog under their own name.

But if you do not want to package, ship, and keep track of multiple items, then drop-shipping is the only way to go. One of the most comprehensive lists of drop-shippers is the Drop-ship Source Directory, at **www.mydssd. com.** You can easily eliminate middlemen simply by using this directory, which is by far the most up-to-date list you will find, and it is quite useful for all your Internet businesses.

While drop-shipping is a legitimate business and can be quiet profitable, many drop-shipping scams exist. A purported drop-shipper may merely be an intermediary who claims he or she is the actual supplier. Also, the goods you are representing may be substandard. You lose an element of quality control when using a drop-shipper, as you are not personally inspecting the items. It is easy to make a poor-quality product look good in a picture. However, when customers get the product, and it is not what they expected, they will not blame the invisible drop-shipper; they will blame you. Avoid drop-shipping frauds and establish an online business or eBay presence by using only reputable, reliable drop-shippers.

A variation of this process is a fulfillment service, which does not supply the products, but takes your products that you have personally selected, stores them, and completes the fulfillment process on your behalf. Numerous reputable suppliers are more than willing to do drop-shipping or fulfillment on your behalf. They may require an account set-up fee that you will need to pay, so you will have to be prepared for some initial investment. Always carefully investigate all related costs before agreeing to anything in writing.

A simple online search is a good way to find suppliers who do drop-shipping, but many companies are more interested in taking money from you than in helping you make money. This is a shortsighted approach on their part because when you make money, they do, too. However, as in all occupations, many do not understand this simple principle. Find a drop-shipper who is reputable, willing to talk to you *in person*, and who will send you actual physical samples of products for your review before you buy in bulk.

Some issues to clarify before starting a business relationship with any drop-shipper are:

- How much will they charge you for the merchandise, including any handling charges they might pass on to you for storing, packaging, and shipping the item?

- Precisely how will the charges be processed? Are you required to pay as you go, as they ship each item, or will they send you an invoice monthly?

- Do they accept returns directly from your buyers in the event the merchandise is damaged?

The advantages of using a drop-shipper is you do not need to have an on-site inventory, you do not need to package and ship anything, and you do not need a place to store your merchandise. It is a great way to do business, but you must be careful whom do business with and what agreements that are made, because it could cost you a lot of money if you are careless. Here are some tips when considering a particular drop-shipper. These are questions you should be asking before you sign any agreement with a drop-ship company:

- Must you agree to sell only their items on your Web site or on eBay, or can you sell other products? Make sure there is no minimum purchase you must sell of the drop-shipper's products.

- Will you have the ability to pick the items you wish to sell from their inventory, or will you be required to sell items they chose?

- Does the drop-shipper provide descriptions and pictures of their products to post on eBay or your Web site?

- What is the process of getting an item shipped? Do they require payment from you first, or will they bill you monthly for the product?

- Do their product prices include shipping, or is this separate? What do they use to ship, and where are they willing to ship to?

- How quickly will the item be sent out to the drop-shipper? Do they have a guarantee?

The way a drop-shipper generally works is as follows:

- You chose the items you wish to sell on eBay and in your store.
- You post the items and place them on eBay for bidding.
- A buyer finds the item and buys it.
- You send the drop-shipper a payment, usually by credit card.
- The drop-shipper gets the order and sends it out immediately.
- You keep the difference between what the item cost you buying it from the drop-shipper and the price the buyer paid.

Many other eBay sellers use drop-shipping companies as the source of the products they sell. Everyone gets the same picture and description of the product. In order to catch the eye of a buyer, you may consider posting your own pictures and descriptions. You need to do whatever it takes to set your business apart from every other eBay store. This takes a little extra work, but this will translate into higher profits later.

Do not be dragged into the trap of trying to sell the thousands of items the drop-shipper has to offer. You will be killed in fees, and your sales will be low. Stick with a niche market. Specialize in certain types of products. Know everything about those products, and be able to talk like an expert about them. Blog about the products you have to sell; get the word out.

Another trap to avoid is when those drop-shippers ask you to pay a fee just to view their catalog. You should not have to pay anything to see the products they want you to sell for them. You should also consider buying a few of the items you are considering selling. Try them out for yourself. You do not want to sell junk, because there is plenty of that on eBay as it is. You want to sell high-end, quality products for a competitive price.

Look for drop-shippers that are offering a healthy number of products and ones that fall into the niche that you wish to sell. Avoid those that boast that they can ship thousands of different kinds of products. Some of these companies are merely a middleman and are buying from wholesalers. This can cause a delay in fulfilling your orders, and they may not be able to offer you the best prices available.

Do not automatically believe claims that their products have a high resale value. Do your research and look at how much the products are selling for on eBay compared to what they claim those products will sell for. Trustworthy companies will not need to inflate their claims; their history and low prices will speak for themselves. You may even find that some reputable wholesalers will also function as a drop-shipper for your company.

You may find yourself in the situation in which after selling your item, you go to the distributor's Web site and find it is not in stock. Do not panic; call the drop-shipper. It is possible they still have the item in the warehouse and simply took it off the Web site because it was running low.

If that is not the case, you will have to contact your buyers and admit that the items they bought are currently not on hand with your supplier. It is imperative you call your customers in this situation; they may not be as angry as they might be if you had just e-mailed this information. It would be wise to offer to refund their money in full immediately, and possibly even send some kind of consolation. Someone else's error may net you negative feedback. That risk is inherent in employing drop-shipping as a routine business practice.

Another resource that is an eBay-certified service provider is Worldwide Brands, located at **www.worldwidebrands.com**. An eBay Radio's product sourcing editor created this Web site, which contains plenty of free or low-cost information. Also available on the site is a membership they want to sign you up for. As with all services that cost you money, investigate before investing and weigh the costs against what you stand to profit.

Online wholesalers

You can find nearly anything online these days. Be careful; anyone can publish a Web site that says they are an Internet wholesaler, and they may just be out to get as many credit card numbers as possible. Do not buy from an online wholesaler who will not give you a physical address and phone number. However, look around online, as many legitimate vendors can get you wholesale products.

One of the most popular Internet wholesalers out there is **www.liquidation.com**. Check out the Web site, and be aware there are many other eBay wholesalers who would be a good resource for products to drive your sales into the PowerSeller status. You should also check out **www.wholesale-central.com** and **www.biglotswholesale.com**. While **www.greatrep.com** sells wholesale giftware and home furnishings, **www.bargainw.com** deals in wholesale dollar merchandise. They have plenty of consumables, health and beauty aids, stationery items, kitchen supplies, candy, toys, cleaning supplies, plastic lines, and housewares.

Buying wholesale can put you into a much nicer profit margin, but there are downsides to buying this way. The most obvious issue is potentially having 5,000 of any one item on hand. Do you have room to store that much merchandise? Is the demand going to be strong long enough to sell that many of one item? You may be smart to pay a bit higher cost per item and not have so much stock.

Before buying cases and cases of an item, check with the manufacturer to see if a newer product line has recently been developed. People may not want an older model if a newer model can be bought with more features. Customers may buy the older model, however, if they can get it at a substantially lower price, making those newer features not worth the extra cost.

Another thing to consider is this: Are eBay buyers going to pay shipping and handling fees for small items? Perhaps you can get 500 baby rattles with a popular cartoon character on them for $0.16 each. These should easily sell for a dollar or more. However, who will pay the shipping cost for one small rattle? Unless it is a very popular cartoon character whose merchandise happens to be difficult to find, you may have a hard time getting people to buy them, no matter how good the deal.

Here is a suggestion: If you have found such a good deal on baby rattles, see if you can snag a deal on some bibs, teething toys, receiving blankets, sleepers, and other baby basics. If you can get together several such items, you can sell them in lots. Make up a package of one or more of each item and sell them as a group (lot). Put in a little creativity, and you might have yourself a nice product. Try getting some tulle (inexpensive netting, like what is used to tie up rice bags at weddings, which can be found cheaply at fabric stores) and ribbon. Arrange your group of items neatly in a circle of tulle (pink or blue), and tie up neatly with a piece of ribbon.

Locate some wholesale gift tags or greeting cards, and include a baby-shower card for the buyer. Presto: a pre-packaged baby shower gift; just sign the card and go. If you are not wild about the idea of venturing into a fabric store to find tulle, locate a wholesaler for wrapping paper and include a package of pink or blue in with the lot. Those little extras are what make an item worthwhile and will build you a grateful customer base.

This is just one example of how you can use multiple items from wholesale lots to create a unique product that will have more appeal than just the individual items alone.

One of the better options for new sellers in terms of drop-shipping is an arrangement with a local artisan or small-town manufacturer. Perhaps you live in Oregon but have a cousin in Baltimore, Maryland, who makes beautiful handmade birdhouses and feeders. He mostly sells them in his front yard. Maybe he even goes to an arts-and-crafts fair a couple of times a year. However, his exposure is limited. That is where you come in.

It would be silly for your cousin to mail birdhouses and feeders to you so you could photograph them, sell them, then re-ship them to the buyer. That is a waste of time and money. Drop-shipping is a good arrangement in this case: You set up the auctions, collect the payments, and send your cousin's share to him. Your cousin ships the item to the buyer directly.

If there is some latitude in your cousin's profit — he generally makes a handsome profit and is willing to share some of it in exchange for your eBay marketing, and he is willing to ship the product before receiving his share of the profits — then this could be a great opportunity for you to create some business for both of you. One way to make sure he gets his share right away is for him to have a PayPal account where you deposit his share (plus the shipping cost he will incur) as soon as you receive payment.

Any such business arrangement, even with family members, should be put on paper and properly documented in a manner suggested by your attorney. You want to build strong, trusting relationships with your drop-shippers, but you also need to make sure all parties are working for the same goal and agreeing on the same things.

Check with any artists or crafters to be sure that they are not making their products from plans or patterns that are copyrighted, nor are they copying a registered or trademarked product from another company. All artistic and handmade items should be made using original ideas and designs of the crafter.

Drop-shipping arrangements can be made with local manufacturing firms as well. Smaller family-owned companies make products all over the country, yet they often do not have the worldwide exposure they would like to have. Set up some appointments to meet with these local businessmen and women and see if you may be able to do business with each other. You may be able to develop an exclusive right to sell their products on eBay, which is always an advantage to you.

When considering all the sources of merchandise available to sell, do not overlook your own ingenuity and creativity. You could be your own best supplier of inventory, whether it is a handmade item or a less-tangible eBook.

Writing and selling eBooks is a growing trend, and one that can definitely be a money-maker if your product is good. If you have some special knowledge of a topic that would qualify you to write an eBook, you can do so with only basic software. EBooks are e-mailed to the buyer upon payment, and Adobe Reader format (PDF files) is the most common format used.

There are software packages available to help you set up your format, add zip with graphics, charts, or illustrations, and other extras that may make your head swim. There are also companies who will (for a fee) assist you. You can even purchase books (paper and eBooks) on the subject as well. Just search "write eBook" in your Internet search engine.

Note to the Reader

WARNING: Read the fine print on any resource you enlist for your eBook venture. Some of them require you to sell and distribute your book through them, or will charge you royalties for every copy sold. Make sure you retain the full reseller rights and copyrights. Be sure that you are the one making the money, not the company that assisted you.

Other types of e-information include booklets, pamphlets, or informational packets. You do not have to have a large enough topic for an entire book for it to be worthwhile to someone else.

If writing is not your forté, then perhaps you have a unique hobby that produces one-of-a-kind (commonly abbreviated as OOAK) products. Perhaps you have made them for family and friends over the years, and everybody has loved them. People have been telling you for years "you should make and sell these; they're wonderful."

Although making items can be time-consuming, many buyers appreciate the efforts of custom-made goods. For one thing, they know their neighbors' children will not be wearing the same exact sweater as the one they bought from your hand-knit supply.

Or perhaps you enjoy woodworking and have a nice workshop set up. Do not hesitate to create some unique items, and photograph them well. Save photographs for a portfolio, which you can e-mail to prospective customers to let them see the other successful projects you have done.

Your handmade items can be made in advance, so you have a supply available to ship immediately, or you may make the items as the orders are placed and paid for. If you choose the latter option, make sure you give a time frame in your auction listing as to the expected delivery after payment is made. If it takes four weeks to make it, be sure your customer knows that. Though this may turn away some buyers, it can help you to avoid investing a lot of time and materials for a product that may or may not sell.

Consider also adding a note similar to the following in every auction:

"If you like my work but have something in particular in mind, or a special request, I'll be pleased to custom-make a product for you for the same cost as the Buy It Now price listed, plus an additional $XX.XX for _____."

State the additional cost you charge for doing custom work and, in the blank space, enter what the extra charge will cover (such as specialty fabrics or yarns needed, higher grade of wood, or special paint colors).

Remember, you must be aware of and follow all copyright and trademark laws when you hand-make items and sell them for profit. This is especially true when making clothing items. There is nothing illegal about buying a copyrighted sewing pattern and making a cute outfit for your niece. But if you use that same pattern to make an outfit you are selling on eBay as your own OOAK creation, then you are in violation of copyright law. The same is often true of knitting or crocheting, quilting, and woodworking patterns. If you have any questions, contact the pattern maker.

Additionally, when using fabrics, you must be sure the fabrics you are using are acceptable for commercial use. For example, fabrics with Disney characters on them are not allowed for commercial use. They generally are stamped along the selvage (finished edge) with a statement such as, "For home use only. Commercial use is prohibited."

If you have any questions about the legality of any particular fabric, contact the manufacturer listed on the selvage or on the bolt's label. The salespeople at the fabric store or your wholesale dealer may also be able to assist you in determining which fabrics are acceptable for commercial use.

For sewers, this can present some problems, such as where to get patterns. There are several good computer software programs that will allow you to create your own custom patterns for commercial use. Unless you can draw patterns you use freehand, you should invest in software to assist you. An Internet search will reveal companies that provide pattern-making services to you for a fee. Compared to the fines you can get for violating copyright laws, this may be the more economical of your options.

Whatever product you personally plan, produce, and sell is also copyrighted. Consider marking your items with copyright information. By law, it is not required that you do so in order for a copyright to be in effect, but it is a smart choice. Use the copyright symbol © and the year it was created, and your name or company's name. For example: ©2006 My Company Name. Doing so will make it easier to defend your rights in the future if it becomes necessary.

TIP

If you are an artisan or crafter who is selling your original product on eBay, be sure to register with eBay's Verified Rights Owner (VeRO) program to protect your rights from infringement by others on eBay.

Now you have some ideas on how to locate merchandise to sell or have been inspired to produce your own product, whether through eBooks or

OOAK merchandise. Spend as much time as you need on this step, because what you sell ultimately determines your profit.

Once you have made the contacts necessary to secure inventory or a drop-shipping relationship, or you have secured a supply of wholesale materials to produce your product, then you are ready to tackle the next set of decisions.

Checklist of Factors to Consider When Obtaining Merchandise
✓ I have made a list of subjects that I am proficient in or have special knowledge about to consider as possible product lines.
✓ I have done some research to determine if the things I know about are being bought regularly on eBay and, if so, approximately how many people are selling these items.
✓ I have evaluated how much space I have at my disposal for storage of inventory to help me decide if I can work with wholesalers who sell in bulk, or if I should consider a drop-shipping relationship with a supplier.
✓ I have made a list of local manufacturers or distributors who may be sources of merchandise.
✓ I have considered the pros and cons of purchasing used items locally (rummaging, estate sales) and decided if I will include these as a merchandise source.
✓ If I am planning to create custom products for sale, I am aware of all copyright laws and how they may apply to the items I am making.

CASE STUDY: SUGAR AND SPICE SO YOUR STORE WILL LOOK NICE

For years, Amber (eBay user "sweet-peas-and-bumblebees") was an eBay hobby-seller who used the online marketplace to resell her children's used clothing and other things around her house that were no longer in use. Because her family's finances did not depend on her making money on eBay, she did not get serious about selling until 2005.

What prompted Amber to start an eBay Store and populate it with very cute and creative merchandise? She is not really sure anymore, but she had tried to sell her custom-made product online before and did not have much luck. This time, however, her stick-with-it attitude has prevailed, and now she is running a swinging business.

As Amber puts it, she "loves baby clothes and shoes," so even though her main product is neither, she could not help but get into that line, even if just a little bit. In addition to the new children's clothing and infant shoes displayed on her store, Sweet Peas and Bumblebees, Amber creates custom graphics and storefront packages for eBay Stores.

Some of her design packages include the *Sugar Cookie, Forever Funky, Ladybug Lane*, and *Ric Rac Pink & Black* themes. Various designs feature a scrolling marquee, a logo, up to 20 category buttons, a button for users to click and "Add Me To Your Favorite Sellers," and buttons to redirect the looker to feedback, the About Me page, or to Contact Seller.

For a low price that is well within reach of every new eBay Store owner, business went into the red a little at first. She utilizes one method that many sellers use: purchasing items in the off-season and storing them.

Amber sends users the complete HTML code. All they do is copy and paste into eBay's page for designing the store, and it is generally available in less than a week.

Users can add additional graphics for a small fee and move things around somewhat from the template. And if sellers have something a little different in mind, then for a little more money, they can have a storefront custom designed for them.

With nearly a dozen storefront package deals available at any time and new ones being designed regularly, new store owners are sure to find something useful. Amber also designs auction templates and store logos. All of her products come with free unlimited technical support offered by this one-woman storefront show.

Coming up with new designs is not difficult for Amber, even though she has no formal education in graphics. She uses Paint Shop Pro to make her products, which she said seems to come naturally to her. About five years ago, she started teaching herself, and through trial and error and a lot of practice, she said she has come a long way.

This is not the first time Amber has marketed her graphics ability, and she has never had this much success. She saw that there was a need for her product. "There aren't a zillion people out there selling graphics," she said. About selling children's clothing, she said "everybody and their brother sells clothes." But in graphics, she said she feels she has a unique product at a good price.

One mistake she sees was in pricing her product almost too low to start with. There is only so much a mother can do in one day, and at $15 per storefront, Amber was swamped when she first began selling them on eBay. It did not take long for her to raise her price so she actually was getting paid a little wage for her time. However, they have continued to sell at their new price. "I guess my talent is valuable," Amber said, seeming surprised that she is still busy after several months.

There are a number of positive aspects about selling graphics; one is that she does not need a lot of money tied up in inventory. Children's clothing and shoes, however, can be a very different story. Purchasing initial inventory is expensive, Amber said, and can even set business. Because she has also been an eBay buyer for more than four years, Amber knows well how buyers feel about shipping charges. "Over-charging for shipping is a huge turn-off to buyers," she said. Apparently, Amber's customer service skills extend to more than just her shipping- price policies. Her 650-plus feedback score boasts an over 99 percent positive rating.

As long as she has kids, Amber will be selling clothes, and as long as there is a need for her storefronts and auction templates, she will make graphics for eBay users. And she may even be coming up with some new graphics surprises in the near future — but she is not giving out any hints just yet.

Chapter Six

Nail Down the Details

Follow Suzy as she completes her first auction for the antique waffle iron.

After the Auction

After a few days of anxiously checking to see how often her waffle iron had been viewed, Suzy got her first bid. The opening bid was, naturally, her starting price of $4.99. This will comfortably allow Suzy to "break even," and she is thankful that at least her fees will not be wasted. She continues to monitor her item and about a day later, she has a second bidder. The automatic bidding system does not allow Suzy to see how the bids climbed exactly, but she now has a bid of $6.05 on the waffle iron. Considering there are numerous other similar items currently available with no bids, she is pleased hers has bids.

The auction ends a couple of days later with many more lookers but no more bids. Though Suzy had hoped to have a final sale price closer to $9.99, she accepts the reality of auctioning: The bidders who are currently looking are the ones who determine the final sale price. This does not sour her attitude, but she does decide she will be more particular about antique waffle irons in the future. In reviewing the other auctions, both current and past, she has seen some photos of beautiful and ornate waffle irons that are apparently capturing the attention of collectors. If she can snag one of those at a future auction, she will definitely have a better idea of its value.

Invoices

Although eBay will send the winning bidder an e-mail notifying him or her of the won auction, Suzy will also create an invoice to send to the buyer. The invoice outlines all the details of the transaction, including the exact shipping cost. It also reviews the payment policies based on what she has entered into eBay's template.

TIP   You can create customized e-mails to your winning buyers. Just go to your "Preferences" link on the My eBay page (left-hand column under "My Account") and click on the link to "Edit" under "Logos and Branding." Use the form provided to give the default message some of your personality. Be sure to click the box at the top that reads, "Include my custom message in this e-mail" or it will still send the default message. (Note: This is the same as the PayPal customized end-of-auction e-mail, so if you have done it in one place, you do not need to re-do it in the other).

To create an invoice, Suzy must first go to her My eBay page. Under the header "Items I've Sold," the auction for the waffle iron will be listed. eBay's system automatically moves items from your "Items I'm Selling" section to the appropriate section ("Unsold Items" or "Items I've Sold") once the auction is complete.

Sending an invoice is as simple as clicking on the blue link in the drop-down menu of options (on the right-hand side of the screen). Doing so will open a new page where Suzy can double-check the information (such as the shipping information, which the system will fill in based on the information from the shipping calculator that Suzy used when she listed her item).

At the top of the invoice form that eBay creates, notice also that the buyer's address may or may not be listed. Sometimes, you will get just a ZIP code, but not the full address. Do not worry; you will get the full address once the transaction is complete. If there was a reason you had not filled out the shipping calculator when listing your item, you will be able to use the ZIP code now to determine what your actual shipping costs will be. You can then fill in the shipping options and prices to the right, so the buyer can choose which they wish to utilize and pay the appropriate amount. Chances are, if you have been buying on eBay already, you have received these invoices yourself and are familiar with them.

Double-check the payment information in the box on the bottom left, and consider typing in a brief "Thank you for your purchase" message. You can also encourage the buyer to pay promptly by reminding them of how fast you ship once payment is received. This lets them know that if they are willing to put in a little effort (paying quickly), you will reward them by making an effort to get it shipped just as quickly. Buyers appreciate little gestures like that, and often it is mentioned in their feedback.

A copy of the invoice will be sent to your e-mail, although you can un-check a box if you do not want a copy. If you have logged the various items during the transaction (such as listing fees, sold price, and Final Value Fees) in your spreadsheet or ledger, then there is no reason why you would need to have a copy of the invoice. The amount of e-mail generated by each transaction can be overwhelming, so you will soon decide what you really do want to keep. If you want to keep a hard copy of the invoice, then click the link toward the bottom that reads, "preview the invoice" and print that screen.

Once Suzy has sent the invoice to her buyer, she can finish boxing her item, taping it securely. Now, she must do what sellers dislike most: wait for the payment to arrive. At this point in the game, sellers want to be paid for their hard work, clear out that inventory, and get on with the next auction. Waiting for payment can be frustrating, but unless you institute only fixed-price listings with an "immediate payment required" feature, you will just have to wait it out.

Most eBay sellers have developed a payment policy that is displayed in their auction description, and it is reiterated in their invoices. However, you will have to accept that some buyers simply do not read the details, no matter how many times they are presented with them. Here are some common payment issues you may encounter with your customers:

Basic Ways to Receive Payment

Most sellers have set a timeline by which they expect payment to be received. And most buyers respect those timelines. Be prepared, however, for the inevitable: a buyer who drags his feet.

Perhaps the buyer has received an unexpected bill in the mail or had a sick pet who needed vet care. Emergencies happen to everybody at one time or another. Be sure to communicate with your buyer if the deadline is near and no payment has been received. Let them know you are concerned and ask if there has been a delay in payment, so you can work out other arrangements. A buyer who has truly had something unexpected happen will be grateful for your consideration and do what they can to make the payment as soon as possible.

If, however, a buyer has second thoughts or decides he does not really want your item after all, anything could happen. They could try to back out of the sale, they could lie to you about a payment in the mail (that really is not), and — in a worst-case scenario — they could try to turn the tables by claiming that you must have received a mailed payment by now and that you are the one dragging your feet or refusing to ship the item.

Encountering buyers like this can be a real headache, and it can make sellers bitter and negative. There does not seem to be a way to predict which buyers will be like this, either. A buyer can have perfect feedback then suddenly you are the unfortunate seller who has an issue with him or her.

If this buyer continues to avoid payment, he turns from a slow payer to a non-paying bidder. In this case, you have options.

Getting paid first

The first thing on your to-do list is choosing how to receive payments. Do not wait until after you have posted an auction to think about these things, as items may sell quickly, leaving you with a buyer waiting to pay and no idea how you want that done. If you put something such as "payment and shipping to be determined by the end of the auction" in your item description, people will know you are new, and they are hesitant to do business with people who simply do not know what they are doing. Keep in mind that at this stage, you are trying to become a PowerSeller, so you need to look as professional as possible.

There are numerous ways you can receive payments from your buyers, and each has its pros and cons. Being aware of all the options can help you make an informed decision that will lead to your company's policy on payments. How you accept payment is up to you, but it is wise to maintain the same policy, regardless of the auction item.

The six basic ways to receive payment are cash, personal checks, money orders, cashier's checks, escrow services, and PayPal.

Cash

Cash may seem like a logical choice, but few sellers will accept this payment type, even though they can avoid any PayPal fees and other nuisances, such as check-clearing time, by doing so. For one thing, if the seller never receives the money, the buyer may not believe it and might accuse the seller of receiving it and not shipping the product. It is too risky a venture, and not worth the hassle. When sellers do accept cash, often you will see this notice in their payment policy: "Cash at your own risk."

Personal checks

Personal checks are another payment form not commonly accepted on eBay. When sellers do accept them, they commonly have a disclaimer in their payment terms stating that they will hold merchandise for ten days to assure that the personal check has cleared. Most buyers accept this requirement.

The good thing about having a buyer send you a personal check is that, as with cash, you avoid any fees from electronic transfers. For the buyer, it is cheaper and easier than going out of their way to purchase a money order or certified check. However, for many PowerSellers and high-end sellers, this option may be too time-consuming to track.

Money orders

A better option to personal checks is accepting money orders and certified (bank) checks. Money orders are less secure than bank checks, but both are still considered more secure than personal checks. Most sellers do not hold off shipping until these items clear.

Note to the Reader

WARNING: There have been many reports of counterfeit Postal Service money orders in the past few years. The Federal Deposit Insurance Corporation (FDIC) Web site has a special bulletin about counterfeit money orders and how to determine whether a Postal Service money order is authentic. See www.fdic.gov/news/news/SpecialAlert/2005/sa2305.html for this bulletin.

There are numerous companies that sell money orders, so a good policy is to ship all items after your bank has accepted the money order for deposit. Your bank will be happy to examine any money orders for you. It saves you and them time and aggravation should the money order be returned.

Cashier's checks

If you do want to accept checks, then cashier's checks are normally considered an incredibly safe form of payment, although most people do not want to pay the extra fees for them unless you demand it. If you are selling an expensive item, consider asking for only electronic payments, such as PayPal or a cashier's check. It is always possible that even this type of check can be counterfeited, especially if it is from a bank from a different country that you have never heard of. The best way to make sure is to ask your bank to look at it.

Escrow service

Another way to secure payment for those expensive or rare items is by using an escrow service. An escrow service is a third party who receives the money from the buyer and holds it while the seller, knowing that his or her money is secured, ships the product. When the buyer has had a chance to inspect the purchased item, he notifies the escrow service to release the funds to the seller. There are fees involved, and the process can take time, but eBay recommends using an escrow service if the auction price is more than $500. Search eBay's Help Directory for "escrow" to see a list of suggested escrow companies and read more about the process, fees, and terms.

PayPal

The final and most commonly used payment option is the electronic payment company, PayPal. This system performs most of their functions directly through the Internet. PayPal, found at **www.paypal.com**, works by obtaining funds from the buyer's bank account, credit card, or debit card. Buyers can choose the funding source(s) they wish to use. Although this can cause some major headaches for sellers, it is worth learning how PayPal works and what its policies are. The good news is that PayPal and eBay are linked, so payment is a smooth process that does not require signing off one service and opening another. Even shipping can be done through PayPal.

PayPal has changed their policies and offers in the past year or so. You can now use PayPal for your eBay transactions without having to upgrade to a new level of membership. They offer extra tools to make the connection between eBay and PayPal seamless. They offer shipping and tracking options and will automatically send this information to your eBay account. When you use this service, it will ask whether you agree to connect your accounts, but it is worth the time and effort and is relatively simple.

There is a catch: PayPal will deduct a commission before depositing the money into your PayPal account. For sellers who have $3,000 or less entering their accounts every month, that fee is a flat 2.9 percent + $0.30 for each transaction. The 2.9 percent is taken from the entire amount of money transferred to you from the buyer — including any shipping and handling charges and sales tax you collect. If you are selling an item for more than $3,000, the percentage deducted is much less.

Monthly Sales Price per Transaction	
Amount Sold per Month	Fees You Owe to eBay
$0.00 USD - $3,000.00 USD	2.9 percent + $0.30 USD (per transaction)
$3,000.01 USD - $10,000.00 USD	2.5 percent + $0.30 USD (per transaction)
$10,000.01 USD - $100,000.00 USD	2.2 percent + $0.30 USD (per transaction)
> $100,000.00 USD	1.9 percent + $0.30 USD (per transaction)

TIP

If you have a buyer bidding on multiple items from you, ask them to hold off paying until all the auctions they are bidding on have ended. Then, they can pay all at once, and you will only be charged the $0.30 transaction fee once.

If you want to have the funds in your PayPal account transferred to your bank account, there is no charge, but the process could take several days. This makes it almost easier to purchase postage and business supplies through retailers who accept PayPal payments. PayPal does offer a newer service of a credit or debit card. You must apply for the credit card, but the debit card is free and works much the same as your bank debit card. You are given a PIN number and can access funds that are in your PayPal account instantly.

PayPal and credit cards

If you display the PayPal logo in your listings and state that you accept Pay-
Pal payments, you cannot state in your listing that PayPal payments made
via credit card will not be accepted. This policy can be found at **http://
pages.eBay.com/help/policies/seller-non-performance.html**.

Having a PayPal account is essential when running an eBay business, especially if you wish to be a PowerSeller. Trying to manage and direct buyers to
different accounts all the time will not only add to the chaos, but will add
to your recordkeeping and accounting tasks as well.

If you wish to sell items from your Web site, you may wish to consider Web
site Payments Standard or Web site Payments Pro.

Web site Payments Standard

- Works with all major online shopping carts
- Includes "Buy Now" buttons
- Allows you to accept donations
- Allows to you use gift certificates to make purchases
- Allows for subscriptions and recurring payments
- Includes Virtual Terminal, which allows you to accept phone and
  fax payments
- Allows your buyers to sign up for PayPal
- Allows you to create custom checkout pages for a consistent look
- Allows you to accept multiple currencies
- Provides a record of your PayPal transactions and the ability to
  download your logs into programs such as QuickBooks
- Provides a log of monthly credits and debits on your account
- Allows for advanced search for transactions
- Includes the ability to refund customers
- Includes integrated shipping services
- Includes a sales-tax calculator
- Includes fraud and chargeback protection
- Provides instant payment notification

- Allows you to withdraw funds with your PayPal debit card
- Includes a "Mass Pay" option
- Allows you to send money to and request money from anyone with an e-mail account

Web site Payments Pro

The Pro version contains all the standard features, in addition to the following:

- PayPal shopping cart
- Auto return feature to bring buyers back to your Web site after they pay
- Encrypted Web site payments
- Payment data notification
- The ability to build new applications on your site

The standard version of Web site Payments is free, and the Pro version costs $30 a month to use.

Brief explanation of PayPal features

PayPal logo and taglines: PayPal can add these automatically, or you can manually insert a set of logos. Go to the "Auction Tools" tab in your account for detailed instructions on setting up either of these options.

End-of-auction e-mail to winning bidder: This is a nice service because even if you are not online to see your auction ending, PayPal will notify the winning bidder, and then, if you have already set up your shipping options properly, the bidder can pay immediately via PayPal if he or she wishes. This slick feature benefits PayPal, too; with PayPal being the first in line to accept payment, buyers do not have to think of choosing one of the other options.

History log: The history log lists every transaction for the previous three months sorted by date. To access it, click on the "History" tab in your account. You can select from several different options for searching the history from searching by transaction type to searching by date.

Downloadable log: This is an excellent way to speed along your record-keeping. Download this log monthly and keep it with your monthly sales ledger. Backing up your data in your sales and inventory ledgers is always wise.

Monthly statement: Sign up to get a monthly statement by going to the "Profile" tab and clicking "Link," then go to the site to print it monthly; new statements become available on the 15th day of each month. Keep these just as you would keep your monthly bank statements. Reconcile them by comparing the totals with your ledger, and if there is any discrepancy, you can compare your downloaded log transaction by transaction.

PayPal statements are only available for three months back, so if you forget to print one, do not wait too long, or it may be gone.

Refunds and fee credits: If you need to make a refund to the buyer, go to the specific transaction. If it is not listed on the "My Account" tab page, then click the link at the bottom of that box that says "All Activity." This takes you to a screen where you can pull up information from the past three months. You can make refunds for up to 60 days after the transaction first took place. Simply click on the transaction you wish to see, and click the "Refund" button. PayPal will walk you through the rest of the necessary steps.

If you refund the buyer's entire payment to you, PayPal will refund you the fees they charged. They do not offer a refund of fees if you only make a partial refund to a buyer.

Buyer and Seller Protection provided by PayPal: Thoroughly read all the information on PayPal's Web site about Buyer and Seller Protections, as the information here is just a snapshot of the programs. You will find detailed discussions about these features under the "Auction Tools" tab when you are logged in to your account.

Buyer Protection is available with all account types, but in order for the buyer to be protected, the seller must have done certain things first.

Some of these requirements include:

- Your eBay feedback score must be at least 5.0 with 98 percent or better positive feedback.

- You must be a verified member of PayPal.

- You must be a seller in one of 20 listed countries; the United States and Canada are included.

- Your account must be in good standing.

- You must have the "Buyer Protection" icon displayed in your Seller Information box on eBay.

- You must use a shipping service that allows you to track the shipment, in case of a claim that the item was never received.

Buyers also have requirements they must meet, including time limits; they must make their claim within 45 days of the PayPal payment. The buyer also must have paid using the seller's e-mail address, as stated in the listing.

A buyer might file a claim if they never receive the item or, as PayPal's Web site terms it, if the item is "significantly not as described." Merely being less than thrilled is not an excuse for filing a claim. Buyers are limited in the number of claims they can make per year, as well. Of course, buyers and sellers are always encouraged to work things out themselves first without resorting to filing claims, which should always be a last resort.

PayPal cares about the sellers they serve, as well. They offer a Seller Protection plan that helps prevent fraud. They work hard to prevent fraudulent chargebacks and will also help you fight a chargeback if you have sufficient documentation to prove that the chargeback is not necessary. Sometimes, PayPal can respond quicker to resolve a situation than eBay can.

Some tips that PayPal offers to help you defend yourself include the following:

- Use tracking tools with every shipment. These can include Delivery Confirmation, which is required for every shipment when you purchase postage through PayPal; insurance; and actual "tracking" (if you use UPS, FedEx, or other carriers).

- Ship to the buyer's confirmed address only. Be suspicious of buyers who want their items sent to different addresses, especially in different countries. In the transaction details, it will say "Confirmed" after the address.

- Check buyers' eBay feedback for a broad view of their reputation.

- Check to see whether the buyer's PayPal account is verified, which means that PayPal has confirmed his or her bank account.

You can check the status of a buyer right from the transaction page. Simply click on the link for "Details." Look for this:

Payment From: Seller's Name (the sender of this payment is Verified).

All users should become familiar with the "Profile" tab on their account pages. Here, you can manage every detail of your account and even see what other services or features you may not be using, such as creating custom templates for invoices. It is worth spending a little time clicking all the links just to learn about how PayPal can work for you.

With more than 78 million accounts, PayPal is by far the largest online payment company. And because it is an eBay company, it is quite easy to use with eBay. It is available in 45 countries and in six different currencies. Plan to accept PayPal for most of your payments. Get to know all the options, and use all the tools available to you. If you make it work for you, your account fees will be well-spent.

Getting a handle on payment choices is a large task, and one you should have under control before you start your first auction. Trying to scramble and set things up after the fact will not help you project a professional image.

Refund policy

There are plenty of eBay sellers who state prominently in their "About Me" page and on each listing, "All Sales Final." This is a policy that may discourage some people from bidding at all. If a customer has never bought anything from you, he or she does not know you at all, has never met you, and is considering buying a product based only on a description and photograph — not having actually seen it in person. You are just a page on the Internet, and customers have plenty of reason to be distrustful.

Of course, you have no intention of being dishonest, but you have to communicate that to your bidders through friendly policies. You will not get that many returns (unless you are selling substandard goods), so you do not have much to worry about. Every physical store in the world builds a certain number of returns into their pricing structure. It is inevitable that once in a while, something may get broken in shipping, or when it arrives, it may not be what the buyer expected. Instead of imposing a strict "no returns" policy, create something a little friendlier. Create a return and refund policy stating you will graciously accept returns within a set time — for example, 30 days. Be sure to state clearly in that policy how shipping fees will be handled and what you expect your customer to do to facilitate the return and refund.

Another detail that takes some thought and planning is choosing your shipping provider(s). There is no rule for which provider you must choose. The three most common shipping providers are the U.S. Postal Service^SM (USPS), Federal Express (FedEx), and United Parcel Service (UPS), although there are several others. Here is a brief look at each provider's basic features, the tools they offer eBay sellers, and some of the intricacies of shipping internationally. *How to list a buyer's shipping options in auctions was covered in Chapter 2.*

You will have to be flexible to a certain degree when it comes to shipping. Some buyers may have only a post office box, and neither FedEx nor UPS will deliver to them. Others may have a very rural address that is difficult to find, making the USPS a better choice. Additionally, with USPS there are different levels of pricing, from the economical Parcel Post all the way to the zippy (and pricey) overnight services. Buyers may not care if they do not receive the item for two weeks as long as they can save money on shipping costs. So be prepared to offer as many choices as you can without being counter-productive.

Another decision you will have to make is how frequently you will ship items. This varies greatly based on what shipper you use, if they will do home pickups of packages, or if you have to haul them to the shipper. Some sellers pick certain days of the week they will ship (such as Monday and Thursday), while others ship every single weekday. Strike a balance between your capabilities and the customer's needs. Obviously, buyers want their items shipped fast, preferably within one business day of sending payment. Determine what is feasible for you, and make sure you state your shipping schedule clearly in your auction listing.

U.S. Postal Service (USPS)

The U.S. Postal Service (USPS, found at **www.usps.com**) has worked hard to secure a piece of the Internet shipping pie. They are a preferred shipping provider for eBay and are integrated with eBay's shipping calculators (when you set up auctions) and PayPal.

Whether you plan to take your packages to the post office yourself or purchase postage online through the USPS's Web site or PayPal, you will need to know how much shipping is going to cost. Buyers are accustomed to having shipping costs stated outright, or being able to use the shipping calculator, right in the auction listing, to determine their choices and costs. Gone are the days when "Contact seller for shipping quote" is the standard phrase on all auctions. Buyers want accurate information before bidding, in most cases.

There are a couple of reasons for this. Mainly, buyers need to weigh the cost of shipping against going to a local store and purchasing the item. Sure, you may sell an item not available in just any store, but odds are it is available elsewhere, even if only online. If your shipping costs are not competitive with another Web site, you may lose the sale. Comparing shipping costs is standard in Internet comparison-shopping nowadays.

The second reason is that a buyer wants to assess your shipping and handling fees. When you add a shipping and handling fee while setting up the shipping calculator, the buyer does not see this fee separately; it is all tabulated in the total cost given when they enter their ZIP code into the calculator.

However, many buyers are not fooled by the fact that they cannot specifically see the shipping and handling charge. If you are selling a paperback book and the media mail quote comes back at $8, the buyer is going to know you heavily padded your shipping and handling. There are differing views on shipping and handling charges, and you will need to make your own decisions about what your policy will be.

See what other eBay sellers have to say about shipping policies and how they handle their shipping and handling charges. Join the eBay discussion boards and ask others to share their feelings about the topic. Then, make up your own mind about how you will handle this choice. *Shipping and handling charges will also be discussed more in Chapter 9.*

However, it is imperative for you to know what the item you are selling will cost to ship. This can be done easily on the USPS's Web site under the "Calculate Postage" link. This easy-to-use tool prompts you for the necessary information, which generally is the type of item (envelope or box), the weight, and the ZIP codes of origin and destination.

Then, it will present you with all your options and the applicable costs; it is as simple as that. Bookmark this tool and use it to calculate postage on any item where you know the destination ZIP code.

 If you want to offer flat-fee shipping (same price for everybody) via USPS, use their online calculator and enter a From ZIP code on one end of the country (such as New York City, NY 10001) and a To ZIP code at the other end (such as Beverly Hills, CA 90210). This will give you the maximum postage needed for that package coast-to-coast.

This tip was offered by eBay seller Linda (user ID "LindaCatNH") who lives in New Hampshire. When she calculates shipping this way, she enters her ZIP code, then a ZIP code in California. That is about as far away from New Hampshire that you can get, postal zone-wise, she said. Add a note in your auction for buyers in Hawaii and Alaska that the cost will be recalculated before they pay.

Linda's customers know her as an honest seller, partly because she has occasionally had a buyer who happened to be in a neighboring state, or even closer. If the buyer is that close, she sometimes recalculates the flat-fee shipping cost and refunds a portion of the shipping fee.

Generally, you will not know the destination ZIP code until your auction is complete and the buyer has been identified. When setting up your auction, if you have an accurate weight for the parcel, use that to set up the shipping calculator. Then, the buyer can enter his or her ZIP code themselves and get an accurate shipping quote.

Obviously, in order to get an accurate shipping weight for an item, you will need to have it boxed up with the packing material (crumpled paper, packing peanuts, or bubble wrap) already in as well. It may not be wise to tape up the box just yet; a bidder may want an additional photo, or you might later put in a thank-you note or a receipt for the buyer.

One of the first items that you will need to purchase for a successful eBay business is a modern, digital, postage-type scale. These items are reasonably priced (they start at about $18) and can be easily found at an office supply store or on eBay. Giving your customers accurate shipping quotes right in the auction listing is simply the easiest and best way to go. When you weigh the box, add 2 ounces or so to the weight on the scale, and use that as your shipping weight.

For your boxing needs, the USPS has a line of co-branded boxes you can obtain for free (co-branded, meaning they have an eBay logo as well as the USPS logo on the box). You can choose from three sizes, plus two sizes that are flat-rate boxes (meaning the price is the same for shipping regardless of destination or weight). There are certain restrictions on all these boxes, so be sure to read up on them on eBay's Web site. All of these boxes are free for sellers to obtain (on eBay's site), but note that they cannot be used to ship items for any other mail class than Priority or Express (depending on the particular item), nor can they be used for anything but mailing auction items.

Other USPS (not co-branded) items (including tubes, labels, and Delivery Confirmation forms) are available on the USPS Web site. Generally these items are free, but the boxes, tubes, and envelopes are for Priority or Express mail only. You will still have to supply your own boxes for other mail classes or for items that do not fit into the standard box sizes.

You can also purchase USPS postage (including extras such as insurance and Delivery Confirmation) through PayPal, then track the package from your PayPal account as well.

If you purchase Priority postage, there are no fees in addition to the actual postage and insurance fee. Delivery Confirmation is free with Priority Mail, and only $0.13 for other mail classes (as opposed to $0.55 if you were to take that same package to a post office and purchase postage there).

When you purchase postage online through PayPal, you also have the opportunity to schedule a home pickup by your local post office. This is especially nice if you do not live a stone's throw from a post office, or if you will be away from your home but want to ensure the boxes are shipped.

If there will be bad weather, or if it is not safe to leave an unattended package near your mailbox, then you may have to get creative. If you have a covered porch, you can call your local post office and give them instructions on where the package will be (or tape a note to your mail box), or get a plastic storage bin with a tight-fitting lid and set it next to your mailbox.

For people who live in condominiums or apartment complexes, often the manager's office will serve as a drop-off location for outgoing packages.

Call your local post office and ask them for suggestions as well. They are happy to help you in any way possible, and they want to make sure your items get to their locations securely and quickly.

A few quick ideas about shipping supplies: Linda in New Hampshire (eBay user "LindaCatNH") has a good suggestion for obtaining free boxes if you are shipping items that do not fit in the free boxes from shipping providers, or using services such as Parcel Post or Media Mail. She said she is not ashamed to go "Dumpster diving" for boxes that have been discarded by retailers, but she also notes that most store owners are happy to have her take them even before they are put in the garbage to avoid having to recycle or dispose of them themselves.

To make a box appear less like a case of frozen peas and more like a new container, she separates it at the glued side and flips it inside out, re-taping it securely. This gives her a clean slate for the postage and address label and also gives the box at least one more use. Recycling is important to Linda, and she hopes her rejuvenating efforts pay off and that people continue to re-use that same box.

Packing materials such as Styrofoam peanuts or bubble wrap can be expensive and environmentally unfriendly. Your local newspaper may sell "end rolls," which are basically the end of the huge roll of paper used to print newspapers on, for a reasonable fee. This paper has not been used, so there is no ink to get on your hands or on the merchandise. The rolls vary in size. Check with your local newspaper or printing presses about end rolls or other materials you could recycle into packing materials.

TIP

Even your ordinary junk mail can become packing material. Purchase a small shredder (not one that does cross-cut shredding — just the one that shreds in strips) and shred your junk mail as needed. Do not use anything with sensitive information on it. When you need packing material, just reach into the container and grab a handful.

If you have kids, this is a good way for them to earn allowance, plus they can feel like they are helping you with your business. Let them make an invoice for their fees, and you can teach them how to do business themselves.

Many eBay sellers have found creative ways to store any packing materials that come into their homes (or friends and families' homes as well) to re-use for their auction shipping. Go to the eBay community tab (on the top toolbar) and check out the discussion boards. There is even one dedicated to packing and shipping questions. If you do not find what you are looking for on the first couple of pages, then ask a question; you will get plenty of suggestions on how to obtain, recycle, and store shipping materials.

If there is one thing that the USPS does not do as well as their competition, it is tracking. Delivery Confirmation and insurance, while nice for the protections they do provide, are not considered "tracking." Because you do not receive any verification that the package arrived (you merely use your Delivery Confirmation receipt or Insurance receipt as a tool to ask for proof of delivery if the buyer claims they did not receive it or it was damaged), you do not even know if the package arrived until the buyer leaves feedback (or contacts you otherwise). or sellers who like to be privy to every little detail, this can be annoying.

Tracking is available only for Express Mail packages. For other classes, you need to purchase a signature confirmation or return receipt, which will add significantly to your shipping costs. Though they do not provide tracking, at least you are notified when the package is delivered. But if you are shipping an item via Priority, Parcel Post, or First Class, and you must know when it arrived, these are your only options, other than going to another shipper.

Shipping with USPS

Pros

- A preferred shipping provider of eBay, they have a variety of tools fully integrated into the buying and selling of online goods.

- It is integrated into eBay's shipping calculator and PayPal, which allows potential customers to determine whether they should buy something from you, or whether it would be cheaper to drive to a store and pick up something equivalent.

- You can purchase your own postage through the USPS Web site or PayPal and print it on your home computer.

- You can purchase insurance and get Delivery Confirmation straight from your PayPal account.

- Priority Mail comes with no additional fees besides the cost of postage and insurance.

- Delivery Confirmation is free for Priority mail and is only $0.13 for other mail classes.

- Their Web site offers a "Calculate Postage" link so you can calculate the estimated postage for the customer; thus, they do not have to look it up.

- Free co-branded (both eBay and USPS logos) boxes for Priority and Express mail classes that come in three different sizes.

- Two sizes of flat-rate boxes, meaning the price is the same regardless of destination or weight for Priority and Express mail.

- All these boxes are available free to sellers, but only for Priority and Express mail, and only for auction items.

- When you purchase your postage through PayPal, you have the option of scheduling a regular pick-up time from your local post office at your home, which can help immensely if you do not live close to the post office, or if you are going to be away from your home or office and still want your products to be picked up.

- For rainy days, you can even get a covered plastic container and make arrangements for the carrier to take your packages out of that instead of stacking them by the mailbox.

Cons

- For other mail classes besides Priority and Express, you purchase all your own packing materials.

- Insurance and Delivery Confirmation is just your receipt to prove that you did actually ship it. If the customer claims they did not receive the package, you have no way of knowing whether they received it. Also, you will not know whether the customer received the item in question until they leave feedback. If they do not leave feedback, you can only assume that as long as they do not complain, then all is well.

- Only Express mail allows for a version of package tracking. For all other mail classes, a signature confirmation or return receipt is only available for a price, and if you are particular about managing the details of your customer fulfillment, this can get expensive.

Federal Express (FedEx)

Federal Express (FedEx) focused on the overnight-delivery market in the early years of its business, but now it also serves the world's slower shipping needs with its FedEx Ground service in addition to their standard overnight service. Their Web site, **www.fedex.com**, can direct you to all your shipping options. Go to the "Welcome Center" (left-hand side of home page) and click on "New Customer Center" to set up an order and learn about what FedEx will do to gain you as a customer.

Their Web site is easy to use and has organized drop-down menus to let you navigate quickly through the tasks you will need to perform. Their online tracking system is excellent, letting you see details such as when the package arrived in a certain location, and even when it is out on a truck for delivery.

FedEx also has shipping materials available online or at any FedEx location.

Their online calculator walks you through simple steps, asking you how soon the package needs to be delivered, general weight, and other information. It gives you sample prices based on examples (such as New York to Los Angeles, 1 pound, $X.XX). Although it may not be an exact quote for you, it gives you an idea of what ballpark you are looking at.

Paying for your FedEx shipments is made simple by a variety of choices. You can be billed monthly or can set up your account to do an electronic funds transfer (EFT) to pay for a shipment. There are other options as well, which you will learn about when you set up an account.

If you will use FedEx on any regular basis, it is worth getting an account and handling all the options online rather than going to a physical location.

Shipping with FedEx

Pros

- They have the most user-friendly of the three Web sites, with clear drop-down menus that direct you to your shipping needs.

- They offer various incentives for switching over to them.

- You can get an account with them, which has a variety of positives, such as the ability to choose to be billed for all your shipping needs once a month instead of every time you ship something, which simplifies things.

Cons

The cons with FedEx are the same as the cons for UPS.

To cut costs and maximize profit, your best bet is to determine which shipping company will offer you the best rates for each of your shipping needs.

The United Parcel Service (UPS)

The United Parcel Service (UPS, found at **www.ups.com**) is not about to be outdone when it comes to online services. Their user-friendly Web site boasts all the great features of their competitors: online tracking, online shipping calculations, drop box locations, paperless invoices, and small business solutions. From their home page (**www.ups.com**), click on the "Business Solutions" link, then the link that reads "I am a small business owner" to learn about the benefits UPS offers to be your shipper of choice. Just a few of the tools they offer are:

- Storage of your customers' addresses online. If you have many repeat customers, this could be a nice time-saver.

- Advanced tracking tools for business owners.

- Arrangement for pickup.

- Creation of shipping labels for up to 20 packages at a time on their site.

- E-mail notifications of deliveries, so you do not have to check tracking.

Shipping with UPS

Pros

- They have a user-friendly Web site with tools for small business owners.

- They will store your customers' addresses online for you if you want. This will significantly increase your productivity if you have many repeat customers.

- The tracking tools for business owners are more easily navigated than the USPS tracking system.

- You can easily arrange for pickup on their Web site.

- You can create up to 20 shipping labels on their site.

- You get e-mail notifications of all your deliveries so you do not have to keep tracking them.

- They offer better rates than USPS for shipping large, bulky items.

Cons

- You need to supply your own shipping materials.

- They are not quite as integrated as USPS.

Although the USPS seems to have the lion's share of business on eBay, the other shipping companies have some features that make them worth looking into. Depending on your product, you may find that one shipper far exceeds the others in ease and service. Like the USPS, you can purchase and print UPS labels right from your computer, for both domestic and international shipments (including the customs forms). Especially for items that are too large for USPS requirements, this handy feature makes UPS competitive with the USPS.

All three shipping companies can also assist you in your international shipments. For sellers who are just starting out, the mere process of shipping internationally could make your head swim. However, with some patience and practice, you will soon be writing up U.S. Customs forms like they were last week's grocery list. eBay's policies state very clearly that it is the responsibility of the seller to be sure their items are legal to sell in any foreign country they are offering to sell in.

Do not let this policy scare you away from considering international sales. It is not difficult to determine what is prohibited or restricted in other countries around the globe, although every country has its own rules about what its occupants may import. To get a handle on what could otherwise be a very confusing topic, bookmark and check the USPS's Index of Countries and Localities Web page, which lists prohibited and restricted items for import, at **http://pe.usps.gov/text/imm/immctry.htm**. If you discover that your product is prohibited or restricted, then it is not acceptable for you to even offer to sell it to the country with the restriction or prohibition.

EBay has the answers to many common questions about international selling and shipping, including an International Selling Toolkit for you to download. A 10-page PDF file is part of this list of tips. See **http://pages.ebay.com/global-trade/index.html** and **http://pages.ebay.com/international-trading/sellertips.html**.

The USPS's International Shipping Manual discusses shipping with the expectation that you are utilizing the USPS's products and services. But regardless of what shipping company you are using, the Index of Countries and Localities will be useful to any seller who ventures into international shipping. If reading the information in the manual is more confusing than reading a foreign language, then print out the information for the country you need to ship to and go to your local post office. Someone will be able to explain the relevant items you need to know for that country; however, note that if your post office is generally a beehive of activity, call ahead to see when their slower times are, or ask to make an appointment. Much of the information in the index will not apply to your occasional eBay shipments. The more educated you are about this topic, the less frightening this will be.

For example, who knew you cannot sell a watch to a buyer in Mauritania? Or that you simply cannot ship photo albums of any kind to Italy? Checking these lists against any countries that you are considering shipping to will save you time. If your product is prohibited in one country, it may well be in many others.

If you choose not to offer international shipping, it is polite to state that policy in your auction listing or templates. A simple statement is sufficient; for example, "We are only able to ship to locations in the United States," or "We are not able to ship internationally at this time."

Though most international bidders will respect your policy, there may be one who will either not read your listing closely enough or will bid and, if they win, hope that you will go through the trouble to ship it to them anyway. *What to do in this case is covered in Chapter 9.*

If you are willing to delve into international shipping, be sure to fill in the international shipping calculator when you set up your auction, so buyers will be able to see up-front what the costs will be. Another detail to make clear in your auction text is that any duties (taxes paid to the country of destination) are the buyer's obligation. Most international buyers understand this, but it does not hurt to cover this base, in case you get a novice. For their part, buyers may be able to determine what their Customs fees will be in advance of bidding. This should always be strongly suggested.

Regardless of what shipping company you use, you will have to provide documents for Customs. All packages sent to other countries must have certain information, such as a declared value of the contents, so standard forms have been developed to provide that information.

USPS Form 2976 Customs Declaration CN 22 — Sender's Declaration (green label) (also known as the short form) is used for shipments weighing less than 4 pounds. USPS Form 2976-A Customs Declaration and Dispatch Note — CP 72 (which is the multi-part longer form) is used for parcels over 4 pounds. When using this second form, you will also need to use a 2976-E Customs Declaration Envelope. You can get these forms at your local post office, or order them from their Web site (if you do a lot of international shipping) at **http://pe.usps.com/text/imm/immc1_008. htm#ep732466**.

Although the USPS and other shipping companies may have their own forms, they cover similar information, so once you are familiar with one version, the others will be easy to use as well.

Tips for filling out Customs forms:

- Fill them out in English. If you are fluent in an officially recognized language of the destination country, you may provide a translation for the "contents" section along with the English (U.S. Customs officials need to be able to read it, too).

- Describe the "contents" briefly, with no abbreviations or American slang.

- Fill in the "value" in U.S. dollars; the Customs agents will do any conversion if needed.

- Make sure you have checked that your item is not prohibited or restricted.

- Do not forget an address label; Customs forms will not double as an address label.

- Attach the completed form to the lower-left side of the package top (same side as address label).

- You may be required to enclose the recipient's name, address and/or telephone number inside the package; check with your shipper for details.

- Insure your package, if at all possible.

The USPS's Web site allows you to fill out the customs forms online at this link: **http://webapps.usps.com/customsforms/welcome.htm**. This page also has a link to the Index of Countries and Localities already mentioned, as well as a rate calculator available right there. The lookup of postal codes is also built in, so you do not have to go searching the site for the tools you will need to complete the form. Both forms are available on that page, as well as the Military versions (for mailing to APO/FPO addresses).

FedEx and UPS also assist in completing Customs forms online and printing them. This saves time when you drop your package off, and is necessary if your package is being picked up at your location. These two companies, however, offer mostly "expedited" shipping in foreign countries. Unless your buyer wants the item fast and is willing to pay for it, you may not find any useful choices with these carriers, but it does not hurt to ask.

TIP Some countries require that a copy of the invoice be included in an envelope with the Customs form, even though you have declared the "value" of the item on the form. Be sure to check this out before heading to your shipping company's location, or you may waste yourself a trip; you can also make it a policy to include one with every international shipment.

International buyers have been known to ask sellers to lower the value of the item to reduce their tax assessment (duty) in their own country. But it is illegal (and against eBay's policies) to misrepresent the value of the item for this purpose. The value of the item is exactly the price they paid for it (minus shipping and handling they paid). Your invoice should reflect exactly what the buyer paid.

Marking the item as a "Gift" is also against everyone's rules. The only time this might be appropriate is if you are sending a replacement for damaged goods. However, check with your shipping company to see how they would suggest you mark the package in this event.

If you are selling an item that is new and has a price tag with a significantly higher amount than the actual sales price, you may remove the price tag if the buyer wishes. This is so the buyer can avoid over-paying taxes should the Customs agent open the package. Customs agents may do this at their discretion; removing price tags that do not reflect what they buyer paid is not illegal.

For more information about eBay's policies regarding international sales, including numerous helpful links to agencies and Web sites that are able to assist you with special situations and general information, see **http://pages.eBay.com/help/policies/international-trading.html.**

Now that you have covered payment and shipping options, let us move on to something a little more exciting: promoting yourself and your business. How you choose to portray yourself and your business has a lot to do with your future success, so choose wisely based on your product, your budget, and your own personal preferences.

Ship right away

Even though it may seem pointless to make a trip to the post office to ship a small, $1 item that a customer just bought, it will mean something to your customer. Get into the habit of making this trip at least once a day, especially when a customer has placed an order. Try to consolidate your trip as much as possible, but do not delay shipping for days just because you only have a few items to send. Shipping is just as important as any other eBay business function.

It may seem like it is a better use of your time to wait until you have several items ready to go out or to do it once a week or so; resist the temptation to do this. Your customers take the recommended shipping times quite seriously. If it says two to four days, then by day five, they are getting a bit upset. If you make them wait a week, you are almost sure to get a nasty comment, a negative feedback rating, and a customer who will not buy anything from you again. Set a time each day that is your post office time — when you will drop off any merchandise that is ready to be shipped. Do this every day, and use e-mail to let customers know when their product has been shipped.

There are a number of stores, such as Mail Boxes Etc., that will ship from different shipping services such as the USPS and UPS. Find one in your community, and you can cut your traveling down significantly.

Schedule regular pickups

Once you have a high volume of outgoing products, you can save plenty of time by printing out your own postage on your computer and scheduling regular pickups of outgoing mail. As long as you have an account with a post office, FedEx, or UPS, they will come to your home and pick up boxes.

Do not worry about the logistics of shipping, because eBay wants you to succeed: When you succeed and are making money, they are also making money. They want to help you in any way possible to sell more products efficiently, and for the best prices possible. Repeat customers for you also mean repeat customers for them.

If you have not done so, go to eBay's shipping center. If you follow the instructions found here, you will be able to estimate your shipping, print out shipping labels, and even track your shipments; they also have tips on shipping. As mentioned previously, they can even order shipping boxes for free that have the eBay logo printed on them from USPS.

Should I…

…buy seller's insurance?

Insurance is meant to protect the seller, as they will be held responsible for damaged or lost products. Items infrequently get lost, though, so you can save money by only insuring products that could potentially break during shipping or that are expensive to begin with. You can save a small fortune in insurance fees if you only insure items that you are genuinely concerned about being damaged. It is your responsibility if something gets broken, not the buyer's responsibility. This point can be argued, as they can also buy insurance, but if the product is faulty, it is your business that will pay in the long run with bad feedback and lost customers. If an item is returned, then you are also losing money because you have paid for shipping and eBay fees for an item you may not be able to resell.

…outsource my shipping?

A fulfillment center is an organization that specializes in sending out other companies' products. They have their own warehouse and trained staff that will make sure all your products get to where they need to go quickly and efficiently. If you have a high volume of outgoing goods, outsourcing your shipping may be a good idea. Many eBay PowerSellers have found that outsourcing their shipping has saved them time and money. If you are thinking about hiring a fulfillment center to store, pack, and ship your goods, then you might want to consider whether you have enough outgoing products to make outsourcing your shipping cost-effective. Based on the outsourcing options available to you, will it cost you less to ship through an outside agency based on the rates for their services? If so, then you should outsource.

Outsourcing may not work if you are selling unique items. If you have the type of business dealing in, say, antiques, and your inventory will be changing all the time, outsourcing will not be practical. It would cost you extra just to send the items to the fulfillment center. On the other hand, if you are selling bulk lots of PEZ dispensers, then a fulfillment center may be a better option.

Pros to outsourcing shipping:

- **Lower cost.** Because fulfillment centers deal in high volumes, they are able to pack and ship for much less than it would cost you. They take buying in bulk to a whole new level. Instead of buying a carton of envelopes, they are able to buy envelopes by the truckload, which significantly lowers their overall costs.

- **Less work.** They will run the warehouse for you, and you will not have to deal with renting a warehouse or other real estate to store and pack your goods. The major advantage to this is that it allows you to work from home, even after your product volume has expanded beyond what your home can handle.

- **Organization.** They have advanced inventory systems with bar codes, which will enable them to ship items more quickly and accurately than you can.

- **Regular reports.** Most fulfillment businesses give their clients regular reports on the status of their products. This takes care of the business of keeping track for you. All you need to do is put all the reports they send you into a three-ring binder or file folder — no more filling out pages in a notebook or spreadsheet.

Checklist of Things to Consider When Choosing Shipping Providers	
✓	I am aware of all the possible ways to receive payments, including the pros and cons of each, and have decided on which ones I will accept in my eBay business.
✓	I will be fair when adding a handling charge to the cost of shipping.
✓	I have (or will) purchased a digital scale for determining the weight of items so my customers can obtain accurate shipping quotes right in the auction body.
✓	I have or can locate sources of reclaimed or recycled materials for packing to save the cost of purchasing new materials, if possible.
✓	I have researched international shipping and made a decision about whether I will offer this option. If not, I can always offer it later.

CASE STUDY: IS THIS WHAT PAVLOV HAD IN MIND?

When people in White Bear Lake, Minnesota, have a garage sale, they only hope that Joe (eBay user "whitebears") is in the neighborhood. Although he said he developed "more selective ways to build inventory" for his eBay sales in recent years, Joe still has a "soft spot for those neon-colored signs that dot the neighborhoods on Thursdays, Fridays, and Saturdays."

It started in 2000 with some clutter. There was not enough to have a garage sale, not to mention the deterrence of cold weather in Minnesota late in the year. Joe had heard about a new Web site, Half.com, and thought he would try to sell a dust-gathering pile of videos that were no longer viewed by anyone in the family. Despite his naturally skeptical nature, he found that they sold well and plunged ahead with clearing the entertainment center of even more dust bunnies. About that time, he also listed a few items on eBay, trying his hand at the auction format.

By spring, he made the decision to "forge ahead as a small-time entrepreneur" and began spending weekends picking up bargains in books, videos, music CDs, and other interesting items. He was testing the markets and learning what sold well. He bombed out on the books, but found he had a knack for the videos and CDs. Some might call it his "light bulb moment," but for Joe, it was more like hearing a bell ring.

His interest in garage sales, moving sales, thrift sale, estate sales, andthe like quickly turned into a real buying frenzy. Joe recalls those earlyyears: "I suspect my family thought I had gone wacko, salivating likePavlov's dog any time I saw a 'sale' sign on the side of the road." At hispeak, Joe would hit 40 to 50 garage sales a week.

He has pared down the rummaging, but certainly not eliminated it from the lineup of merchandise sources. While Joe started by selling VHS videos, the market has taken a serious downturn in recent years because of the DVD format's popularity. But he still sells VHS tapes and has plans to continue to do so. "There are a lot of eBayers and others out there who say the VHS market is dead," he said, but he does not see it that way. "Selfishly speaking, I don't mind seeing people say that, because it keeps them from taking up space in my niche market. The VHS market is not dead, and probably is not even on life support."

His strength in this market lies in the knowledge of what truly will sell and what will not. A typical garage sale with 50 VHS tapes might yield only two or three that are worth his investment. Because he has been selling VHS tapes for five years now, he knows what 5 or 10 percent of those available are collector's items or have what he calls a "niche viewership." This is not something that a new seller will know without some prior experience in this market, Joe said.

Though Joe feels that the fixed-price format of Half.com or other similar sites can often yield a higher profit margin, those sites are not really conducive to selling some of the other items that he picked up here and there as he rummaged throughout the Twin Cities. "The more sales I went to, the more I would pick up trinkets or novelties or sports memorabilia, another market that I had a modicum of interest and knowledge in, and list those items on eBay and wind up turning a profit," he said.

Over time, his knowledge base became quite diversified, and he found he was doing as much business in all those other areas as he was in CDs and VHS videos. Nowadays, his CD and VHS inventory accounts for less than half of his sales.

One of Joe's growing areas of merchandise is in the collectibles: everything from pewter figurines and trinket boxes to Elvis memorabilia. He tries to tap into the nostalgia of the baby boomers and looks for things he knows will be of interest to them, such as games, dolls, and other items that were popular during their growing-up era.

A personal interest in what Joe calls "old paper" includes things like sheet music, documents, old postcards, and magazines. One of his favorite paper goods is stereoview cards — if you recall the opening story of this book. He finds these items "interesting from a historical perspective — as well as often highly profitable."

Although every businessperson wants to make profit, Joe feels that it is not just about selling the right things to the right person. Joe's business philosophy is simple: "Any business should have two main goals: First, turn a profit, and second, serve the customer. You absolutely cannot achieve goal No. 1 in the long run without achieving goal No. 2. And beyond that, customer service is more than good business; it's just plain the right thing to do," he said.

In order to gain satisfied customers, Joe's policies are honest and straightforward:

- Give honest, courteous, prompt, cordial, and professional service — always.

- Respond to e-mails in one day (or less, if at all possible).

- Ship quickly and at a reasonable cost to the buyer.

- Fully disclose all defects and other conditions of sale in every listing.

- If a buyer has a problem, work with him or her to come to a solution.

- Offer a no-questions-asked money-back guarantee.

For the rare buyer who is out to "strong-arm" him, Joe relies on his thorough knowledge of eBay policies and uses eBay to his advantage when he is in the right.

His willingness to work with buyers to achieve their satisfaction has been a big hit with international bidders, who often have to hunt far and wide to find sellers who are willing to go that extra mile for them. "I opened my auctions to international sellers two or three years ago, and it was one of the best business decisions I've made," he said. "There's no question I sell more, and sell at higher closing prices, because I ship internationally."

He has not run across many troubles with international shipping, with an estimated 99 percent of the buyers being polite and appreciative. Payments generally arrive promptly from international buyers as well, he notes. He does make it clear to international buyers that he will not mark their item as a gift as a way for them to avoid paying duties. That does not jibe with his overall policy of honesty.

Advice from Joe:

- Get involved in the Community Discussion Boards: "They're invaluable."

- Take time to randomly read feedback of other sellers: "You can see how people deal with each other, or fail to deal with each other."

- Keep talking to an unhappy customer: "Ninety-nine-plus percent of problems can be worked out just by keeping open the lines of communication."

- Don't be afraid of your items not always selling: "You lose some and you win some, but more often than not, you win."

In the long run, Joe said his only regret is that he did not start his online sales venture sooner. Though his business nets him a part-time supplemental income, it has given him full-time joy and satisfaction to know that he is now a PowerSeller with a feedback score exceeding 2,600 and 99.9 percent of his customers reporting their satisfaction. Pavlov might not give a hoot, but it sure makes Joe proud.

Chapter Seven

Advertising — Toot Your Own Horn

I f you are still reading, you are obviously serious about getting your business off on the right foot. Though these tasks are a time-consuming aspect of "being your own boss," doing research (such as reading this book) and taking time to set things up properly is really the only bona fide way to go about this.

Next on our ever-growing list of details is how to advertise yourself on and offline.

If you were starting a traditional business in your hometown, there are numerous steps you would take to spread the word, but placing an ad in your local newspaper probably is not going to get the word out to 135 million people worldwide.

So how are you going to let the entire eBay community know you are there, ready, willing, and able to sell? Even small things can make a difference, so consider using all the resources you have available at little or no cost to you.

Free Marketing Strategies

First let us take a brief look at the free marketing strategies you should be employing. eBay offers every seller these five free ways to make your listings stand out.

Cross-promotions

This is the box at the bottom of your listing that says "Other Great Items From This Seller," and it does not cost you anything to have it. To get it, go to your "My eBay" page and click on Preferences (under My Account) and click the link that says "Promoting Similar Items on eBay Pages and E-mails." Edit your promotion preferences here. If you are utilizing all the cross-promotions available, it will say "Participate in cross-promotions" and then "Yes in all available areas" after that. That is it: free help from eBay to drive lookers and buyers to all your other listings.

One of the places your cross-promotions will be displayed include in the e-mails sent to non-winning bidders letting them know they did not win the auction. When someone places your item on their "Items I'm Watching" page, he or she will also see some of your other cross-promoted items. Even when a buyer pays an invoice through PayPal, he or she will again be shown a choice of your merchandise.

Check out my other listings

Even though eBay will automatically add a box that displays your other auctions, it is at the bottom of the auction page, and sometimes it is just not noticed. So while you are writing out your auction text, make sure to add a link to your other listings.

Cross-promotion connections

You can make arrangements with other sellers to promote each other's items. This is great if you sell widgets, but not the specialty cleaner that keeps your widget looking new. You should cross-promote with the sellers who sell complementary items, not competing items. Check out the information under "My Account" and "Cross Promotion Connections."

"About Me" page

Every eBay member has the opportunity to create an "About Me" page at no cost. Some post pictures of pets, local tourist attractions, or themselves, giving their customers a "face." Others are more businesslike, sharing information about their merchandise or customer-service philosophy. If you have not yet made your "About Me" page, do so soon.

To create your page, go to "Community" (on the top toolbar) and scroll to the bottom of the page; you will see a link inviting you to create a page. The step-by-step instructions walk you through a series of boxes where you type in your text, make your choices, and preview your page.

You can use your own HTML, if you are lucky enough to know it already, simply by clicking on the "HTML" tab.

If you are like many new sellers and do not know much HTML, you can use the drop-down menus to choose your font type, size, and color. The buttons for bold, italic, underline, numbering, and bullets are all standard. The buttons should look like those in most word-processing software.

Spend a little time making your page interesting. Do not use a font that is too small, nor too large. All-capital letters will make it appear as if you are shouting. Use different colors for the different sections, such as personal information, business information, policies, and customer service.

You can also link to photos that you have stored online, or your company's logo, if you have one already. Even if you just post basic information, it is a start. Surf eBay and look at other seller's pages (there is not a way to search "About Me" pages; you need to just click on the "Me" logo after any seller's name) and get ideas for your own page. Do not steal any logos or photos, though.

Personal information should be friendly and interesting, but not too personal. You do not want to offend potential customers by stating any views on controversial topics. Additionally, for security reasons, it may not be wise to get too detailed about where you live, or the identity of other family members.

Pets, however, are an opportunity to share photos and discussion. Also, your travels, the seasonal scenery in your part of the country, or a photo of your workshop might be appropriate. If you make your product by hand, show an item in different stages of completion and perhaps a description of how the item is made with care and attention to details.

Business information you might want to share could include your mission statement (from your business plan) and your customer-service philosophy. If you have not yet put one to paper, here is a good time to do so. Your statement might read something like this:

> *Our goal is to serve all our customers in a timely manner with fair prices, speedy delivery, and service after the sale. We want to make every customer a repeat customer. If there is anything about our service that you feel needs improvement, feel free to e-mail me personally at WillysWidgets@e-mailprovider.net.*

If your product has any exemplary features or has won any awards, praise, or good reviews, cite these and the source that you got this information from. For example:

> *Our widgets are made by the finest facility in North America. The Widget Review (July 2005) states, "these widgets out-perform every other model on the market. You can't go wrong when you invest in this easy-to-maintain and quiet-running model."*

eBay will also ask you to choose if you want any current items listed to appear after your text. You can even choose how many items you want to provide links to. Additionally, you can have your last ten, 25, or more feedback comments displayed, with a link inviting the reader to go to your member profile and view all your feedback.

Sellers are proud of good feedback, and you should always take the opportunity to share your well-deserved rating. *Chapter 9 gives more information on feedback.*

You will also be able to insert links to Web sites, including your own company's site, with certain restrictions that are clearly laid out (click the link on the "About Me" creation page), and HTML images. To further personalize your page, you can choose from one of three layouts, then preview your information in the chosen layout. If you want to see the other layouts, simply go back and re-choose.

TIP

Editing your page follows the same process. To edit your page, go to the page and scroll to the bottom. There you will find a link directing you through the editing process. Keep your page current, and edit it any time you have a new product line or an announcement to make about your business. Also, try changing photos seasonally; this helps those looking at the page know it is current.

When your page is complete, eBay will provide you with a link to your new "About Me" page, which you should make a point of writing down. Add it to your e-mail templates or signature so each business e-mail you send can point prospective customers to your page, which highlights your product and your feedback.

Linking to and from eBay. Promote your eBay Store, your "About Me" page, and auctions on other Web sites, or via your e-mails. In addition to using your "About Me" page link, you will be able to link people directly from their e-mail to your store when the e-mail is opened. When you link from your "About Me" page, make sure you are within the requirements of eBay's policy; linking from your "About Me" page to your own personal Web site (or domain name, see below) is important.

You cannot link from your page to another auction site that you also may sell on; it must be to your own personal Web page. However, on that Web page, you can link to other Web sites where you auction. Check out eBay's policies thoroughly before linking; you certainly do not want to offend the company that is helping your business get a good running start.

Linking is an important part of Internet marketing via e-mail and message boards, which are also considered free marketing techniques. Remember to use e-mail to its full potential. It does not cost anything to add links to your eBay Store, your "About Me" page, or your personal Web site in an e-mail. Use the signature section to place this information in every e-mail, so you do not have to retype or copy and paste the links every time.

Start saving your customers' e-mail addresses right away. Use your address lists to announce new products or other big news from your business. You do not want to bombard your customers with e-mails, as you may then be relegated to their "blocked senders" list, but you do not want them to forget you, either. Seasonal e-mails can be a happy medium. For every season, e-mail your customer list with a new announcement, product promotion, and a wish for their happiness in the months to come until you e-mail them again. But make sure to express your sincere desire to do business with them again.

Do not forget the "opt-out" message, reviewed in Chapter 2. All businesses must be sensitive to customers who do not want to receive e-mail, so keep your own list of those who contact you and wish to opt-out. Also include a statement about what you do with your collected customer e-mail addresses. Be sure to let customers know you value their business and have no intentions of ever selling, renting, or trading e-mail addresses with anybody else.

If you are looking for a way to supplement your own customer database, you can purchase e-mail address lists that are generated from "opt-in" clauses on Web sites. These are generally considered more reputable sources of e-mail addresses than some other lists you can buy, but beware — it still may be regarded as spam by the recipients. Be sure to make an e-mail title clearly indicating that you are not spam. Many companies also offer to actually do the e-mailing for you, using opt-in lists they have on file. But there are scam artists posing as reputable marketing companies who simply send spam with your company name attached to it. Tread very carefully when contracting with any other company to do the e-mailing for you.

For the most part, at least for now, obtain your e-mail list from your own customer base and guard it carefully. Your customers will thank you for protecting their privacy and not adding to the spam in their inbox every day.

Another possibility for your seasonal e-mail is to use a newsletter format, with advice on other products compatible with yours or of a general nature. For example, Willy's winter e-mail might be a newsletter format with a list of the "Top 10 ways a Widget or Gidget can make your life easier during the winter months," along with general tips on how to conserve electricity and cut heating bills. Even though widgets and gidgets may have nothing to do with heat or electricity, this information is almost universally applicable in the winter.

Sprinkle little tidbits of interest in a newsletter: a very brief poem, humorous quote, or anecdote from one of your customers (feature a customer's comment or quote every time, and you may find your customers start giving you material, just hoping to be featured in the newsletter).

To make a newsletter universally readable by your customers, use software that will transpose your format into a PDF file. There are reasonably priced programs available to do this (of course if you are using Adobe Acrobat, you will not need a separate software), and one of the best is found at **www.pdfonline.com/convert-pdf**.

This software is available for free. You will have to tolerate a pop-up box every time you use it, asking you to purchase the product. But even if you choose not to purchase the additional products, the basic product will convert your Publisher file, Word document, or most any other file to a PDF format.

You will also need some graphics for your newsletter. Microsoft products contain built-in connections to their Web site where you can search through thousands of clip art and Web images. There are many clip art studios that you can purchase at any software retailer that are also worthwhile. When comparing, make sure you purchase one that allows you access to the company's Web site and any new clip art that is produced after the discs you purchased were made.

Because your newsletter will be sent via e-mail, you can offer special discounts to these valued customers. Insert a link to a current product in your store and offer a discount, such as free shipping, for those who buy in the next 48 hours. Instruct them to delete the shipping charge during the eBay checkout process. You can compare their e-mail address to those on your list and make sure they are customers who had received your newsletter (and not a new customer who accidentally deleted the shipping charge).

Internet chat rooms and message boards can also be a way to spread the word about your eBay business. Check around for eBay-related sites that are not affiliated with eBay. There are dozens of Yahoo! groups devoted to eBay, some of which exist only for members to post their listings, specials, and links to their store. There is no cost involved to you — just a few minutes of your time to post the information.

Try looking for message boards and chat rooms devoted to your particular product, as you will probably not generate much interest in your heavy metal music sales if you are posting ads on a board of senior citizens who are looking to buy travel-related products.

These suggestions are not all-encompassing in regard to marketing yourself for free. Check out the eBay community discussion boards on this topic and you will learn some tricks of the trade without having to figure them out the hard way.

But few businesses can survive solely on free marketing. Though it is important to utilize every possible opportunity you get to advertise your business for free, you will probably have to pay for some services as well. There are marketing ideas worth paying for.

As with the free marketing ideas, eBay offers for-a-fee services. If you are using eBay as your primary selling tool, you will probably also utilize every possible option eBay offers to market your business and products.

The eBay Store

Probably one of the most common tools used by sellers is the eBay Store. The fees for having your own eBay Store are reasonable, if you were to compare the price for renting a traditional store space or regularly placing ads in the local newspaper. Once you are a registered eBay seller and have earned a feedback score of 20, you are eligible to open a store. *Learn more about how feedback is calculated later in Chapter 9.*

eBay suggests you open a store when you are ready to sell regularly (this is not really a good choice for the occasional seller because there are ongoing fees) and when you have sufficient inventory (a regular product stream). The basic eBay Store can be purchased for as low as $15.95 a month, with the first 30 days at no cost to you.

There are three tiers of eBay Stores:

Basic:
- $15.95/month
- Must sell at least ten items/$100 per month

- Can be for a secondary income or hobby
- Can be able to use Selling Manager for free
- Limited space, e-mails, and customer service

Premium:

- $49.95/month
- Is the most common type used by a PowerSeller
- Must sell at least 50 items/$500 per month
- 24/7 customer service
- Able to use Selling Manager Pro for free
- More e-mails and listings you can manage
- More space for photos

Anchor:

- $299.95/month
- Must sell at least 500 items/$5,000 per month
- Has all the features of Premium with increased space for pages and photos
- Store name frequently appears in "Shop eBay Stores" area of matching search results

If you are interested in what each level of store has to offer, you can access this information at **www.pages.eBay.com/storefronts/start.html**.

Benefits of your own eBay Store

The benefits of having your own eBay Store include:

- A professional presence on eBay that says, "I'm not just an occasional seller."

- Lower listing fees for store inventory items (details below).

- Longer listing times (or never-ending listings) for store inventory.

- Categorization of your merchandise of your choice; five pages in your store.

- A place to showcase all your listings, including current auctions.

- Selling Manager software use for free.

- Cross-promotions in more places for store sellers.

- Linking for a domain name directly to your store.

- Final Value Fee credits if your off-eBay referral buys from your store inventory.

- Accounting Assistant (software that works with QuickBooks).

- Free-email marketing tools.

- Sales reports for your store and other listings.

- Special features for upgraded store types (Featured and Anchor Stores).

Having an online presence is important, and having a permanent storefront is one way to achieve that. Whether you have the basic or the Anchor Store, you can use eBay's tools (or your own HTML) to create a store that showcases your merchandise. It takes time to set up a store that "looks" zippy and professional, but if you take the time to read all the associated "Help" files and utilize the built-in tools, you will soon have a great-looking, unique store.

Your store will show all your current listings, whether they are fixed-price listings, auctions, or "store inventory" listings (which are sold through Buy It Now only). But what do you choose to put into inventory, and what do you select for auction?

There are differing theories about this, and it will depend on your product. If you primarily sell the same products over and over again, then you should always run some auctions. When lookers do a search from the home page (at the top right), they will see auctions (including fixed-price listings) in their results, not store inventory.

If a looker's search turns up 30 or fewer results, then up to 30 "store inventory" listings will appear after the auction listings. If the search turns up more than 30 results, a link at the bottom of the page will let buyers know the same items can be located in eBay Stores. The looker just needs to click the link to be taken to a page of store listings.

If a search turns up no auction or fixed-price listings matching the searcher's criteria, but there are store inventory items that match, then up to 30 of the store inventory items will be displayed with a gallery photo (a photo that is displayed in the actual search result, as opposed to the green camera icon that normally displays, unless you pay the extra fee for the gallery photo).

So what is the difference between a fixed-price auction and a store inventory item? The difference is primarily the number of days that it is available for sale. Fixed-price auctions run the same as regular auctions: for one, three, five, seven, or ten days only. In your store, you will be able to set up your inventory items to be for sale for 30, 60, 90, or 120 days, until you cancel it. You can convert any store inventory item back to an auction item at any time, if you wish to do so.

Why would you want to have a listing never expire? This is for items you always stock or always produce. But do not start mentally adding up the listing fees just yet; when you list store inventory items, the listing price is currently $0.12 for a whole 30 days. The Final Value Fees are higher for store inventory items, though. *See the charts of eBay Store fees at the end of the chapter.*

Do not forget that your store will not get the same type of exposure as auctions in the buyer's basic search (there is no way for buyers to specify that they want to search store inventory only, or in addition to auctions), so you would be wise to still run auctions. Think of them as a tool to drive people to your store.

This is not to say that stores are entirely without their own promotion. Your store will be listed in the directory of all stores, which can be easily accessed from the home page. Some people prefer to buy from a store, rather than wait it out in an auction, so they search by going to the eBay Stores page first.

On the eBay Stores page, the buyer can search by store names or by matching items. For Willy, if buyers want to find out who is selling widgets in an eBay Store, they can search "widget," and the search will return a list of stores that currently list a "widget" in their inventory. This is the only place eBay lookers can go to search specifically in store's inventory.

But do not rely on buyers to always search the eBay Stores page. Write a sentence or two to include in every auction text, suggesting that the looker could find more variety and choice in your store. Save your text in a word-processing software and insert it into every auction, and make sure to put it in your Turbo Lister templates. The point is to get lookers to check out your store, even if they are not as interested in the auction item once they have seen it.

However, there is an important warning: Let us say you want to promote your store in every one of your auction listings, as suggested above. That is a great thing to do, but you have to be sure you do not engage in what is known as "keyword spamming." In short, your invitation to view your store cannot, for example, refer to your store items by brand names or even keywords.

Your invitation must be generic in nature. You cannot say, "Be sure to view my store for more great items, including Louis Vuitton purses, Manolo Blahnik shoes, Gucci bags, and more." Even if that particular auction is for one of those designer purses, you cannot list other brand names in your auction text, not even in an invitation to view your store or other auctions.

Let us say your auction is for a Gucci handbag; the invitation to your store can say, "Be sure to visit my store for more great designer items." You did not mention purses, any particular designer, or brand names.

You may wonder why this is such a major issue on eBay. See it this way: An unscrupulous seller will insert popular keywords in his auction text, so when a looker searches "Manolo Blahnik," the seller's auction will show up in the search results, even though their auction has nothing to do with that keyword. They do this in an attempt to gain more exposure for their items.

This is not really fair to the looker who is not interested in the other item being misrepresented, and it seriously affects the integrity of eBay's database and search results. eBay is constantly on the lookout for violations of this policy, but it cannot be in all places at all times. It is up to all sellers to be aware of this underhanded method of promoting listings and to make a commitment to never engage in keyword spamming.

Be sure to play fair and promote your store in a way that showcases your integrity as a seller. Buyers look for and appreciate honest, trustworthy sellers.

When you use appropriate cross-promotions to attract buyers to your store, they have to merely glance at the left-hand side of the screen to see the neatly categorized list of all your items. Perhaps they are not interested in spare bike parts, but you have also picked up a nice wholesale lot of porcelain dolls. If they see a category for porcelain dolls, they can avoid paging through all your items and go straight to what they are interested in.

When you are a store seller and your looker bids or buys, you also have cross-promotions presented to the bidder/buyer. Of course, one of the best ways to promote your eBay Store is to get a domain name (for example, Willy might want to get **www.widgets4sale.com**) and then have it go straight to your eBay Store when anybody on the Internet clicks on it. There are costs to a domain name, but they are fairly reasonable, especially if you do not actually have a Web site there. Think of a domain name as a portal for now, with the potential to be yet another selling tool (an off-eBay Web site) in the future.

One good reason to get a domain name is this: eBay will give you credits on Final Value Fees on sales of your store inventory (not auctions, even though they too are listed in your store) if the buyer got to your store through your own marketing efforts. So, that domain name you are considering can actually pay for itself if people use it to get to your store and then make a purchase. Be sure you understand eBay's policies on this very well so you meet all the requirements properly.

Remember that your buyers will not know which type of service that you have. It is up to you to customize your store and make it look professional while making it easy for buyers to browse through. Here are some areas to pay attention to, as you can change and modify them according to your and your buyers' needs:

- You can change the store design. This includes the name, theme, gallery view, and the order that your items are sorted in.

- You can customize your pages. You should have a policies page that answers questions about your policies, such as shipping and payment.

- You should make sure that it is clear where you will ship to and where you will not.

- If you are collecting sales tax, make sure you have this included on your policies page. This will depend on the state you are selling from and selling to.

- Include customer service and return policies. You should also state your contact information and when customer service is available; mention what your time zone is.

- You can name up to 300 different custom categories that allow your buyers to browse in specific areas for items. This helps make your store unique based on the types of items that you have for sale.

- You can use promotion boxes on your eBay Store that allow you to give your store a different look every month and when you are placing items on sale.

TIP When you have an eBay Store, consider advertising it locally the same way you would advertise a brick-and-mortar store: newspaper, the yellow pages, and radio ads. These may be especially effective if you also have a Web site address (domain name) to advertise along with it.

There are also four additional goodies you will be able to use free when you open a store: Selling Manager (free with your store), Accounting Assistant (works with QuickBooks), e-mail marketing, and Sales Reports.

eBay Store tools

Selling Manager

Selling Manager is a program that makes your "My eBay" page's "All Selling" tab slicker, more productive, and more useful. It is a strongly suggested selling tool for medium- and high-volume sellers. It usually costs $4.99 per month, but it comes with a free 30-day trial, so consider trying it for the 30 days before you open your store.

One of the nice features of this program is its ability to track your sales contacts. Selling Manager can help you with that e-mail database you are planning to keep. It also includes some nice e-mail templates, plus templates for invoices and shipping labels. You can even create templates for feedback comments that you can store and use for your customers.

This software will archive four months of your listings, unlike the standard in "My eBay," which shows only those listings for 60 days back. There is also a tool to help you download your selling history, which can be helpful for your bookkeeping. For those of you who set up your books in Quick-Books right away, Accounting Assistant will interface with QuickBooks to make all those tasks easier.

E-mail marketing

E-mail marketing is crucial, and because you will have Selling Manager keeping track of all your sales contacts, you can use the free e-mail marketing techniques to send up to 100 e-mails monthly to your contacts if you have a basic store; upgraded levels get more. If you need to send more than 100 e-mails through this system, there is a $0.01 charge for each additional e-mail.

Although this may not be a cost-effective way to send out thousands of e-mails a month (when you only have the basic store), take advantage of it, at least monthly, until your contact list reaches 100 buyers. eBay provides a step-by-step guide to help you set up your strategy and system.

Sales reports

Sales reports are a good way to get a quick glimpse of your overall sales, the percentage of your sales that come from auctions versus store inventory, or the sales for each of your store's categories. The features and freebies of the basic store are good for the fee charged. Sellers who immerse themselves into their eBay selling and learn to use all the tools available to them — there are even more than what we are able to cover here — will not regret paying their eBay bill at the end of each month.

At some point, you might be successful enough to upgrade to a Feature Store. Priced at $49.95 per month, it is still not unreasonable because you will be privy to these additional benefits:

- Your store's name and brief description will be rotated among all Feature Stores and shown on the eBay Stores page in the center (not top box, but the one below it).

- You get up to ten pages you can fully customize by category or price, by promotions and specials, a dedicated home page, and so on.

- The ability to minimize the eBay header on all your pages, giving you more room for your own information.

- Traffic reports that give details about what buyers are looking at most, and where they entered your store from (for example, your own domain or eBay).

- More detailed sales reports than with the basic store.

- Your inventory listings are more likely to appear at the bottom of the page where a buyer searched for auctions with certain keywords.

- $30 per month to use on eBay's keyword program. *Learn more on this in the next section.*

- Selling Manager Pro is included free ($15.95/month value).

An Anchor Store will give you premium exposure and services on the eBay Stores home page, but this venture will cost $299.95 per month. Suffice it to say, this is something to write down and post on your wall as a goal: "I Will Someday Upgrade to an Anchor Store."

Keywords

When buyers search for listings, they type in words they think might be in the title of something they want to purchase. If they are in the market for a very expensive watch for Grandpa's retirement gift, they might type in "Rolex" or some other high-end brand name of watches. In that case, Rolex is the keyword that connected the buyer with Grandpa's new watch.

eBay allows sellers to bid on the right to have their store's advertising displayed when their chosen keyword is searched by buyers. Have you ever noticed that if you perform a search for "Rolex watch," then just above the first auction listing, a couple of boxes visibly stand out and try hard to entice you to check out those Rolexes? If you click on one of the boxes, you will be taken to that particular seller's store, more than likely.

This is how the higher-volume sellers who can afford more than the minimum advertising in their budget keep their merchandise in the front of your vision (or in this case, at the top of the list). They also can then make a sale without having an auction at the top of the list (which, by default, shows auctions ending first or the "best match").

Many top sellers swear by this technique, and when you have a Featured or Anchor Store, you will have an allocated amount of money to spend on the keywords program. You are only charged for your banner at the top of the page every time a customer clicks on it. So although your banner might display 15 times in a 24-hour period, you will only be charged the fee for the two times that it was used to enter your store.

You can also purchase keyword banners if you only have a basic store, but there is an up-front fee charged in addition to the per-click fee. When you have your store set up, go to the "Manage My Store" link and click on "Purchase Keywords" to learn about the fees and restrictions.

Google has a keyword per-click program called AdWords. Once you start using keyword banner programs and feel you have a sense of how to best use your keywords to drive business to your eBay Store (or your domain name, which in turn drives customers to your eBay Store), then look into this program as well at **www.adwords.google.com**.

Your own domain name, as already described, can be used without an actual attached Web site; it can be used as a stand-alone product that merely refers potential customers to your eBay Store. But once you have the income (and time) to devote to setting up and maintaining an off-eBay Web site, then you should look into getting your own Web site or store.

The cost for this can vary greatly depending on a number of factors, such as your ability to create the site yourself (using a software such as Microsoft

FrontPage®, Adobe® GoLive®, or Adobe's Dreamweaver®), or have a friend or family member who can assist you with this task.

If you prefer to hire someone to get it done, you may find a big price difference when you check with several companies. Sometimes small in-home businesses will create sites cheaper than "the big guys." Just be sure you get the best Web site and hosting deal for your money, including features such as a secure server with a shopping cart. There are companies online that will design an original site for you as well, so do not limit yourself to only local companies (although keeping your business local may be something you want to do).

Your hosting company will also be able to submit your site to all the major search engines, so people can find the site when they search for applicable words. One good trait about Web site search engines is they will also search the content of your site, so matching phrase and words will be shown, not just matches in your site's name.

Affiliated marketing

Having your own Web site can lend itself to yet another new marketing opportunity: affiliated marketing. This is a method where you loan out space on your site to another company's banner and, in return, if customers go to the other site via your site, you get a per-click fee or a percentage of the profits when the customer purchases something. Affiliated marketing is popular and should be considered when you get to this level of sales and marketing. Be sure to check into having your banner ad on other Web sites as well.

You can use your Web site for a variety of purposes; you can conduct product sales on your site, in addition to an eBay Store. You can also use your Web site as an information portal, merely providing information about your product and directing all sales back to your eBay Store.

Willy might set up a Web site to sell his widgets and gidgets without paying eBay fees. But because he can earn some credit on his Final Value Fees
by directing his Web site traffic to his eBay Store, he may also choose to
focus on maintenance of your widget or showcasing the newest models of
widgets and gidgets, which can be purchased in his eBay Store. Either way,
when a potential buyer searches the Internet for "widget," "gidget," or any
other related word, they will be directed to Willy's site. These are just a
couple of ways that you can add a Web site to your existing sales approach.

Business cards and giveaways

Other less-expensive but worthwhile marketing items are business cards
and giveaways. Business cards have become downright cheap in the past
decade, and you can even print them yourself on cardstock (and then cut
them out by hand), or buy pre-perforated paper that will let you quickly
separate them. Search for companies on the Web that have volume discount pricing; however, ask about the weight of the cardstock they use, as
it can vary. You do not want to pass out business cards that are not much
thicker than regular paper. Standard cardstock comes in thicknesses starting about 65-pound weight. Make sure any business cards you order are at
least that weight or higher.

If you get a good deal on business cards, order them in a large quantity and
be liberal about passing them out any chance you get. Tack a few up on the
bulletin board at your local grocery store, gas station, or anywhere else you
are allowed to leave these items. Do not litter, and do not leave them in
places where solicitations are not welcomed, as that will decrease your professional image. In addition to business cards, you can order literally thousands of products with your company name, eBay Store name, Web site
address, or company logo on it. You can pass out everything from baseball
caps to pens, pads of paper, and small toys, all with your information on it.

Pass these items out to your family and friends as well as at gatherings such
as parades (simply walk through the crowd — you do not have to be in the
parade itself), and community gatherings (picnics, your son's T-ball game,

school programs, or the county fair). Do not make a pest of yourself, but if you are excited about your product, your store, and your business, people will want to hear about it and pass the word along for you. You never know where your next customer will come from.

> **TIP**
>
> These are also nice items to tuck into an order, as a way to encourage your buyers to come back soon. You could also send along a business card with a message on the back, "Pass this card on to a friend who will receive a 10 percent discount when they order." and then when you get a customer who mentions having a card of yours, ask which customer gave it to him or her. Then you can send the referring customer a thank-you e-mail with an invitation for 10 percent off his or her next order as well.

Newspaper and radio advertising

Other traditional advertising methods might serve a purpose for you, such as newspaper and radio advertising. If your product is heavily used or highly desirable in a particular geographic location or among specific populations (such as in warm climates or during the summertime, or if it is popular with college students), then consider ads in targeted, appropriate publications. If your product is popular with college students, contact college newspapers, which often have reasonable rates and are starved for advertisers. Trade journals are a good place for ads if your product is applicable to one particular field, such as for use by medical professionals. Regional magazines that are published for a local readership may have good advertising rates, and they will help target your audience in that region.

Local radio stations might be willing to pursue an advertising campaign for you. Look into sponsoring a particular hour of the day, such as rush hour, where people stuck in their cars might be more likely to listen in. Try offering a product as a prize once a day to "Caller No. 5." Pay to have the station's DJs wear shirts and hats with your company logo at local functions, and pass out some of your giveaways to the crowd. There are many ways radio stations can help you build your company's name locally, and though you may not have but a small percentage of your sales locally, if everyone in your county knows about your company, they will be more likely to refer friends and family to your site as well.

These ideas are just some of the ways you can advertise your eBay business, ranging from the free to the frivolous. Name recognition is what it is all about; even if people cannot always remember your name or your phone number, if you can implant your Web site address in their subconscious, you have succeeded. Now that you have some ideas on where to obtain your merchandise and how to set up payment, shipping, and advertising plans, you are close to starting up the actual business of selling. Take a quick look at the differences between your old eBay status (as a looker, buyer, or occasional seller) and your new relationship with eBay: serious seller. You are now a virtual store owner.

Store Type	Monthly Fee
Basic	$15.95
Featured	$49.95
Anchor	$299.95
1st 30 days	always free

Length of Store Listing	Insertion Fee	Additional Surcharge	Total Per Item
30 days	$0.02	None	$0.02
60 days	$0.02	$0.02	$0.04
90 days	$0.02	$0.04	$0.06
120 days	$0.02	$0.06	$0.08
Good until canceled	$0.02 / 30 days 'til canceled	None	$0.02 / 30 days 'til canceled

Insertion Fees		
Price	30-day Duration	Good 'Til Canceled*
$1.00 - $24.99**	$0.03	$0.03 / 30 days
$25.00 - $199.99	$0.05	$0.05 / 30 days
$200.00 and above	$0.10	$0.10 / 30 days

Good 'til canceled listings are charged every 30 days.

**Store inventory listings have a minimum starting price of $1.00.*

Note: *Fees for store inventory are based on the duration, not the quantity. See eBay's policies to gain a thorough understanding of store fees, as this is merely an overview.*

Final Value Fees	
Price	**Final Value Fee**
Item not sold	No fee
$1.00 - $25.00	12.00% of the closing price
$25.01 - $100.00	12.00% of the initial $25.00 ($3.00), plus 8.00% of the remaining closing value balance
$100.01 - $1,000.00	12.00% of the initial $25.00 ($3.00), plus 8.00% of the initial $25.01 – $100.00 ($6.00), plus 4.00% of the remaining closing value balance $100.01 – $1,000.00
Over $1,000.01	12.00% of the initial $25.00 ($3.00), plus 8.00% of the initial $25.01 – $100.00 ($6.00), plus 4.00% of the initial $100.01 – $1,000.00 ($36.00), plus 2.00% of the remaining closing value balance ($1,000.01 – closing value)

All the other features and extras offered by eBay (listing designer and bolded title) and all the photo options have different pricing for store inventory as well. You can find the complete breakdown of store fees at **http://pages. eBay.com/help/sell/storefees.html**.

Checklist of Things to Consider When Planning Your Advertising	
✓	I have set up my eBay preferences to utilize cross-promotions effectively.
✓	I have created my "About Me" page.
✓	I have set up a place to securely store my customer database so that I can e-mail specials or newsletters to my customers.
✓	I am aware of the benefits of opening an eBay Store and will consider doing so when I have a regular product stream and the financial ability to move ahead.

✓	I understand eBay's policies against keyword spamming and choose to be an ethical seller who will not engage in this behavior.
✓	I understand that I can advertise on sites like Google for a per-click fee when my budget will allow me to do so.
✓	I will consider a domain name for the purpose of directing traffic to my eBay Store and ultimately to have as an e-commerce site, when I am financially able.
✓	I will utilize common techniques such as business cards, giveaways, and local advertising to help drive customers to my eBay business.

CASE STUDY: THE CHICKEN … OR THE EGG?

When considering an online business, one of the first decisions people make is where to sell: Get a Web site first, or sell on eBay first? Web site … eBay; eBay … Web site? It is like trying to figure out which came first: The chicken or the egg? For small businesses that do not already have a retail presence, eBay presents the perfect opportunity for the new business owner. However, the right Web site at the right time can also be a good way to start.

For those who choose to start with eBay first, they often hope their business will expand and they will eventually have to rent a retail space. Maybe they hope that they will someday have their own Web site, in order to expand their reach to sellers. Steven, an eBay seller in the Seattle, Washington, area, did things in the reverse order. He began his online business by selling his products through his own Web site and decided that, to expand his business, he would add eBay to his market as well.

Steven had some distinct advantages, of course, such as already having many of the items and processes in place that many new eBay sellers need. Because he already had an e-commerce site where he sells his designer-inspired sunglasses, eyewear accessories, biker glasses, and other complementary items, he also had a business structure in place. He already had a product stream, thanks in part to his brother who directed him to some wholesale contacts he had established for his own business. Prior work experience with some local companies had given Steven the knowledge to build his own Web Site.

So why would someone with his own Web site even need to sell on eBay? "I decided to sell on eBay to assist and increase my sales and help promote my e-commerce site as well as getting rid of old stock on hand," Steven said. "With eBay's huge traffic and exposure, it was just a win-win situation."

Even though Steven has been an eBay member since October 2002, he had previously sold his unused household and personal items, much like any run-of-the-mill hobby buyer and seller. When he decided to expand his sunglasses-selling business into eBay in December 2004, he did have to learn a bit about the differences of selling this way as opposed to through his own Web site.

"One of the things I had to do is get a system down that is not as prevalent on my Web site," he said. "I had to make time for listing items, leaving feedback, studying competitor's auctions and pricing, and learning what the most effective strategy is for the number of items you list via auction and items listed via store inventory."

Steven's store, Celebrity Glasses, showcases a large variety of sunglasses and accessories categorized in numerous ways for the browser who wants to consider many different styles. His personal e-commerce site, **www.fightclubsunglasses.com**, helps build brand recognition for him as well. These two selling outlets keep him busy, and crowded. Believe it or not, he manages both of these businesses out of his one-bedroom apartment. The lack of space would make some people ornery, but Steven takes it with a grain of salt. "I store my own inventory, package my items, and ship everything from home," he said. "Needless to say I am hurting for room, since my apartment looks like a small warehouse."

He also manages both sites and all aspects of the business entirely on his own — something that he admits "can get a bit overwhelming." Managing two businesses simultaneously would be just that for most people, but Steven has managed so far and will continue to do so. He is pleased with how his business has grown. He has also managed to achieve some goals in quick order. In just six months, he rose to PowerSeller status with over 99 percent positive feedback. His current goals include maintaining that level of sales and customer satisfaction as well as moving up the PowerSeller ladder. In addition to becoming a PowerSeller, Steven was pleased when he hit the 500 mark in his feedback score.

Maintaining a high level of sales is not always a given, and Steven knows it. Especially when he wants to keep both of his business avenues profitable, he realizes that having a creative angle and a high-quality product are two things that will set him apart from other sellers with similar or even identical merchandise. In addition to a high-quality product, Steven tries to keep his product lines fresh and current with the trends

Another important aspect of customer service is making sure the item arrives safely. He uses a special bubble wrap and crush-proof boxes to ship. Though he has things pretty under control, Steven does admit to botching a few details here and there. One mistake, he said, is that he used to list items on eBay that he had not actually yet received in stock. A late shipment from a supplier or a damaged shipment that had to be replaced could wreak havoc for his eBay business when members bid and paid but did not receive the item. To make sure that does not happen anymore, he only lists items and quantities that he has in his possession.

For some sellers, finding the right auction-creation software is not as easy as downloading Turbo Lister. Steven tried Turbo Lister, but it just did not meet his needs. He has been reviewing several other available products and is now using Auctiva tools. For keeping his financial records straight, he uses spreadsheets that he created in Microsoft Excel®, but he hopes to move to specific accounting software in the near future. Inventory can be tracked right in his eBay Store.

You could say that eBay has been a good move for Steven, who said, "Unlike other sellers, I profit from every pair (of sunglasses) I sell, even when you factor in the fees eBay charges as well as my merchant account." This does not happen by magic, however, and he also notes that in order to make a profit, new sellers would be wise to research and find a product that gives the ability to mark up substantially, is easy to ship, and, of course, that they have easy access to — yet is hard for competitors to access.

That is a rather large order for someone who is considering delving into the world of online selling. But Steven has shown that with persistence, creativity, and hard work, it can be done.

Chapter Eight

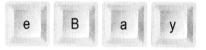

Join the Club

Moving From a Looker or Buyer to a Seller

Open a seller's account and verify your identity

When you join the ranks of the millions of eBay sellers around the world, the first thing you will have to do is open a seller's account. There is really only one difference between the seller's account and the account you had to look or buy from eBay: You will have to verify your identity to eBay and provide some financial information.

You can usually verify your financial information by providing a credit card number and information about your checking account with any U.S. bank. There is no cost to become a seller, so your card will not be charged, and no withdrawals will come out of your checking account, unless you also designate one of these accounts for paying your monthly eBay invoice.

If you have already set up your business checking account, be sure to use that account information for your seller's account setup and also arrange to have your invoices paid automatically from that account.

If you do not have (or do not want to provide) a credit card number for verification purposes, you can choose to become ID Verified, which means that for a $5 fee (charged to your eBay account), the secure system will cross-check your name, address, and telephone numbers against various databases to help prove that you are whom you say you are. Even if you will use a business address and telephone number for your customers' information, use your home address and phone number for this process.

Once you have completed the verification process (actually, this is a good thing to do, even if you register as a seller by providing credit card information to eBay), you will have the ID Verified symbol in your profile.

Starting a PayPal account

There are a few other tasks that you should complete before starting up your first auction, including starting a PayPal account if you have not already been using one for your purchasing on eBay — and, if you have, setting up a second one. eBay will prompt you to do this when you set up a seller's account. Use your business checking account information in PayPal as well so that you can transfer funds from your PayPal account when needed.

> **TIP**
>
> When eBay sends you an invoice (via e-mail), you do not have to wait for the funds to be withdrawn from your checking account. If you have funds in your PayPal account, go ahead and pay your eBay invoice if you want.

Review your preferences

Now that you are an eBay seller, review your preferences to be sure they accurately reflect the way you want to receive information and view your selling information. Go to "My eBay" and click on "Set Preferences" under the "My Account" header. When the next page opens, on the right-hand side, you will see a link that says "show all"; click this to see all the preferences laid out on the page.

For instance, if you have located a Web site to store your photos on (so you can enter multiple photos without paying extra fees to eBay), edit the category "Use this picture service," and enter the site or service you will use. If you do not want buyers to be offered an eBay checkout, then you will have to change the pre-set "Yes" to a "No" by clicking the "Edit" link at the top of that section.

At the bottom of the "Selling Preferences" section, you can edit your preferences for blocking particular bidders and buyers. In case you ever want to block whole groups of people from your auctions (such as those with unpaid item strikes against them, or those in a foreign country you do not ship to), then this is where you will need to make that change.

It is not very common that sellers opt to block all bidders who did not already have a PayPal account. This would be useful if your *only* payment option is PayPal (although you need to really consider the needs of your customers before making such a drastic decision), and you do not want to be bothered by buyers who ignore your requests for PayPal only. Some buyers will ignore information such as that and just assume or hope that you will accept their payment form once the auction is over.

In order to block certain people or groups of people from your auction, visit the following link: **http://pages.ebay.com/services/buyandsell/biddermanagement.html**.

You can also require that bidders be pre-approved before bidding. This is not a commonly used technique in selling, except under special circumstances. See **http://offer.eBay.com/ws/eBayISAPI.dll?PreApproveBidders**.

TIP	Take a few minutes and click on all the possible details you can change or edit, just to see if you fully understand what all your options are. You will also find links to explanations of these items.

If you have already decided you will use some of eBay's software applications, such as Selling Manager or Turbo Lister, then download those and spend some time getting to know them before you begin posting auctions. *Review Chapter 2 for a descriptions of setting up an auction step-by-step using the traditional auction setup.*

Contractual duties to eBay as a seller

Even though you have not even received your first invoice from eBay yet, review some of your contractual duties to eBay as a seller. If you did not take the time to actually read your User Agreement when you first created an eBay account, take the time to do so now. There probably will not be anything earth-shattering in there, but you will have a better understanding of how eBay views their relationship with you, the new seller.

In particular, item No. 3 of the user agreement clarifies the actual position of eBay as a service. It states:

> *Although we are commonly referred to as an online auction Web site, it is important to realize that we are not a traditional "auctioneer." Instead, the site acts as a venue to allow anyone to offer, sell, and buy just about anything, at anytime, from anywhere, in a variety of pricing formats, including a fixed-price format and an auction-style format commonly referred to as "online auctions" or "auctions." We are not involved in the actual transaction between buyers and sellers. As a result, we have no control over the quality, safety, or legality of the items advertised, the truth or accuracy of the listings, the ability of sellers to sell items, or the ability of buyers to pay for items. We cannot ensure that a buyer or seller will actually complete a transaction. Consequently, we do not transfer legal ownership of items from the seller to the buyer, and nothing in this agreement shall modify the governing provisions of Ca. Com. Code § 2401(2) and Uniform Com. Code § 2-401(2), under which legal ownership of an item is transferred upon physical delivery of the item to the buyer by the seller.*

And in item No. 15:

> *You and eBay are independent contractors, and no agency, partnership, joint venture, employee-employer, or franchiser-franchisee relationship is intended or created by this agreement.*

Simply put: You are on your own here — eBay has set up the tools for you to do your business, but it is your duty to operate within the law and the rules set up by eBay.

Though eBay will assist in facilitating communication between buyers and sellers in the event of a conflict, they ultimately are not required to "fix" the problem, as stated in item number 3.4 of the User Agreement:

> *Because we are a venue, in the event that you have a dispute with one or more users, you release eBay (and our officers, directors, agents, subsidiaries, joint ventures, and employees) from claims, demands, and damages (actual and consequential) of every kind and nature, known and unknown, suspected and unsuspected, disclosed and undisclosed, arising out of or in any way connected with such disputes.*
>
> *If you are a California resident, you waive California Civil Code §1542, which says: "A general release does not extend to claims which the creditor does not know or suspect to exist in his favor at the time of executing the release, which if known by him must have materially affected his settlement with the debtor"*

In particular, sellers have the following duties when they list an item for sale on eBay:

- You must be the legal owner of the item or have permission of the legal owner, and you must be of legal age to enter into contracts (18).

- Your item must be described as accurately as possible, and honestly, with all terms of sale disclosed in the listing.

- You cannot put content on the site that does not specifically deal with the item you are listing.

- You must use the appropriate categories for listing items; you cannot put something in a category that is currently "hot" just so people will see it.

- You must not knowingly sell prohibited items (a comprehensive list is on the site).

- If you are selling multiple items (Dutch auction), all the items must be identical.

When your listed item receives bids or sells, your obligations are these:

- If you receive even one bid at or above your minimum price (or your reserve price), then you must sell the item at the highest bid, even if it is the minimum price, unless:

  - The buyer fails to follow through with your pre-set requirements (such as paying within a certain time frame).
  - You cannot verify the buyer's identity.
  - If the listing falls under the Non-binding Bid Policy (such as real estate auctions).

- You must not fail to provide the goods as described in a timely manner by:

  - Refusing the payment. *See Chapter 6 regarding eBay's policy on PayPal credit card payments.*
  - Failing to ship the item.

At all times, you have the following obligations:

- You are not to commit any type of fraud on eBay or its users, including:

  - Manipulating the price of any item.
  - Interfering with another seller's auctions or sales.
  - Shill bidding (artificially raising the bids on your own items, by either bidding with another user ID or having a friend bid on it).
  - Canceling listings to sell directly to someone who found your product through eBay.
  - Offering to sell or buy off-eBay to avoid fees.
  - Fee-avoidance techniques; see **http://pages.ebay.com/help/policies/listing-circumventing.html** for a thorough explanation and online tutorial on this topic.
  - Falsely claim a "Final Value Fee credit"; see **http://pages.ebay.com/help/policies/fvf-abuse.html**.

- You are not to commit any fraud upon the owner of a copyright, trademark, or owner of intellectual property, including:

  - Selling items by using a brand name in the auction, when the actual item is a knockoff or imitation.
  - Selling items made using a copied or copyrighted pattern, design, or instructions.
  - Selling handmade items using materials that have copyrighted designs (i.e. fabric with Disney characters, stating in your auction that this is a Disney item, when it was neither made by nor endorsed by Disney).

To assist owners of intellectual property and copyrights from infringement of their rights, eBay has created the Verified Rights Owner Program (VeRO). The 5,000 or so participants have registered with eBay as intellectual property holders or copyright/trademark holders. If you misrepresent a product in your listing and the owner of the copyright, trademark, or intellectual property you have incorrectly used or misused notifies eBay, then your listing could be revoked. If you repeatedly infringe on the rights of others in this manner, your eBay privileges could be revoked. eBay takes the rights of copyright/trademark holders very seriously.

For example, say Willy sells his widgets and gidgets that are made for him by Acme Widget Manufacturers of America. Acme's main competitor is the Winning Widgets of America Corporation. Let us say Willy has found that even though the widgets are pretty much identical in every way, he sells them faster if people think that they may be made by the Winning Widgets of America Corporation.

He does not actually say that Winning Widget makes them; he merely implies it by making an auction titled, "Widget, Winning My Auction is Easy." Now, perhaps anybody who was not a widget connoisseur might not even know that "Winning" is an indirect reference to another company that makes widgets or, specifically, the company that did not make the widgets that Willy is selling.

But the avid buyers of widgets know, and so does the Winning Widgets of America Corporation. In fact, they are a registered VeRO program member, and they regularly scan the listings of every seller who has the words "widget" and "gidget" in their listings, looking for any unscrupulous sellers who are looking to capitalize on their Winning product's name.

Willy, being the honest seller that he is, did not realize that he was infringing on the rights of the other manufacturer. He was just trying to make a zippy title, and knowing most widget buyers are familiar with the Winning name, he added it to assist searchers in finding his widgets. OK, so eBay will be forgiving… once. But the Winning Widgets of America company will be watching his listings for a while, just to be sure.

For a complete breakdown of the VeRO program, copyright infringement issues, and intellectual property, see these eBay pages:

- **http://pages.eBay.com/help/confidence/vero-rights-owner.html**
- **http://pages.eBay.com/help/policies/questions/vero-ended-item.html**
- **http://pages.eBay.com/help/policies/replica-counterfeit.html**
- **http://pages.eBay.com/help/sell/trademark.html**

TIP — In the above example, Willy was not only violating the Winning Widgets of America Corporation's trademark rights, but also engaging in keyword spamming. By inserting the other company's name (even part of it) in his title, he was inadvertently causing the search results of potential customers who were searching for widgets made by Winning Widgets to display his listing as well. *Keyword spamming is covered in Chapter 2 as well.*

There are a number of other equally important items in the User Agreement, so take some time out to read up on them. Even if you have every intention of being an honest, upright seller, it is always good to be familiar with this information, in case you ever need to refer to it later for a question. You want your customers to take your eBay business seriously, so you need to make sure you take seriously your obligations to eBay and your customers. Review and print (for future reference) the detailed information about all of eBay's policies for sellers at **http://pages.eBay.com/help/policies/listing-ov.html**.

Other Areas of eBay

Now that you have reviewed your duties as a seller, turn your attention to a few more specifics about eBay that you may want to keep in the back of your mind, should the opportunity arise for you to turn these places into potential markets for your product.

eBay Motors

This site is dedicated to selling cars, boats, motorcycles, and vehicle parts. The format is almost identical to eBay.com. Make sure you read all the policies and rules before you begin selling, because there are some differences. You can access the site at **www.motors.eBay.com**. Many of the cars, boats, motorcycles, and vehicle parts are listed by people who are private parties. Dealers also sell on here, but they usually place special or hard-to-find items with special accessories. The bidding and selling structure is pretty much the same as it is on eBay.com.

Half.com

This site is dedicated to selling print and multimedia items, such as books, DVDs, video games, and CDs. There is no bidding involved, and there are no bidding fees, either. This is quite advantageous if your products fall into these categories. You can sell your items for any amount you like, but Half. com does give you a suggested selling price once you put the information about the book in the listing. You can do this by using the UPC or ISBN code on the product. The following is what Half.com suggests selling your products for, according to their condition. The percentages are based on the retail price of the item.

- Like New: 50 percent
- Very Good: 45 percent
- Good: 40 percent
- Acceptable: 35 percent

You should be aware that your item *must* have a UPC code or ISBN number that is recognized by Half.com's catalog. If you cannot locate the number, or they do not have it in their catalog, you should consider selling the item on eBay.com instead.

There are no listing fees. However, should you sell an item on Half.com, they do take a commission. Here is a breakdown of their commission structure:

- $0.75 to $50.00 = 15.0 percent
- $50.01 to $100.00 = 12.5 percent
- $100.01 to $250.00 = 10.0 percent
- $250.01 to $500.00 = 7.5 percent
- More than $500.01 = 5.0 percent

These rates are determined per item sold and do not include the price of shipping. Payments to sellers are sent twice a month to the place designated, such as a direct deposit to a checking account. Shipping is handled a bit differently than it is on eBay.com. Half.com charges a flat rate and reimburses the seller this amount in their twice-a-month payments. They have two options for the buyer — Media Mail and Expedited. They can get a slight discount if they buy more than one item at once. Be aware that what Half.com charges the buyer for shipping and what they reimburse the buyer are two different amounts. To find information regarding shipping rates, go to **http://pages.half.eBay.com/help/policy/shipping_p.html**.

StubHub

This site allows people to buy and sell event tickets. You can buy and sell tickets on eBay.com, but StubHub works a little differently. First, there is no auctioning involved with StubHub — you set the price for what you want to charge for the tickets. This can have advantages and disadvantages. You will get what you want for your event tickets, but you may have fewer interested buyers.

The way it works is that if a person wants to buy your tickets, he or she will pay for them on the StubHub site. You will have 48 hours to confirm the sale. If you do not respond, or you no longer have the tickets, StubHub will help the buyer find alternative tickets. If you do have the tickets and confirm, you then have to send the tickets immediately. You will be paid seven days later by check or PayPal after StubHub confirms that the client received the tickets. StubHub guarantees that the buyer will receive his or her tickets in time for the concert, and you have to ship accordingly. The good news is that the buyer pays the shipping, and StubHub will send you the FedEx sticker to mail the ticket.

Before you set up business as a ticket broker for StubHub, be aware that there are laws concerning the resale of tickets in certain states. You can check **www.stubhub.com/help-top-questions-seller** to see what the current state laws are. Some states only allow you to sell the ticket for $3 over the face value of the ticket, so unless you were getting the tickets for a fantastic deal to start, you will not make much of a profit.

Kijiji

This site is owned by eBay and is a classified advertising site. You can list-advertise your products on this site for free, much like the classified ads section of a newspaper or like **www.craigslist.org**. This site has some designs that are similar to eBay when viewing products, except this site is not set up for bidding. You can search by city and state when you first log on. Then you can search under various categories like housing, personal ads, or for sale items. You can also search for items by keyword. This site is worth checking out, **www.kijiji.com**. You can sell your items to different regions, and it is especially helpful if you have a retail store. It is not moderated like eBay is, and the buyers contact you directly. If you have difficulty selling particular items on eBay, this may be your solution. If you sell locally, you also eliminate shipping costs.

MicroPlace

This eBay-owned company has jumped on the bandwagon of microloans. If you have some extra cash, and you want to make some money while helping people out, you should check out this site at **www.microplace.com**.

MicroPlace works as follows: People are in need worldwide and in poverty situations. They would not qualify for a regular loan to help them work or start a business. Micro-lending takes the investments of many people and organizations and lends this money to people in these dire situations. You make your money back as they pay back their loan. There is some risk involved, as with any loan situation. You should look at the details and clauses of the contract before loaning any money. The good part is that you are not loaning large amounts of money to a couple of people; rather, you are loaning small amounts to many different people.

Placing the information that you invest part of your profit into the working poor on your site helps boost the class of your business. It shows people that the money they are spending on products sold by you is going to a good cause. The best part about it is that you are making a small profit by helping others in need.

ProStores

This eBay-owned site is for those ready to set up a Web store. They offer competitive prices when compared to other online Web site servers. They have a variety of different levels of Web sites and services available, depending on the needs and size of your company. The nice part about using this site to set up your store is that it is eBay-friendly, and they offer you a unique Web address. Once you set up the site, ProStores automatically imports your live eBay listings and other settings. You can access this site at **www.prostores.com/ecommerce_eBay.html**.

Skype

Nothing says cutting-edge like the ability of your customers to chat with you online, regardless of how far apart you live from each other. Skype is a free service that allows you to make audio and video calls around the world. If the call is from one Skype user to another, the call is free. You can also call cell phones and landlines for about 2 cents a minute. Skype offers an incoming number and voicemail for either $18 for three months or $60 for a full year.

Your buyers can look for the Skype logo on your listing and click the "chat" button, which is in a text format, or the "voice" button. It will let them know when you are online to answer questions. As a PowerSeller, you can indicate whether you want to be contacted with chat or voice on the "Sell Your Item" process.

Having this option available makes your buyers more confident that you can be contacted and that you are a real person selling an item. You can connect with previous buyers easily and make them repeat customers more easily. You do not even have to be online to receive a Skype call, as there is a forwarding function that allows you to receive your call almost anywhere.

Setting up Skype on eBay is not difficult. First, you need to make sure you have the latest version of Skype. You can find the free software at **www.skype.com**. You must create an account on Skype; this is free, unless you add other services. You can link your Skype account to your eBay account by going to your eBay account and looking for "Skype" in your eBay preferences.

Under your preferences in the "My eBay" tab, select "Member-to-Member Communications." It is here that you can "Add" a Skype name to update your preferences. On your Skype account, click "Link my Skype account to eBay."

Once you have added Skype to your preferences, open Skype, and click Tools > Options > Privacy. You need to make sure that you select the "Allow my status to be shown on the Web" check box. As you create a new listing, you should add your Skype name so buyers can contact you quickly via Skype.

eBay Business

eBay Business is another specialty site accessed from the home page that shows listings of industrial equipment and supplies. The listings are divided among general industrial categories, such as Agriculture & Forestry,

Construction, Food Service & Retail, Industrial Electrical & Test, Industrial Supply, and Manufacturing & Metalworking. Some of the categories (such as Agriculture > Tractors and Construction > Trailers) have a $20 insertion fee in this section, so check out the categories that have higher fees before listing here. Search "eBay business fees" in the help directory to learn more. It can be accessed at **http://business.shop.eBay.com**.

Want It Now

Want It Now has been a fairly recent addition to eBay's plethora of innovative ways to keep people visiting — and buying from — their site. Want It Now is full of listings from potential buyers stating what they want to purchase but have not found in the auction listings or stores (or did not want to take the effort to look for).

You can search by general categories or type in a specific word or phrase (just like searching for auctions) and see what pops up. You may find your buyer this way, instead of having them find you. It can be accessed at **http://pages.eBay.com/WantItNow**.

Everything Else

Just when you thought you have seen it all on eBay, you will stumble across the Everything Else category, where you will find zany sub-categories such as "mature audiences," "mystery auctions," and "weird stuff." Not just ordinary weird stuff, either: eBay manages to have three categories of weird stuff: "the slightly unusual," "the really weird," and "the totally bizarre."

"Mature audiences," as a category, probably does not need any explanation as to what type of merchandise is available there. However, in order to even enter that portion of eBay, you must be ID Verified and go through an additional sign-in session, or agree to the terms of use and have your information verified. If you have products you wish to market in this area, the general auctioning public will not see them, to protect minors. This can make it somewhat difficult to market items in this area, so unless your item is explicitly "adult" in nature, you may want to list it in non-mature-audiences categories first.

Mystery auctions are just that: a mystery. In this type of auction, the bidder purchases something, such as an empty cardboard box of a certain size or shape. However, the contents of the box (which are a mystery) are given to the buyer as a gift, at no additional charge. These auctions often cite "eBay rules" that they are following, but the "Help" files do not contain any such reference. So whether this is part of the whole storyline or simply an urban legend of sorts is, well, a mystery.

The outrageous stories that go along with these boxes are like online soap operas. They seem to take on a life of their own, and some of them have developed almost a cult following. There are jilted lovers disposing of their former flame's possessions, ex-roomies who were stiffed on the lease, and even babies hawking goods. Some people even try to turn it into a real mystery: You will receive this envelope with instructions on where to locate a treasure. Whatever the sob story (real or fictitious), there seems to be a certain fad-like following.

Hints are often provided every time the auction reaches a new level of bidding, such as with every $50 increment. It is inconclusive whether these auctions really do bring any amount of business (or whether the buyers even pay for them), so do not pin your hopes on getting rich by posting these auctions. However, if you need a good laugh after a long morning of posting auctions and updating your accounting files, this might be your source.

The weird categories, however, may indeed be the strangest things to hit the Internet auction sites. There are plenty of just plain-old-stupid auctions, and even auctions that really are not weird at all, but that have truly interesting items.

Like the mystery auctions, there may not be much actual business value in listing here, but they are good for a giggle once in a while. Note that despite eBay's policies against having sexually explicit material on the general site, the "weird" categories can contain much of that material, so be cautious about letting minors explore these categories.

A recent foray into the "weird" turned up a Buy It Now offer for purchasing 1 square inch of land in a particular state. The price? Just $9.95 plus $1 to ship your authentic deed to you. Another weird item: A set of plastic wall hooks that screw into wood. They are shaped like a human appendage and cost just $6.95, plus $4.95 shipping.

If those items are too mundane for you, try bidding on a pewter-colored statue of the Grim Reaper. Looking for the most unusual jewelry? Try on an enchanted ring from India, or a necklace with a pendant carved from the eggshell of a large bird. If you are searching for something profound, you can purchase a prayer, or a bobble-head of a major religious figure.

You might only be able to conclude that it is true: eBay is the world's marketplace, including just about anything for just about everybody on the planet.

Seeing the Big Picture

Getting back to business, you will need to hone some tactics before you start auctioning. You will need to be adept at searching current and past listings, so you can do some price comparisons to know how to price your auctions. Another useful skill is learning to navigate quickly around your "My eBay" page.

And even though your mind may be spinning still from the discussion about the User Agreement, there are a few more policies you need to be aware of, including eBay's list of banned items.

Searching current and past auctions

Searching current and past auctions is not terribly difficult, but you will likely do a lot of it — unless you sell the same merchandise repeatedly. It is worth learning the tricks to good searching. When you do a basic search, you may be confronted with ten pages of results you do not have time to page through. Narrowing your search and utilizing keywords will help you find the listings you need to compare.

Basic keywords are those that would be in the title, such as the brand name (Levi's), the manufacturer (Apple), or the year made, size, and color. Think of how you plan to title your auction, and search for those same words. Do not make your search term into a full sentence, though, as your results will have to match every word in your search.

If you have a wholesale lot of infant sleepers to sell, your basic keywords might include "infant sleeper," "baby sleeper," or "newborn pajamas." When you search multiple words, simply leave a space between the words. This tells the search engine you want the title of the auction to contain all those words, in any order. If you want the word order to remain the same as your search (useful for a title of a book), then insert quotations around the phrase.

Perhaps you are not picky about the word order, but you want to find listings for any down jackets — but not green ones. So you might search "down jacket –green" or "down coat –green." Put the minus sign before the word you do not want to get results for.

Suppose you want to find those same jackets, but not green or purple ones. Your search would then be "down jacket –(green,purple)" or something similar. Insert the terms you do not want to see in parentheses separated by a comma but no space, and put the minus sign directly before the parentheses.

Willy wants to find past auctions of widgets, either made by Winning Widgets of America or Ace Widgets of America. So he will search this way: "widgets (winning,ace)" to include all widgets where either Winning or Ace was also used in the title.

If you are looking for a word that may be misspelled, use the beginning of the word and an asterisk (*) to search for all titles containing that string of letters: adv* will bring up listings for anything with advanced, advertising, adventure, advantage, or advent in the title.

TIP   eBay will automatically include items in your search you did not specify, such as common misspellings or two spellings for the same basic word (grey/gray), or add an "s" to the end of your term (boot/boots) to give you more results. If you do not want the search engine to do this, put your term in quotation marks. eBay provides a list of keyword search category expansions that you can view on the Web site. Just search the help directory for this term.

Other tips from eBay:

- Search titles and descriptions by checking the box below the search field.

- Be specific. Searching "doll" will get you an overwhelming number of results. Searching "porcelain Cinderella doll" will get you a lot closer to what you are looking for.

- Try searching with and without the "s" on a word that could be plural.

- Do not use punctuation in a search unless it is part of the term (for example, Dr. Seuss).

- Browse categories where you might find what you are looking for, and study the titles for ideas to assist your searching.

Navigating your My eBay page

Navigating around your My eBay page is not rocket science, but there are a few things you might not be familiar with. It seems everywhere you click on eBay, there are dozens more links with even more information and even more links. You just do not have time to explore every link, so perhaps you have not seen some of these spots in My eBay.

When you click on "My eBay" (from the top toolbar), you will be taken to your Summary page. Notice to the right side of the page is a link called "Page Options." This is the quickest way to review all the available content on this page. Change it up to suit your needs; it does not have to be the way eBay set it up by default.

For instance, if you get to the point where you have many auctions going at once, you can opt to have up to 15 items shown. You can also move around the order of the items on that page. If current auctions are more important than actions you are currently watching or bidding on, then move selling auctions to the top of the page. You even have choices in what columns of information you want displayed. For the current auctions, you can display the number of unique bidders that auction had. This lets you know if there are several bidders, or perhaps just two having a bidding war. There is not any strategy involved in knowing this — just pure curiosity.

Notice that each section has its own "Page Options" link, in case you want to just change that particular section. Additionally, each section listed in the box on the left-hand side of the page is customizable to suit individual needs. You will spend a lot of time on your My eBay page, so it may as well be user-friendly.

On your current listings, notice that each item has a drop-down menu at the end that says "Sell Similar." This is a shortcut to starting another listing of similar nature. It does not have to be an exact duplicate because you can edit or change anything in the listing, including the category it is listed in, the price, duration, or description. It saves time in areas such as shipping policies and general information.

Other drop-down menu options include revising that listing, adding to the description (meaning to revise just the item description portion of the listing), ending the item listing, or ending promotions on the item. Some of these features cannot be accessed when the item has a current bid on it, or if the listing ends in the next 12 hours.

Current listings are shown both on the Summary page and the All-selling page. On the all-selling page, it also shows your previous listings that did not sell. The drop-down menu on those items offers to re-list the item with the opportunity to revise anything in the listing you choose before it is resubmitted to the active listings. *Re-listing is also discussed in Chapter 9.*

In order to qualify for a re-list refund (if your item sells the second time around, eBay will refund your second listing fee), you must have initiated the re-list from this screen. That is the only way eBay can track that it is the same item/auction.

Spend time clicking on all the customizable sections of your pages, and get to know the options. When your My eBay pages serve you most efficiently, then you know it is customized correctly.

eBay's banned-items list

One of the more important eBay's policies you should familiarize yourself with is eBay's banned-items list. The list contains more than 80 categories where all or some of the items are restricted or prohibited. There are the obvious items, such as human remains and counterfeit items, but did you know that used clothing is allowed for sale only if it has been properly cleaned according to the manufacturer's instructions? Used cosmetics are never allowed to be sold because of the U.S. Food and Drug Administration's rules. The lists are too comprehensive to reproduce here, but spend some time reviewing any category that is applicable to your product line. Search eBay's help section for "banned items overview."

Other informational lists you may want to review (or print out for reference) are the eBay Glossary and eBay Acronyms. There are a number of terms and abbreviations that are unique to the Internet and online auctioning, and you need to understand and use them appropriately.

eBay's Banned Items list can be located at **http://pages.ebay.com/help/policies/items-ov.html.**

The Glossary is located at **http://pages.ebay.com/help/account/glossary.html.**

The Acronym list is found at **http://pages.ebay.com/help/account/acronyms.html.**

Keeping your eyes on the enemy

In addition to all the other tasks that you will juggle as a small business owner, you will be smart to keep an eye on the enemy — your competition. This is not to say you cannot be friendly with other sellers; by all means, do not alienate them, because they may be the only ones who can answer a query you place on the message boards.

However, it is always a good practice in business to know what your competition is doing. On eBay you can view your competition's listings and compare their prices, their shipping rates, their warranty, or other customer-service policies. Make sure you are adequately updated on your competition, because you can bet potential buyers will do some of the same comparing.

> Do not ever take or use photos or item descriptions from another listing to use as your own. This is a violation of that seller's intellectual property rights and could be reported as a VeRO violation. This also applies to the "look" or "feel" of someone else's About Me page.

Check out the competition regularly. There are a few shortcuts for doing this. First, you can add another seller to your Favorite Sellers list and get regular reports on their new listings. Or to see many sellers' items at once, perform a search using your keywords and then save the search to your Favorite Searches list. On your My eBay page, you can quickly pull up your favorite searches with just a few clicks.

Of course, you will probably see your own listings among the favorites in the search, but that is actually a good thing. Try to put yourself in the buyer's shoes:

- What is different about your listing?
- Does it stand out?
- Are the photos previewing properly?
- Are your photos of better quality than the competition's photos?
- Is your shipping cost (or the option to calculate shipping) right on the search page?
- How does your title compare to the other auctions?

If you spend some time honestly assessing your listings against other companies' listings, you can learn a lot. You do not want to copy the competition (and certainly not their photos or text, as that is against eBay's VeRO policy), but you want to make sure your listings are as polished, professional, and informative as theirs.

Staying on Top of Trends

Keeping up with the competition is not the only detail you will need to regularly monitor. Things change on eBay very quickly; new features are added constantly, upgrades to services are being tested, and new educational opportunities are offered.

A couple of spots on the site you will want to become familiar with are the eBay Pulse page (the link is on the left-hand side of the home page, just after the list of categories). This page has information on the top search terms (keywords or phrases) that day, the top five largest stores (by number of active listings at that time), and the most-watched items at the moment. At the bottom of the page, follow the link to the page showing all eBay categories and, from there, you will get to each category's "Pulse" page, showing the top searches in each category and the top-watched auctions in each. Looking within the categories your products are listed might give you some idea of what people are looking for.

The Pulse pages are gaining quite a following. The most watched auctions shown on the eBay Pulse main page are often featured on other Web sites that show unusual or interesting auctions. This has created a desire among many auctioneers to have slicker, fancier sites than the next guy, and more outrageous and unusual auction items, just hoping to be featured on eBay's Pulse page, and then on to other sites.

eBay University and Seller Central

Another way to keep ahead of the crowd is by utilizing eBay University and Seller Central. With eBay University, you can take courses in selling, from beginner to advanced. The Selling Basics course is for the real newbies, and it will prepare you to do basic transactions. For those who are already somewhat experienced with the concept of selling on eBay, there is the Beyond the Basics course. This course will assist you in creating a better-than-basic listing, help you utilize some of eBay's online tools, and familiarize you with PayPal.

For the seller who wants to really delve into the business aspects of eBay, try the eBay for Business course. This will give you additional information about taxes, inventory, accounting and recordkeeping, finding merchandise, and marketing yourself.

The first two classes are available live (check schedule on eBay's Web site for a date near you), online, or via a CD-ROM that can be purchased. The business-level course is currently only available at the live sessions. If you have a chance to attend, you may be able to do more than just learn; these classes are a great chance to network with sellers in your area.

Even if you do not have the time to devote to a whole class right away, check out eBay's Seller Central pages, which can be accessed right from the home page (see the "Helpful Links" box center-right on home page).

The seller central pages are categorized using these headers: Getting Started, Best Practices, Advanced Selling, Category Tips, What's Hot, News & Updates, and Resources. These contain hundreds of pages of information and links. For the benefit of your business, make it a priority to review each of these sections. Schedule time to read, and consider it a cost of doing business every bit as much as paying your PayPal fees. The more knowledge you have, the better seller you will be.

The following are just a few of the do-not-miss places you will access through the seller central:

- *eBay Solutions Directory:* A thorough listing of third-party (not made by nor provided by eBay) software and tools to help you in your eBay business.

- *Square Trade Dispute Resolution program:* For when you and your customer just cannot see eye-to-eye.

- *eBay's Top Seller Webinar:* You can replay the Web-seminar right on your PC.

- *Buyer Behavior Report:* Climb into the psyche of your buyers and learn how to give them what they want.

- *What's Hot:* A category-by-category breakdown of what is selling best on eBay at the moment.

- *Merchandising Calendar:* A heads-up on promotions eBay will be running.

Joining the eBay Community

eBay is not just a bunch of people selling things on a Web site — it is a bunch of people. The fact that they are buying and selling is just one common factor among them. eBay members have been the backbone of this vibrant online community in a way that is unlike any other on the Internet. Here, it does not matter who you are: If you have a question, someone on the message boards will answer it. And it has always been that way. Right from the early days, eBayers have been chatting regularly with cyber-friends on the site's message boards. They are happy to share their stories, triumphs, frustrations, and thoughts about life. These communities are composed of people who know each other only by their eBay user ID — and often not much else.

The Internet has created a phenomenon unlike any other in history. It takes the concept of pen pals to the ultimate level, and eBay has seen its share of online friendships grow throughout the years.

Take, for example, Pamela in Ohio (eBay user "Pamelas_Timeless_Treasures"). This stay-at-home mother began selling on eBay because of the encouragement of another eBay seller named Julie, whom she had met on a message board. Her online friendship with Julie has continued to this day, resulting in the co-authoring of an e-book about eBay, even though they have yet to meet in person.

CASE STUDY: THE BORDER FIASCO

Pamela Vasquez's first auction was the stuff of nightmares — for the buyer.

Pamela (eBay user "pamelas_timeless_treasures") had been searching for a part-time income in all the traditional places, but nothing gave her the flexibility to homeschool three daughters, be home with her husband in the evenings, or be there for the housework or pets. The weak economy in her area did not help, either; even during the holidays, seasonal jobs were hard to snag.

In an effort to gather potential ideas for earning money, Pamela posted an inquiry on an online message board (not on eBay), asking other stay-at-home mothers how they located the best jobs. One encouraged her to consider eBay.

This woman had been so successful on eBay that her husband had been able to quit his job in corporate America to help her with auctioning. Though the story was amazing, eBay was not exactly what Pamela had in mind. But having never really considered it, she was willing to post an item and see what happened.

In November 2003, she entered some jungle-print wallpaper border for auction. Like many new sellers, Pamela hawked over her auction, checking to see if there were any bids or even any lookers. Even though she did not have use for them any more, she found it hard to believe that *nobody* wanted the borders, even for her opening bid amount. She checked the auction on the last day and, discouraged, did not bother to even look at it again after it had ended.

Taking that as her cue, Pamela decided that eBay was not her cup of tea and began to explore other ideas again.

About eight weeks later, she happened to check a rarely used e-mail address and, to her shock (and utter embarrassment), found a rather anxious message from someone she had never even heard of. The message was clear: Where is my wallpaper border?

She did some quick checking on eBay and discovered that in the final hours, her auction had indeed sold. The buyer had even paid via PayPal, and somehow she had never been notified. That rarely used e-mail address was the culprit: It was the one on file for eBay and was the one she had used regularly when she had first become an eBay member.

Now she was in a serious bind: eight weeks and a buyer who had real cause to be angry with her, all because she failed to realize that her eBay correspondence would be going to that address.

Pamela explains how she handled the situation. "I immediately e-mailed her, apologizing profusely," Pamela said. "I explained what happened and told her I would even drive the borders to her home if it would get them there sooner."

The buyer, who lived approximately one-and-a-half-hours away, was very gracious and understanding. She was remodeling a child's bedroom and needed the borders, but was willing to wait a couple of more days for the regular mail service. But Pamela's offer to drive the borders to her made an impression. Despite everything, she left positive feedback when the transaction was complete.

"If the buyer had not been so understanding and positive about the entire fiasco, I do not think I would have continued to sell on eBay," Pamela said. Among other lessons learned through this experience: Keep your eBay contact information up-to-date. Pamela learned early that if she did everything possible to remedy the situation, the average customer would be understanding and work with her in return.

When recalling this incident recently, Pamela went to her records and located this buyer's e-mail address. Even though it had been almost two years since the transaction, she again e-mailed to thank this person for her patience and understanding. "I let her know the impact that her kindness in (that) situation has had on my life — it has been significant."

Although it took Pamela time to really get serious about selling on eBay, she has been at it regularly since March 2004. She primarily sells used books for children and homeschooling families. Great literature is a passion for her children, who love to peruse Mom's pile of eBay inventory and see if it is something they would rather add to their own collection than let her sell. Pamela tries to foster a love of learning in her girls, and literature plays a big part in that effort.

She finds her merchandise at a variety of places: library book sales, rummage sales, and thrift stores, to name just a few. Recently, she has started taking in consignment merchandise for people who do not have the time or interest in learning how to work on eBay themselves.

When she started selling regularly online, Pamela felt that if she could contribute $400 to her family's income every month, she would be happy. It took a couple of months to meet that goal, but once she did, she has been steadily padding the family budget ever since.

There are things she wishes she had done differently, of course. She initially did not do enough research to determine what the proper price for her items should be. She lost plenty of money by not knowing how to price items and by not utilizing proper keywords so buyers could locate her items easily. "Had I done my research differently, I would have used different keywords and not had to pay for that very expensive lesson," she said.

She also had to learn about off-eBay resources that offer options to increase sales, such as storing photos online and utilizing HTML to offer multiple photos in a listing. But even though there has been a learning curve to eBay and mistakes made along the way, Pamela did have one big advantage that many eBay sellers do not: a community of other eBay sellers who offered advice, tips, and encouragement.

The woman who initially encouraged Pamela to sell on eBay, Julie Anna Schultz, also hooked her up with a large group of sellers who have their own group discussion board on the Yahoo! Groups site.

Having other people who learn your name and give personalized advice was a great benefit to Pamela; she knew she was not alone in this venture. Now that she has nearly 400 auctions under her belt with a greater than 99 percent positive feedback score, she still credits much of her success to the members of that group. In fact, she is so convinced that having a group of people for support is so beneficial that it is the first thing she would suggest to anybody who is considering eBay as a job.

Chapter Nine

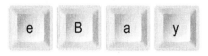

Your Item Sold… Now What?

Now the Real Work Begins

Congratulations on selling your first auction! This is a monumental step on your road to officially becoming an eBay seller. But, do not pat yourself on the back just yet because your work has just begun.

Now, you have to deal with the buyer, and most importantly, get the item to the buyer in a quick manner. Remember, selling items is the reason you got into this eBay business, but your ultimate goal is to become a Power-Seller, so your customers' satisfaction is just as important as the actual sale. Positive feedback is crucial to reaching that goal. So, here are a few things you may encounter once your item has sold.

Happy to Combine Shipping

If you have stated a shipping discount policy on eBay, then you may have to wait for payment up to the number of days you allowed in your policy per chance the same buyer wins another auction.

Combining shipping can also bring about some unique issues, especially for buyers who wish to pay via PayPal. If the buyer wins one auction and you send him or her an invoice, they may pay it, then two days later win a different auction and expect you to give them a combined shipping discount. In the meantime, you have paid two transaction fees to PayPal. This also says nothing of the fact that you may have already shipped the first item.

It is ideal if the bidder lets you know he or she is bidding on other items so you can wait and send them one invoice for all items won, with one shipping charge. You will also incur only one PayPal fee this way. But you must also do your part to let buyers know NOT to pay an invoice if they plan to bid on multiple items. Good communication is probably the best way to avoid this potential fee-gobbling issue.

What if a buyer does not inform you of this, and sends multiple PayPal payments — but still expects a shipping discount? If your policy is clear that they must pay for all items at the same time, then you are in the right not to give them a shipping discount.

But is this the best thing to do, in terms of customer service, or for your reputation? You will have to weigh the costs and determine if the possibility of a negative feedback from the buyer is worth it. Whatever you do, you should always communicate clearly and calmly with the customer, even let them know you have paid multiple fees because of their multiple payments, rather than just one fee. Suggest an alternative: a shipping discount, but not quite as large a one, so you can recoup some of your excess fees.

Many buyers will be willing to work something out, and may even apologize for their lack of attention to the details. Upon learning they messed up, some buyers will retract their request for a shipping discount. And then there will always be the small percentage who will demand the largest possible discount regardless of any fault on their part.

Money orders are accepted only if...

You may find that you can run into problems accepting money orders, such as buyers who wish to pay via money order and will wait the entire ten days that you state you will allow for receipt of payment. On the tenth day, they will mail the money order. Depending on where each party lives, that means you may have to wait 14 or more days for payment.

Consider creating a policy that states, "If you are paying via money order, please mail it within three days, so that I receive it within the ten days allowed." This will work for some, but do not be surprised by buyers who do not wish to pay any sooner than absolutely necessary.

Unfortunately, this is just one of those things out of your control. Like with any other payment type, communicate with the buyer and express concern that her payment may be lost in the mail. Ask for a specific date the money order was mailed, and the serial number of the money order from their receipt. Hopefully, the buyer will communicate back with the details. If she knowingly mailed it after the deadline (or has not yet purchased it), she may avoid communicating with you until the time frame that she expects the payment to arrive.

You will have to decide what to do in the case where a money order arrives after the date required. Do you send the money order back, file a complaint with eBay against the buyer for not following your policies, and re-list the item? That is probably more trouble than it is worth, since the buyer can always fall back on, "But I did pay for the item." You may come out of just such an exchange looking like a petty person who cares more for rules than your customers.

Items will be shipped within...

If you state in your auction listing that you will ship an item within two business days of receiving payment, make sure that you have noted any exceptions to this rule. eChecks through PayPal can take up to six days to clear, and buyers often do not realize this. So the customer thinks he paid on one date, and in your view, he has not really paid until the funds become available in your PayPal account, several days later. You could end up with an unhappy buyer who feels you were slow to ship. Be sure to communicate with a buyer who has used an eCheck. Tell the buyer you will e-mail him the day that you receive the actual funds (the date the eCheck clears), and that you will honor your shipping policy based on that date.

Another exception you might wish to note: Personal checks need time to clear the bank as well. If you accept personal checks, give your bank a call and ask for a reasonable time frame to expect items to clear.

Non-paying bidders

Even payment troubles often pale in comparison to the headache of dealing with a non-paying bidder. The good news is that most eBay sellers will tell you these people are rare. But that still does not make it any easier to deal with them when you find that your communications are being ignored.

eBay has a set-up procedure for dealing with non-paying bidders. The first step is to file an unpaid item dispute form within 45 days of the transaction, but generally you must wait seven days (there are a couple of exceptions, such as if the buyer is no longer a registered user, or if the buyer is from a country you do not ship to).

To begin the process, click the link to the Dispute Console on the left-hand side of the My eBay page. Then, click the "Unpaid Items" link. You can also read up on the unpaid items policy and process by using the links in the box below this. It is a good idea to thoroughly read and understand the process before beginning.

Once the form has been filled out, eBay will contact the buyer. Depending on whether, or how, the buyer responds to this form, the dispute may or may not be resolved quickly. For buyers who are merely dragging their feet a little, the friendly reminder directly from eBay seems to get buyers in the mood to pay sooner than later. If, however, this person is downright determined not to pay for the item, the process gets a little more complicated.

At any point in the process, the buyer and seller can mutually agree to just forget the whole transaction. If so, the buyer does not get any Unpaid Item Strikes and the seller can get a Final Value Fee refund. At all times during the process, eBay tries to maintain their position as the vehicle by which the buyer and seller can communicate and work together.

At some point in time, the dispute must be closed. Whether there is any satisfaction between the parties, the dispute will only remain active for 60 days. If you open a dispute, it is in your best interest to remain involved in the process and close the dispute within this time frame. If you do not do this and eBay must close the dispute for you, you cannot claim a Final Value Fee credit and — even if the buyer was in the wrong — the buyer does not get a strike.

Leaving feedback in the event of an unpaid item is tricky. Sometimes emotions will dictate your response and you might leave feedback (or a response to the buyer's negative feedback) that later you might wish was not available for all your other customers to read. Even if you must say something negative, you can do so calmly and without compromising your integrity. Feedback will be discussed later in this chapter.

Despite the occasional blip on the eBay radar, the majority of transactions completed on eBay are smooth and hassle-free. You will receive your payments in a timely manner (some of them within 24 hours of the auction's end and, occasionally, even one immediately upon the close of the auction) and in return, you ship in a timely manner.

Shipping the Item

When Suzy receives her PayPal payment from the winning bidder of her waffle iron, she immediately proceeds to the next step: shipping the item.

Because her item was pre-boxed and weighed to utilize eBay's shipping calculator during the auction, all she has to do is get it in the mail.

Suzy has already decided to utilize the services of the U.S. Postal Service (unless the buyer has a special request or the item is too large for the USPS to handle) by printing shipping labels and paying for shipping on all her auctions through PayPal. The following are more than a dozen good reasons why you should do the same:

- You do not have to leave home to ship items; leave them right in/ near your mailbox (protected from weather, of course). This makes it easy to ship every business day (and even Saturdays, for the truly dedicated sellers).

- You can e-mail a message to notify your local post office you have packages to be picked up.

- You can prepare packages for mailing in the evenings or over a weekend; it is easy to specify the next business date for your label.

- You do not have to spend your own money to ship items from your post office (because the money is still in your PayPal account) because the postage is paid from PayPal funds. You definitely should not wait until transferred funds from PayPal arrive at your bank; this will leave you branded as a "slow shipper."

- You can even ship items that were paid via other means (such as a money order). Just use the drop-down menu on the item's line on My eBay and click "print shipping label." You must have sufficient funds in your PayPal account (it is a good idea to leave some if you transfer to your business bank account).

- You get Delivery Confirmation free with Priority Mail and other mail classes (First Class, Parcel Post, Media Mail) for a mere $0.13. That is actually cheaper than your post office, without leaving home or waiting in line.

- You do not have to hand-write a shipping label. You will print a nice label right from your computer, complete with addresses and delivery, confirmation number, plus a receipt for your own records, on one sheet of paper.

- You can print the label without the postage amount displayed, so your buyers cannot easily determine what your handling charge was.

- Your buyer is notified via e-mail that you have created her shipping label and given the delivery confirmation number, without you ever lifting a finger.

- You can include a personal message to the buyer (sent with the delivery confirmation number) stating the ship date or thanking her for the purchase.

- You can determine when your item has been delivered, right from My eBay or PayPal, although it does not display full "tracking" like UPS or FedEx.

- You can create and print international customs forms and shipping labels in the same simple manner.

- You can upgrade to a special printer for the self-stick labels.

- PayPal and USPS will not charge extra fees for this service.

With all these great benefits and features, this should be one of the easiest decisions to make. When you open accounts with FedEx or UPS, you can also create shipping labels right from your computer as well. UPS also works with PayPal, and you can create both domestic and international shipping labels on PayPal's site and pay through PayPal. This gives UPS an edge over FedEx for those sellers who need to utilize carriers other than the USPS (for larger items). Other shipping companies might utilize PayPal, or you can get a PayPal credit card to use with other shipping companies.

Contact the individual carriers to determine who will let you pay with PayPal funds and who will not.

Once Suzy has her label printed and attached firmly to her package, she can place it out in time for her mail carrier to pick it up. To finalize her end of the transaction, she lets the buyer know the package is on its way and leaves positive feedback for the buyer.

TIP Even if your mail carrier comes daily to deliver mail, utilize the online scheduling system so they know to look for your items the next day.

If you choose to take your packages to a shipping location such as the Post Office, a UPS store, or FedEx location, then you will have to determine a shipping schedule. Unless you have a lot of free time, driving to a shipping station every day is not very practical. In this case, set a schedule of days that you ship, such as "every Monday and Thursday" or "Monday, Wednesday, and Fridays." Make sure this is stated clearly in the text of every auction, preferably in your policies that you will copy and paste into every auction.

Some other shipping companies will also schedule pickups of your packages, but be sure to ask about any fees for doing so before actually scheduling these.

Proper packaging

What exactly constitutes proper packaging is a subjective matter. While you might think that your packaging skills are adequate, a buyer might be aghast at how an item was sloshing around in the box. The best rule for packing is to use the smallest container that you have (box, envelope) that will hold the item with just enough room for adequate cushioning (no more than 3 inches around is usually sufficient for all but the most fragile items). Nobody wants to receive a huge box with 90 percent newspapers and 10 percent of the space used by their item. Not only does that leave the buyer with a lot of waste to dispose of, but it can make them feel like they paid postage for many unnecessary shipping materials.

High profile ratings are important to customers, and they will likely not buy from a seller whom they do not think they can trust to bring the online transaction to a satisfactory fulfillment. Follow these basic guidelines to make sure you are bringing all your transactions to their proper fulfillment:

- Do not charge for time, gas, or miles used going back to the post office. That will drive your prices up because you will have to charge more for shipping, and most customers have some idea how much it should cost to ship whatever it is they have bought. Only charge what it costs to ship the item.

- Reuse shipping materials. When you buy things to resell, or you receive inventory, make sure you hold onto that shipping material so that you can reuse it. This will lead to significant savings in shipping costs.

- Buy shipping materials in bulk. The cost of a shipping container may not seem like much, but if you are shipping items every day, you will save significantly if you buy in bulk. Go to your local office supply store and buy all your envelopes, bubble wrap, and packing tape in bulk.

- Be honest about how much it will cost to ship something. Do not surprise customers with "hidden shipping fees" at the end. Because they already want the item, they may still buy it, but they will not be happy with you. Do not forget that if you get too many complaints about excessive shipping costs, eBay could shut you down.

When you print your shipping labels with PayPal Shipping, the address will always be correct — human error is factored out. That is a good thing. If you write or type out labels, then double-check the address. If the item was paid through PayPal, be sure to use only the confirmed address on file with PayPal, in order to qualify for their buyer and seller protection programs.

This can pose a problem when your buyer, due to a time constraint or to save postage in re-shipping, asks you to ship the item directly to his sister in Albuquerque, New Mexico, instead of his own address in Cincinnati. What do you do then? Sometimes, you will have to choose between the seller protection program and customer service.

One way to handle the situation is to *not* print the shipping label through PayPal, but to physically take the package to your shipper's location. Make sure you purchase Delivery Confirmation and even perhaps Signature Confirmation (if your buyer has communicated this wish before you invoiced him, you can add these costs to the postage). Though you still will not qualify for any assistance from PayPal if the buyer claims the item never arrived, you will at least be able to prove that you sent it, and that it did indeed arrive.

This is something you may want to cover in your policies as well. Some sellers have noted in their listings that they will not ever ship an item to any place other than a confirmed address. You will have to decide if this is the same route you will take when dealing with the occasional customer who needs something done out of the ordinary.

Combining shipping can cause a payment delay, but it also can cause other confusion. Most buyers think combining shipping will always save them a lot of money, but it may not be the case. For instance, if you sold two items that, when packaged in small bubble envelopes, each weighed 7 ounces, you would be able to send them each for about $1.75 via First Class Mail, or approximately $3.50 for both. When you put both of those items into the same envelope, they now weigh 13.5 ounces, and no longer qualify for First Class Mail. Your only option now is Priority Mail, which is a minimum cost of $3.85. The buyer actually pays more this way.

Where this can make a difference, however, is if you do not charge any handling charge for items in a multiple purchase.

If you were to charge $2.50 for each of those 7-ounce items ($1.75 postage plus $0.75 handling), then the buyer would be charged $5 in total shipping and handling if you mailed them separately. If, however, you charge a combined postage of $3.85 for Priority Mail, and only charge one handling charge of $0.75, then the buyer would pay $4.35 for shipping and handling. In this case, combining shipping is cheaper for the buyer.

When you decide on a combined shipping policy, you can fill in eBay's shipping discount calculator, which will then create combined shipping quotes for buyers on invoices with more than one auction item.

You can choose from two basic methods of combining shipping:

The flat-fee method

On combined purchases, the calculator will automatically use the highest shipping amount from any of the items, then add a flat fee for every additional item. This only works if you have set up the shipping calculator when you listed the item, but if the buyer purchased three items, and the individual shipping quotes are:

Item	Shipping Quote
#1	$2.60
#2	$3.85
#3	$6.95

The calculator will start with the highest shipping cost, $6.95, and then add your flat fee ($1 in this case) for each additional item. So this buyer would pay a combined shipping fee of $8.95 for all three items, as opposed to $13.40. You can also set the calculator to use the highest shipping price and have additional items sent free.

The combined-weight method

For combined purchases where you have entered each item's individual weights into the shipping calculator (when you listed each item), eBay will add together all the weights and, using the buyer's ZIP code, calculate a combined shipping quote. The combined items will need fewer boxes or envelopes, but you will also likely be using a larger box or envelope, so the total weight may very well differ somewhat from what the calculator determines. However, you can re-package all the items in a different container and revise the shipping cost on an invoice before sending it. If you need to do this, be sure to communicate with the buyer why he or she may not receive an invoice quite as quickly. Most buyers are willing to be a bit more patient in order to get a lower shipping cost.

Local pickups are utilized for larger items that would be impossible or very expensive to ship, such as automobiles and furniture. You should have formulated a local pickup policy along with your other policies, but when it comes to these very large items, it may not be logical to expect the buyer to meet you halfway. In the case where a buyer must really come to your home, take precautions to keep your home, valuables, and family safe.

All shipping companies have rules about what can be shipped (no flammable materials) and in what type of container it must be in (no FedEx boxes sent through USPS, unless the FedEx logo is covered by labels or inked out). These rules can usually be found on your shipper's Web site or by asking a representative at your shipping location.

Different classes of USPS mail

One set of regulations that needs to be covered briefly is the different classes of USPS mail and what is allowed in each type. Gone are the days of Second Class and Third Class mail for super cheap rates. The USPS revamped its classifications several years ago and now features these choices.

Media Mail is the cheapest rate of mail. However, it is restricted to these items:

- Books
- Film

- Manuscripts
- Sound recordings
- Video tapes
- Computer media (CD/DVD-ROMs and floppy disks)

The package cannot include advertising (which is why most magazines are excluded, unless they are not current magazines purchased as collectibles). This class of mail takes two to nine days on average to reach its destination, depending on distance. Media Mail packages can weigh a maximum of 70 pounds.

Media Mail has been heavily abused in the past by persons who wish to mail items at its economical rates regardless of what they are mailing. In the past, if you marked a package as "Media Mail," the USPS staff might not even question its contents. A recent change in rules (which you should find posted at post offices) states that Media Mail packages are now subject to opening and inspection at the discretion of the USPS to cut down on this fraud. eBay sellers should promote a high standard of integrity and not even offer to ship items via Media Mail when they do not qualify.

Parcel Post is more expensive than Media Mail, but often less expensive than Priority Mail. Parcel Post does not have the restrictions of Media Mail, but also does not offer the same services as Priority Mail, such as mail forwarding. In cases where the package weighs less than 2 pounds, the difference may be as little as $0.10. Considering the potential for slower delivery (two to nine days), Priority (two to three days) is often a better overall deal. Where Parcel Post becomes more of a bargain is with a heavier package. Parcel Post packages can weigh up to 70 pounds.

First Class items can be in envelopes or small packages, but there is a maximum weight restriction of 13 ounces. First Class items often can reach their destination in three days or less.

Priority Mail has a flat rate for anything up to 1 pound: $3.85. For a package that weighs very close to 1 pound, that is not much more than

Parcel Post for the same item. If the item is 13 ounces or less, consider First Class unless the buyer would like the package to definitely arrive in two to three days.

Priority Mail packages can weigh up to 70 pounds. For items over 1 pound, the cost is based on a combination of weight and distance. If you mail an item to a town 30 miles away, it would be cheaper than mailing the identical item 3,000 miles away.

Express Mail is the fastest way to get your item delivered. It is also the most expensive option at the USPS. With a weight limit of 70 pounds, you can express packages to anybody in the country with a guaranteed delivery in one to two business days.

Certain items you sell on eBay may merit Express delivery, such as time-sensitive items (tickets to an event) or a last-minute holiday gift. Express Mail uses a flat-fee, with a package up to 8 ounces costing $13.85, or 9 ounces up to 2 pounds for $17.85. Insurance up to $100 is included free with Express Mail, as is full tracking online.

TIP

To see a chart with brief descriptions of the mail classes and their restrictions, go to www.usps.com/customersguide/dmm100.htm.

Insurance and Delivery Confirmation are offered by the USPS for the protection of both buyer and seller. It is important to note that PayPal's buyer and seller protection programs do not replace either USPS's insurance or Delivery Confirmation services. Be sure to read up on PayPal's programs so that you are clear about what they do offer you as a seller.

You have already learned that when you purchase shipping through PayPal, Delivery Confirmation is automatically utilized on every package, regardless of mailing class. There is no extra charge for Priority Mail packages to get Delivery Confirmation, but all other classes are charged $0.13. This makes Delivery Confirmation affordable for all shipments.

Insurance is not included automatically, but it is very easy to purchase it along with your label. Just one click of the mouse insures your package for the appropriate fee (which is determined based on the final bid price of the item).

You will have to determine which items you will require your buyers to purchase insurance for. If there is any way you can build insurance into your shipping quote, do so; buyers like to feel they are getting a good deal when insurance is included in the price.

TIP

PayPal's buyer and seller protection programs are not to be confused with insurance. In order to qualify for assistance through their program, you may have to produce proof that you insured the package to begin with. Read up on all the intricacies of this program so you are aware of its benefits and limitations.

What do you do when an item is damaged in transit and the buyer had not purchased insurance? That is a tricky question, indeed. If your auction policies clearly state that insurance is at the buyer's option, but suggested, then technically you are in the clear, and the buyer should have no claim against you.

However, what if the buyer's "claim" specifically blames you, the seller, for not properly packaging or padding the item? Could this be merely a way to coerce you into refunding their money, when you really were not at fault? Or could this be a type of fraud?

When it comes to any item that has a serial number or other specific identifying marks, it is a good idea to keep a record of those per chance you have a buyer who will try to defraud you. One such scam is to purchase an item identical to one that the buyer already owns (but is broken, defective, or damaged in some way) and then when the newly purchased one arrives, the buyer "claims" that it was damaged or broken. They want to keep the newly purchased one and return the original for a refund.

Any returns or refunds should always be done after the merchandise is received back from the buyer (with return postage at their expense). If there is any reason to suspect fraud of this sort, contact your shipper and eBay for assistance.

Customer service

Like with many other issues, you will have to determine what is best for your business when it comes to issues of damaged merchandise without the purchase of insurance.

Many of these issues have one common theme: customer service. You would think it should be a no-brainer, but this is a topic that can be anything but simple.

Providing good customer service in some ways is easy:

- Do not misrepresent your product or mislead your customers in any way.

- Provide timely and efficient answers to questions; be helpful.

- When the auction ends, communicate with the buyer (via an invoice) within one day or less.

- Thank the buyer often for their purchase and express wishes for future transactions.

- Do not cheat the buyer or overcharge for things like shipping.

- Keep your word about shipping timelines and ship in a timely manner.

- Communicate with the buyer on the date you shipped the item.
- Follow up with the customer by giving good feedback.

As long as the customer is happy, it seems like "good customer service" was smooth and simple. But when the customer is not happy, you still must provide good customer service in a calm and professional manner, to the best of your ability.

If you have been honest all along in a transaction, you have nothing to hide from an angry buyer who merely wants you to be responsible for his lack of purchasing insurance, or who wants to scare you into doing more than is reasonable. In short, some people want something for nothing, and they will prey on an eBay seller (who, to them, is not a face but just a user ID) to get it.

Do what is right in trying to make things right with your buyer, and always remember that although your goal might be to have 100 percent customer satisfaction, it is just that: a goal. It is not the end of your business if you do not make an overly demanding buyer happy. If you ever feel threatened by an angry buyer, do not hesitate to get eBay involved. Sometimes a buyer who thinks nothing of being hostile with you will not have the courage to do so when eBay is involved.

Make a point of always notifying each buyer of the date you will ship the item (and thanks to PayPal shipping, it is a much easier task than it once was). Buyers love to have their item shipped quickly, and when they know the item has been shipped out, they can anticipate its arrival.

Feedback Forum

One very important way to have your customer service skills displayed to future customers is through the eBay feedback forum. When your customers are pleased with your service, most of them will take the time to actually point out what they appreciated about you. Fast shipping, nice-quality products, excellent prices, and value are all things that buyers might mention.

Future customers do look at your feedback, especially when you are newer to selling than a competitor. If they find that of your 25 feedback you have received, 22 people made a point of noting that you shipped very fast, then a potential buyer who appreciates fast shipping might buy from you as opposed to some big corporation whose shipping department may or not get their item out quickly.

Feedback has its flip side, too. You need to give feedback to every buyer who purchases from you. Nothing is more annoying to a buyer who pays in a timely manner than to have to bug the seller to leave them feedback. Sellers can become lax about feedback once they have a very high score themselves. Do not let your company become too busy to leave feedback.

Some sellers have policies about when they will leave feedback. Some sellers bluntly state, "I will not leave you positive feedback if you leave me negative feedback," even if the buyer did nothing wrong. Others say, "I only leave feedback after you leave me feedback."

Feedback is intended to reflect how each party in the transaction has performed. An example of a good policy would be along the lines of the following: "Once you have performed your duty (by paying in a timely manner), then I will leave you feedback. I do not force you to leave me feedback, but I would appreciate it if you did so when I have completed my duties to you."

If the buyer, in turn, is unhappy with your service or product, then he rightly can leave you negative feedback, although it is always best if he communicates with you before doing so to try to work it out. Your fair policies, quick responses to his questions, fast shipping, and good communication throughout the process will build goodwill with your buyers. In turn, he may be more inclined to contact you before leaving negative feedback.

However, think of it this way: if the buyer has never had any personal service from you other than a standard invoice with no personal message, what would give him the idea that he should e-mail you when he is unhappy? If you convey the feeling of being a coldhearted person (with very negative or harshly stated policies and no personalized communications throughout the sale), buyers might think of you more as a company and not a person on the other end of the e-mail.

Good customer service throughout the process will go a long way for receiving good feedback. It seems almost inevitable that you will eventually get a negative feedback, but you do have the opportunity to post a comment or explanation in your defense.

Always try to think of yourself as the buyer. If you have ever, as a buyer, left negative feedback for a seller, then you will know that you felt very justified in doing so. Though there are buyers who utilize feedback in the wrong manner, try to put yourself into your buyer's shoes and work from there. Even after negative feedback has been given, try to work it out. If you can later come to some agreement and salvage the transaction, you can mutually agree to have the feedback removed by eBay.

Good customer service and good feedback go hand-in-hand. Giving your customers high-quality, efficient, friendly, and caring service has benefits beyond the positive feedback. It can bring about repeat customers or referrals — your customers send their friends to your eBay store. The positive feedback it generates is a referral as well. And the bottom line is this: It is the right way to do business.

Re-listing Items and Second Chance Offers

These are auction features. Not all auctions will sell the first time. In fact, sometimes it takes a number of different attempts to sell the same item.

Doing your research and placing items in the right category, with the proper keywords in the title and with an appropriate price, will help you sell your items. But nobody can force the buyers to search the week that your item is listed, and nobody can change the fact that 20 other sellers just happened to list the same item around the same time. Those are all unknowns about eBay that can throw a loop in your well-laid plans to meet a certain sales goal for the week or month.

There are times when things seem to go your way. Some weeks, your auctions seem almost on fire. Those carry you through the slow times and will keep you coming back to eBay as a selling platform.

And when the slow weeks come, learn quickly to take it all in stride. Use the time to read up on all the eBay announcements or take an online course that week. Spend some time finding a discussion board that interests you, join it, and get involved in the discussions. When you have busy weeks and months, there will not be as much time to get involved in the social aspects of eBay, so try to think of your slow times as your time to expand your network and educate yourself to be a better seller. Investigate all those nooks and crannies in eBay that you have not yet had time to look at.

If your items do not sell the first time around, you have the option to re-list them and, if they sell the second time, eBay will refund your insertion fees after the auction ends. The refund only applies to the actual listing fee. You do not have to do anything to request the credit; it is done automatically by eBay. To see if your credit has been applied, check the Seller's Account and view your fees since the last invoice.

In order to receive a re-list refund credit, you must re-list the item within 90 days of the original ending date. Also, the credit is good only if the item sells the second time. If not, you do still have to pay for that second listing fee. You can start a new listing (third listing) for the item. If it does not sell, the fourth re-list will now qualify for a re-list refund credit. eBay does not put a limit on the number of re-lists.

Other requirements to note:

- Only listings in auction or fixed-price formats qualify (not store inventory or real estate listings).

- Dutch auctions and multiple-quantity auctions do not qualify.

- You may lower the starting price or keep it the same as the original listing, but you cannot raise it.

- If the original listing did not have a reserve price, then you cannot use reserve on the re-list. If you used reserve both times, the second reserve must not be higher than the first time.

A re-list refund is also given for auctions that were successfully won by a bidder who did not pay for the item. In order to qualify for this refund, you must complete the Unpaid Items Process, which includes filing an Unpaid Item Dispute and requesting a Final Value Fee credit for the item.

When you re-list an item that did not sell the first time, review every aspect of the listing and see if there are ways you can improve it. It may not have sold due to the roll of the dice, so to speak. Perhaps the buyers simply were not looking for your item at that time. But perhaps there are things that you can do to make sure your item gets its fair share of lookers the second time around. Be sure to reconsider the following details:

- Are your photos adequate? If not, try taking a fresh batch in a different room than the first time, with different lighting or angles. Iron a clothes garment and display on a hanger. Use a contrasting, colored background. Take more close-ups, using HTML to avoid extra fees.

- Does your title drive traffic to your listing? Practice a few searches using the keywords in your original title. Are you coming up with other items similar to yours? If not, then find out why. Once you find other items similar to your own, review their keywords and see if some of yours could be effectively changed.

  - Also, double-check your title for accuracy. If your title describes a "Men's Winter Jacket size XL," is that accurate? If your item description lists it as a size Large, then one part is wrong. Make sure these two things match; if not, you may be inadvertently driving buyers away.

- While you are cross-checking your title and description for accuracy, review the description for typos and confusing information. Make sure you give enough information so the buyer can fully understand everything about this item.

- Review eBay's list of categories to see if there is a more appropriate category you could place your item in. Or perhaps you would be better served by listing it in two categories the second time around.

- Was your starting bid, or fixed price, too high? If your auction was current during a week that 20 other similar items were available, the ones with the lowest starting price might get the most action. Even if the auctions ended at a higher price than your starting price, you might want to consider lowering your starting price, perhaps even to the break-even point.

- Were your handling fees causing you problems? If your item is fairly lightweight and potential bidders can probably guess that it weighs less than 1 pound, your $2.50 handling fee might be glaringly obvious to savvy buyers who know that Priority Mail will cost you only $3.85.

While there is nothing ethically wrong with a reasonable handling fee, buyers chafe against it, so consider eliminating it or building it into your item price. Then, advertise in your description, "Shipping is a low $3.85 for Priority Mail with FREE Delivery Confirmation." (If you purchase your postage through PayPal, that is, you will also get free Delivery Confirmation.)

Second Chance Offer

A Second Chance Offer can also be utilized when a bidder does not pay for an item. Instead of re-listing the item, if you had another bidder who was bidding on the item, you can choose to offer the item to that second bidder for their highest bid.

Or, if you have an identical item to one that sold (and the buyer did pay for) you can offer the second one to the next-highest bidder. This is a useful tool because it saves you from re-listing the item and hoping that the other bidders will see the auction and bid on it. If the next-highest bidder is interested in an identical item, they can purchase it for their highest bid amount. You do not incur any listing fees when you utilize a Second Chance Offer, but you will pay Final Value Fees.

A third occasion when you can correctly use a Second Chance Offer is when you have listed an item with a reserve price that was not met. If you decide you are willing to sell the item to the highest bidder, you can offer it to the bidder this way.

In the "Selling Reminders" section of My eBay, you will find a link to all your recently sold items that are eligible for a Second Chance offer. Basically, any item that had more than one bidder is eligible. To start the process, use the drop-down menu to the right of the item in your Items I've Sold or Items Not Sold section of My eBay.

> **TIP**
>
> If a buyer has chosen not to receive Second Chance Offers, you will be promptly notified as you proceed through the steps of offering the item. If you have reason to believe that the bidder may actually want the item, you can always contact the member through eBay and politely inform them that the item is available for a Second Chance Offer, but that their settings are blocking you from sending them such an offer. If they wish to receive the offer, instruct them to change their settings and to contact you when they are ready to receive the offer. Bidders may not realize that they are not set up to receive Second Chance Offers.

When the bidder receives a Second Chance Offer, she will see a pre-set number of days for which you, the seller, has made the offer available. In order to take advantage of the offer, she must complete the checkout for the item before the time the offer expires. This is so you can offer the item to yet another bidder in a timely manner.

Some sellers theorize that giving the bidder more than 24 hours to decide if she wants your item is asking for trouble. Because buying often involves the current, urgent desire to possess an item, if you give a buyer too much time to decide, she is as likely to pass on the offer as to choose it. If, however, you have built a sense of urgency into the offer (by giving them only 24 hours to pay or pass), then you may ultimately have more luck selling the item.

You do not have to utilize the Second Chance Offer system at all, or you may also continue to utilize it (by going down the list of bidders) until you find a buyer. Keep in mind, though, that each bidder is offered the item at their highest bid — not the final bid of the item. So you must decide at what point you might be better off re-listing the item and hoping for a higher bid price (and potentially claiming the re-list refund credit).

Other things you should know about Second Chance Offers:

- You can only offer them for up to 60 days after the original auction ends. However, unless the item is extremely unusual, rare, or highly desirable, many bidders will have moved on and found something else fairly quickly, so consider utilizing this feature sooner rather than later.

- If you are using this feature due to a non-paying bidder, be sure you have done everything you can to complete the first transaction before moving on to the other options.

- You cannot use this feature for Dutch, or multiple-quantity, items.

- If you have more than one duplicate item, you can send out offers only for the exact quantity of items you do have; in case all bidders wish to buy, you must be able to provide product for them all.

- If a bidder does not respond within the deadline, the seller cannot re-offer the item to that same bidder.

- Be sure to check out special rules for Second Chance Offers if your item was listed in eBay Motors, or the Business & Industrial categories.

- Only the non-winning bidder to whom you have sent the offer can view and purchase it, even though it will show in your Items I'm Selling view.

- You can cancel an offer at any time if the bidder has not yet responded.

Keeping a Customer Database

When you make a sale to a satisfied customer, keep track of the buyer's e-mail address. This can be done in a number of ways, from keeping a simple handwritten list in a notebook to a database set up on your computer. If you have your list on your computer, occasionally print it or be sure your computer's hard drive is backed up regularly; in the unfortunate event of a computer crash, your data will not be entirely lost. *Turn back to Chapter 7 for more information about customer databases.*

A computer database or blank table that is filled in by hand could be as simple as the following:

Name	E-mail address	Transaction date(s)	Purchase types
Suzy Buyer	suzybuyslots@ e-mailprovider.com	1/27/09 5/15/09	1 Widget 2 Gidgets

Do not forget to store e-mail addresses of customers in separate folders in your e-mail program, so you do not accidentally forward jokes and other things you might send to your friends. Many e-mail address book programs allow you to add notes as well, or classify them in some way, such as by the product type they purchased from you.

When you open your eBay store, you will receive Selling Manager basic for free with your monthly fee. This software will assist you in keeping a database that stays on eBay's servers, so it will not be lost in a crash of your hard drive. Although it is hard to imagine eBay's computer system being wiped out, crazier things have happened, so it might be wise to occasionally print or copy that information to another source for safe-keeping.

Protect your customer's information with the same zeal that you expect from sellers who have your e-mail stored. Utilize your database wisely and do not bombard your customers with too much e-mail, or you will be branded as junk mail. Utilize the built-in features of your eBay store for sending custom e-mails and newsletters.

In order to build a repeat customer base, you have to keep yourself in your customer's view. Even though someone may have ordered a pet cockatoo's food from the same Web site for years, the company will mail catalogs on a regular basis. This is wise for a number of reasons: It keeps the company name fresh in a buyer's mind; it gives the buyer a chance to view products he or she may not have seen on the Web site; the buyer can peruse the selection at his or her own pace; and, mostly, it gives the buyer something tangible to pass on to friends and family who have pets and are looking to do business with a reliable company.

While there are numerous Web sites that sell the same specialized pet foods, some people are repeat customers at this one because the Web site is always accessible, the product is always in stock, they e-mail order confirmations as well as a shipping confirmation, and they have always shipped very quickly.

Find a way to set yourself and your company apart from the competition by offering the best in reasonable prices, friendly and helpful service, honest transactions, and speedy shipping. Buyers who need a steady supply of your product will take notice. And buyers who do not need a steady supply will remember you, and all buyers have the potential to send other customers your way.

CASE STUDY: THE BORDER FIASCO

In retrospect, this couple's wedding vows should have been phrased something like this:

Do you take this man to be your lawfully wedded business partner? Do you promise to set up auctions, handle the bids, and box up the product, on weekends and holidays, with a broken foot or a puppy gnawing at your slippers, for richer or for poorer, for as long as you both shall eBay?

Avery Bernstein probably would have answered "I do" anyway, but on that early morning in April, she could not have guessed that within three months, she would have a broken foot and be couped up in the couple's second-story apartment in a new town with few friends. The puppy came later.

Not being one to sit idly and pout, Avery (eBay user "dhb9876") made a proposal of her own to her husband: She wanted to sell on eBay full-time. Daniel did not hesitate; he already knew that his bride had been selling sewing and quilting supplies on eBay throughout her college years. She knew how to get merchandise through wholesalers or manufacturers, and she had the education necessary to keep the business's books properly.

She even still had her business structure in place — it was all set. They just needed merchandise to sell. Daniel, a bachelor until age 39, when he met and married Avery, had accumulated quite a large collection of sports cards — more than 100,000 cards. He had been buying and selling on eBay himself to facilitate the improvement of his own collection, but was willing to do more selling of his collection than adding to it for the moment.

They each had eBay user IDs, but decided that two would be confusing; they needed to be one. Because they were going to start their full-time venture by selling some of Daniel's sports cards, they decided to use his existing ID, as it was already associated with sports-card buying and selling.

So Avery went to work, scanning the cards slated for sale, using descriptions written by Daniel and sending out the goods, all with her foot propped up at first. It gave her something to think about besides her doctor's bills and set in motion a serious business. Within three months of selling full-time, they had qualified as PowerSellers, and the business has been growing ever since. They soon opened an eBay Store, called Dab's Cards And More, and they created a Web site address that redirects visitors to their eBay store.

The first year or so was tough; operating a full-time business with inventory and shipping supplies all over the apartment created the perfect environment for chaos. Things got misplaced a few times, and details fell through the cracks. Moving three times that first year was a definite low point. But those trying times also gave them the opportunity to build a reputation of positive customer service. They were humble and apologetic to customers whose merchandise was mixed up or lost. They made amends the best they could and offered refunds if the customer desired it.

And when they finally bought a house of their own, they set to work making it their business headquarters. Sports cards, quilting supplies, and other items they have branched into for the business have invaded their four-bedroom home. Their basement has been converted into a packing and receiving warehouse. One bedroom is the office, and its closets have been useful in keeping inventory straight.

"If you sell for any length of time, you will ship the wrong thing to the wrong person," Avery said. That is why she has devised a system in the office's closet for inventory. "You don't have to get fancy," she said. She has an "It is Listed" shelf and a "Not Listed" section. Items that can be stored in zippered bags or clear plastic storage containers are kept from dust and pet odors (from their puppy, who can be seen on the store's page).

Not merely content to set up her house in proper business-operating-mode, Avery also schedules her day as if she were going to an office and has a boss looking over her shoulder. Otherwise, she admits, she may just waste away her day and not accomplish much. "If I treat it like a job, it will be a job" is her motto.

Despite being an accountant, Avery keeps the majority of her records in a simple ledger book. She plans to invest in QuickBooks Pro within a couple of years, preferring to wait and buy the professional version she is accustomed to rather than a less-expensive, fewer-features version.

However, her low-tech approach to accounting does not apply to much else. Avery utilizes all the features of Turbo Lister to their fullest potential. She has mastered HTML for posting multiple photos by storing them on a Web site that offers free picture hosting.

Those two items — Turbo Lister and an online photo-hosting site —are what she calls the "must haves" of selling on eBay. Her third must-have is a digital postage scale. Spending time shuffling back and forth to the post office to make shipping quotes for customers is a waste of time. With an accurate scale and the shipping company's Web site, she can accurately determine the shipping costs when setting up an auction.

The couple's shipping policies are in line with their customer service philosophy: Treat the customer as you would like to be treated. They give their best shipping rate to repeat customers who purchase multiple sports cards at one time. They offer international shipping, and they do not charge extra to ship sports cards to Canada, much to the delight of our hockey-loving neighbors. "We would be out of business if we didn't ship internationally," she said.

Customs forms can be time-consuming, Avery admits, but she said that if you learn to do them correctly, you will be rewarded. So far, she has encountered no problems with international shipping, but she does her homework first. For instance, she has learned that you cannot ship cardboard playing cards to Italy. To avoid any possible confusion or problem with customs, they have a policy of not shipping sports cards to that country, even though sports cards are technically not "playing cards."

Their policy of treating customers fairly also extends to foreign governments. They refuse to mark items as a "gift" so that the recipient may not have to pay taxes on it, as that practice is illegal. Additionally, they do not under-value the contents of a package for the benefit of the buyer who wants to pay less tax on it. They mark the value as the actual amount paid. Buyers may not always appreciate their policies, but it shows they are honest sellers, and everybody has to acknowledge that.

Even though they have not always been treated fairly by others on eBay, Avery and Daniel insist on doing the best they can for every one of their customers. It shows, too, with the PowerSellers' feedback rating quickly topping 1,700 with a 99.9 percent positive rating. "I have total faith in eBay; it was founded on the principle that all people are basically good," Avery said.

They may not be millionaires yet, but that is their final answer.

Chapter Ten

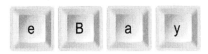

Changes in eBay Policy — 2009

D uring summer 2009, there was quite a buzz about upcoming changes policies in eBay that were due to take effect in September of that
year. By the time this book is printed, those policies will be in effect, but
they still maybe tricky to understand. They are included here in order to
give you a headstart and allow you to begin applying them to your growing
eBay business.

Detailed Seller Rating

A DSR is an indicator of customer satisfaction. A recent addition to eBay is
the ability for buyers to leave an anonymous rating of your businesses performance in four different areas: items as described, communication, shipping time, and shipping charges. A buyer can leave these ratings without
your knowing who left it. The ratings use stars 1 through 5. DSR will not
affect your ratings, but it can affect your eBay reputation and is essential
in your quest to become a PowerSeller. A rating is an overall feeling your
customer has about their experience with you. DSR includes more specific
areas that can give you an idea of where you need improvement.

You will learn how to boost each of these areas. You need to look at them from time to time and look for any trends. You want the average in each area to be at least 4.5 stars in order to meet the eligibility requirements to become a PowerSeller.

The following are some tips to help you keep your DSR scores where they need to be.

Item description: In this area, be careful how you describe your items. You must be totally honest and describe your items as accurately as possible. You may think that adding information or not being totally honest will win you a sale. But though in the short term someone may buy the item, this practice can completely undermine your reputation as a seller. A particular word to be careful about is "new." This adjective should never be used to describe almost-new, refurbished, or used items. New items have never been used before and are in their original packages.

Communication: If you are like many sellers, you might not check your e-mail on the weekends. This is perfectly acceptable, as working all the time can lead to burn out. If this is the case, be sure to let your buyers know your business hours. You should also encourage your buyers to only evaluate your communication skills based on your response time on weekdays, as this is a more accurate evaluation.

Shipping time: Remind your buyers that shipping time is not the same as transit time. In order for them to accurately give you a score, they should look at the postmark on your package rather than when it arrived. It is important to let your buyers know when you ship; drop them a line when you have actually sent their package, and be diligent about sending packages quickly. Remind the buyers that you are not responsible for delays in transit or the time it takes for their payment to clear, as the latter will affect when you will ship a package. Maintaining open, frequent communication about shipping will often increase your average score in this area.

Shipping charges: Buyers sometimes do not see your listed handling charges. It is normal to charge a fee for packing supplies and boxes, and this is over and above the cost of shipping. You should have your handling charges and policies clearly written where your buyers can see them. This can help you avoid any problems and can increase your average score in this area.

The new eBay policy focuses more on removing 1s and 2s rather than increasing 5s from buyer feedback. There will be new maximum number of low scores in order to remain a PowerSeller or a top-rated seller, which is a new designation. Only the scores from U.S. buyers will be counted toward these requirements.

Top-rated sellers are those who provide the best and most consistent buyer experiences. They will be rewarded with 20 percent fee discounts, better search engine exposure for fixed-price listings, exclusive ability to purchase Featured First, and a top-rated seller badge to be displayed on the seller's pages.

In order for a PowerSeller to qualify as a top-rated seller, he or she must satisfy the following criteria:

- Maintain at least 100 transactions in the past year
- Cannot have more than 0.50 percent of all transactions be rated with a 1 or 2 DSR with U.S. buyers on each of their 4 DSRs

There are new PowerSeller requirements and rewards that started in April 2010. The top-rated level PowerSellers will now have more strict requirements based upon low DSR ratings. PowerSellers cannot have more than 1.00 percent of transactions with U.S. buyers be a 1 or 2 rating and, in addition, they cannot have more than 2.00 percent of their DSR ratings to be a 1 or 2 in the areas of communication, shipping time, and shipping and handling charges.

There are new DSR requirements that all sellers on eBay must now follow. All sellers can only have a maximum of 3.00 percent of their transactions be rated with a 1 or 2 and can only have 1 or 2 ratings in 4.00 percent in the areas of communication, for shipping time, and or shipping and handling charges. In April 2010, the numbers become even stricter with low DSRs being only allowed in 1.00 percent of transactions for item as described and, in addition, having low DSRs in 2.00 percent in the areas of communication, shipping time, and for shipping and handling charges. The exception is low-volume sellers who will have to have four scores of 1 or 2 before being penalized. There are penalties for sellers who have low scores, such as lowered placement in searches or limits on selling until their ratings are improved.

Selling Practice Changes

The changes in the eBay policies are an attempt to make sellers more accountable and professional. One of the changes is that charges for shipping insurance will be removed from listings. This practice was overkill because it is the seller's responsibility for the package to arrive safe and intact, not the buyer's. Sellers can buy the shipping insurance themselves but cannot add a separate charge for just shipping insurance. Sellers can, however, add the cost of insurance to their shipping price when appropriate.

There is also a new Seller Dashboard. It will display low DSR and give specific reasons and areas that need to be improved based on those scores.

But not all the policies are set to penalize sellers. There are improvements to the "Best Match" function in searches. In addition, your sales will not be reset by changing the title of a listing or raising the price.

There are new multi-quantity and single-quantity fixed-price listings in the Best Match searches, even without any sales history. This will be enhanced with a New Search Visibility tool that will help sellers evaluate their listings instantly in order to help the seller improve their position.

There are new policies concerning Buy It Now listings that are listed auction-style. The greatest change is that the BIN price will be required to be at least 10 percent higher than the auction start price.

Some features will no longer be available to eBay users:

- Featured Plus
- Border
- Highlight
- Gift services
- ProPack
- Homepage Featured

The Featured First function will only be available to top-rated sellers, and even then it will not show up on all searches. Another feature that only top-rated sellers and PowerSellers will be able to use is the "Great Savings" box, which will feature listings from three PowerSellers instead of just one in the eBay product catalog.

Efficiency Measures

There is a new process to report and resolve unpaid items. Instead of the eBay Resolution Center taking 60 days to resolve an item, it will now be 30 days. In addition, there is a new process with disputes when a buyer makes a claim of not receiving an item or receiving an item that was different from the listing. This process will reduce the time of disputes by streamlining the process and the number of pages that need to be filled out.

If you were ever worried about international sales, eBay has made it easier. eBay will no longer count DSRs from foreign buyers. You will also have control over which countries you do not wish to ship to. You can specify that you are willing to ship to some foreign countries, just not all foreign countries.

The new eBay system will also allow you to track shipments and Delivery Confirmation numbers for more carriers. The shipping information will be more readily available for buyers to see, so it will improve DSR scores for Sellers. The exception is that local pickup will not have any shipping DSR, as it will be turned off on the feedback.

These are the highlights of the many changes in eBay. In order to keep abreast of these new policies, visit **http://pages.eBay.com/sell/July-2009Update/overview/index.html**.

Appendix A

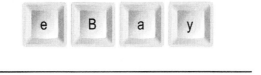

DBA Form

Statement of Intention to Conduct Business Under an Assumed or Fictitious Name

The undersigned party does hereby state his/her intention to carry on the business of _____ , at the business location of _____, in the City of _____ , in the State of _____ , under the assumed or fictitious name of: _____.

The owner's name, home address, and percentage of ownership of the above-named business are as follows:

Name:

Address:

Percentage of Ownership: 100 percent

Signed on _____ , 20_____

_____

Business Owner Signature

_____

Business Owner Printed Name

Appendix B

e B a y

State-by-State List of Sites for Starting a Small Business

Note: Web addresses do change occasionally,; these URLs were accurate as of the publishing date.

A

Alabama: **www.alabama.gov/business/startbusiness.php**
Alaska: **www.aksbdc.org**
Arizona: **www.azcommerce.com/Webapps/SmallBusVR/intro.asp**
Arkansas: **www. asbdc.ualr.edu/**

C

California: **www.ss.ca.gov/business/resources.htm**
Colorado: **www.coloradosbdc.org**
Connecticut: **web.ccsu.edu/sbdc**

D

Delaware: **www.delawaresbdc.org**

F

Florida: **www.floridatrend.com/small_biz.asp**

G

Georgia: **http://www.sbdc.uga.edu**

H

Hawaii: **www.hawaii-sbdc.org**

I

Idaho: **http://business.idaho.gov/ICL/alias__business.idaho/ tab-ID__4947/DesktopDefault.aspx**

Illinois: **http://business.illinois.gov/step_by_step_guides.cfm**

Indiana: **www.isbdc.org**

Iowa: **www.iowasbdc.org**

K

Kansas: **www.accesskansas.org/businesscenter**

Kentucky: **www.ksbdc.org**

L

Louisiana: **www.lsbdc.org**

M

Maine: **www.maine.gov/portal/business/starting.html**

Maryland: **www.mdsbdc.umd.edu**

Massachusetts: **www.mass.gov/portal/index.jsp**

Michigan: **www.gvsu.edu/misbtdc**

Minnesota: **www.deed.state.mn.us/bizdev/start.html**

Mississippi: **www.mssbdc.org**

Missouri: **www.missouribusiness.net/sbdc**

Montana: **http://sbdc.mt.gov**

N

Nebraska: **www.nlc.state.ne.us/nsf/Faq/businessinfo.html**

Nevada: **www.nsbdc.org**

New Hampshire: **www.nhsbdc.org**

New Jersey: **www.nj.gov/Business.html**

New Mexico: **www.smallbusinessnotes.com/stategovernment/new-mexico.html**

New York: **www.nyssbdc.org**

North Carolina: **www.nccommerce.com/servicenter/blio**

North Dakota: **www.nd.gov/businessreg**

O

Ohio: **http://business.ohio.gov**

Oklahoma: **www.okcommerce.gov**

Oregon: **www.sos.state.or.us**

P

Pennsylvania: **www.paopen4business.state.pa.us**

R

Rhode Island: **www2.sec.state.ri.us/faststart**

S

South Carolina: **http://scsbdc.moore.sc.edu**
South Dakota: **www.usd.edu/sbdc**

T

Tennessee: **www.tsbdc.org**
Texas: **www.business.gov/states/texas**

U

Utah: **http://business.utah.gov**

V

Vermont: **www.vermont.gov/doing_business/start_business.html**
Virginia: **www.yesvirginia.org/startbusiness/default.aspx**

W

Washington State: **http://access.wa.gov/business/start.aspx**
Washington, D.C.: **http://brc.dc.gov/index.asp**
West Virginia: **www.wvsos.com/common/startbusiness.htm**
Wisconsin: **www.wisconsinsbdc.org**
Wyoming: **www.wyomingentrepreneur.biz**

Bibliography

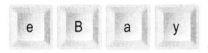

Shareholder.com. eBay Inc. First Quarter results. **http://files.shareholder. com/downloads/.../eBay_Q109_EarningsRelease.pdf.**

Blacharski, D. & Lujanac, M. How and Where to Locate the Merchandise to Sell on eBay: Insider Information You Need to Know from the Experts Who Do It Every Day. Florida: Atlantic, 2007.

Blacharski, D. eBay's Secrets Revealed: The Insider's Guide to Advertising, Marketing, and Promoting Your eBay Store With Little or No Money. Florida: Atlantic, 2007.

Editors of Socrates, Business Plan Book, Advice From the Experts. Chicago: Socrates, 2006.

Peragine, J. eBay Income Advanced: How to Take Your eBay Business to the Next Level — For PowerSellers and Beyond. Florida: Atlantic, 2009

Peragine, J. How to Open & Operate a Financially Successful Wedding Consultant & Planning Business: With Companion CD-ROM. Florida: Atlantic, 2008.

Peragine, J. How to Open & Operate a Financially Successful Personal Training Business: With Companion CD-ROM. Florida: Atlantic, 2008.

Pinson, L. & Jinnett, J. Steps to Small Business Start Up, Everything You Need to Know to Turn Your Idea into a Successful Business. Chicago: Kaplan, 2006.

Sitarz, D. Sole Proprietorship, Small Business Start Up Kit. 2nd Ed. Carbondale: Nova, 2007.

Author Biographies

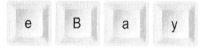

John Peragine:

John was born in Miami, Florida, in 1970. He grew up in the Tampa Bay area, but attended the North Carolina School of the Arts, in Winston Salem, for high school. He attended Florida State University and earned a bachelor's degree in psychology from Appalachian State University. He finished his master's degree and Ph.D. in Natural Health at Clayton College of Natural Health in spring 2002. In August 2007, he took the plunge. John had been a social worker in child protective services for far too many years, but had been toying with the idea of being a writer. He had written for a few national magazines and received positive responses for his work. He decided to quit social work and took a chance at writing full time. Luck was on his side, as during his first year, he was assigned to write seven books for Atlantic Publishing Group, Inc. Since then, he has completed numerous freelance projects, including writing for magazines, and creating workbooks, eBooks, articles, ghost-written books, blogs, and more. He is now working full-time and hopes to get fiction completed and published soon. More information can be found at **http://johnperagine.books.officelive.com.**

Cheryl Russell:

Cheryl L. Russell holds a Bachelor of Arts and a Bachelor of Science from Winona State University in Minnesota. She first began using eBay as a casual buyer and began selling while at home raising her two youngest children. In addition to occasionally selling on eBay and being a full-time mother, Cheryl puts her education to work by freelance writing. She enjoys reading, designing custom dresses for her daughters, and other creative pursuits. Cheryl and husband, Fred Miller, live in southwest Wisconsin with their three daughters, six pet birds, and a pair of chinchillas.

Index

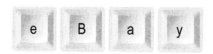